SHAKESPE...

A...

MUS... St J...

D1375759

Jost Amman, 'Poorly rewarded musicians'. The serenaders, playing cittern, violin, lute, and flute, are doused by the woman under whose window they perform. The motif has a precedent in an earlier engraving by Dürer for the *Ship of Fools*.

THE ARDEN CRITICAL COMPANIONS

SHAKESPEARE
AND
MUSIC

DAVID LINDLEY

The Arden website is at
http://www.ardenshakespeare.com

This edition of *Shakespeare and Music*
first published 2006 by the Arden Shakespeare

© 2006 Thomson Learning

Arden Shakespeare is an imprint of Thomson Learning

Thomson Learning
High Holborn House
50–51 Bedford Row
London WC1R 4LR

Typeset by Gray Publishing, Tunbridge Wells, Kent
Printed in Croatia by Zrinski

British Library Cataloguing in Publication Data
A catalogue record for this book is available from the British Library

Library of Congress Cataloguing in Publication Data
A catalogue record has been requested

ISBN 1-90343-618-4 (pbk)
13-digit ISBN 978-1-90343-618-9 (pbk)

ISBN 1-90427-171-5 (hbk)
13-digit ISBN 978-1-90427-171-0 (hbk)

NPN 9 8 7 6 5 4 3 2 1

CONTENTS

PREFACE

There are many different books which might appropriately be written under the title *Shakespeare and Music*, and it is worth defining what is and what is not being attempted here. This book is concerned primarily to explore the ways in which music in Shakespeare's plays might have been comprehended by the audiences at the Globe and Blackfriars theatres in the sixteenth and seventeenth centuries. It focuses, therefore, on the particularity of musical events – instrumental and vocal – as they occur in the plays, attempting to place them within the period's wider cultural understanding of music both as a symbol and as something experienced in the world beyond the theatre.

The book does not engage with the fascinating musical afterlife that Shakespeare's plays have engendered, from adaptations in the eighteenth century through to the operas of composers such as Verdi and Britten, or the musicals of Cole Porter and Bernstein; nor does it take in the musical commentaries on Shakespeare's plays and characters in overtures and tone-poems by Elgar, Tchaikovsky and many others. It takes no cognizance of the countless fine settings of songs from the plays for solo singers or for choirs, nor does it consider the vast body of popular music with more or less tenuous links to Shakespeare. The story of the music inspired by Shakespeare is at least as interesting a phenomenon as that of the many literary appropriations that have been increasingly studied in recent years, and reflects, as they do, the ways in which Shakespeare achieved an iconic cultural status.

This study does not deal, either, with the related but distinct question of the place of music in the performance history of Shakespeare's plays themselves. This is a real and significant gap in current criticism – music, although a vital part of theatrical experience, is all too often left to one side in the increasing number of valuable treatments of the plays' stage history. In order for such a study to be written, a good deal of primary research will need to be done amongst the archives of theatre companies – and the material will not necessarily be easy to find, since music is often the least well-preserved of all the traces of past productions. This, however, seems to me one of the most challenging and important areas for further research.

In approaching the subject in the most straightforward of ways I inevitably attempt to build upon the work of my predecessors, and especially upon the constellation of still-valuable studies published in the 1960s and 1970s. The work of Gretchen Finney, John Hollander, Peter Seng, Frederick Sternfeld and others laid secure scholarly foundations, and my debt to them is profound. Given the great mass of Shakespeare criticism it is inevitable that I will have benefited from critics I have read, but whose work has so sedimented in the mind that I am no longer conscious of its influence, and, equally, that I will have missed any number of studies that I ought to have read. I have deliberately been sparing in the citation of secondary material, so as not to overburden the text (or the reader) in what is intended as an introductory account. This does not diminish my sense of indebtedness to the legions of Shakespeare scholars who have directly and indirectly influenced my thinking.

More immediately, however, I wish to acknowledge my particular thankfulness for help and support to a variety of people and institutions. The Arts and Humanities Research Board Study Leave award made the writing of this book possible. The support of the School of English at the University of Leeds and of my colleagues has, as always, been of immeasurable value. I am grateful, too, to the participants in a conference on Shakespeare and Music, organized jointly with the Leeds School of Music, for a lively weekend which sparked many ideas. I am especially beholden to Martin Butler, Ian Harwood, John Jowett, Michela Calore and Christopher Wilson, who all generously made their work in progress available to me. For assistance with matters musical I thank Peter Holman, and, especially, Richard Rastall, who kindly read and commented on a draft of Chapter 2. Susan Anderson read the first two chapters, and I am grateful for her ability to spot the obscure and tangled, from which the final version has benefited. The General Editors, Paul Hammond and Andrew Hadfield, together with the anonymous publisher's reader, all made valuable suggestions – and saved me from many errors. I wish to thank the production team at Arden Shakespeare for their careful assistance in preparing this book for press. I am grateful to Jessica Hodge and Giulia Vicenzi, and their successors Margaret Bartley and Philippa Gallagher; to Helen Oakes and especially to Helen Parry for her attentive copy-editing.

Most of all, however, I must declare my overwhelming gratitude to Bridget Lindley, who has borne the stresses and strains of the book's composition with constant patience. Without her encouragement, and her tolerance of my total neglect of duties domestic, the book would not have been possible at all.

LIST OF ABBREVIATIONS

All references to Shakespeare's plays are to the *Arden Shakespeare Complete Works*, edited by Richard Proudfoot, Ann Thompson and David Kastan (revised edition 2001), save for *2 Henry 4*, *Richard 2* and *Pericles*, where I have used the most recent Arden 3 editions (by David Kastan, Charles Forker, and Suzanne Gossett respectively). Throughout I have used 'Arden 2' to refer to the edition, produced in the series between 1951 and 1982, and 'Arden 3' to the third series, which began publication in 1995 and is still ongoing. Quotations from old-spelling texts are given in the form in which they appear in the cited edition, save that I have routinely normalized i/j, u/v, and expanded &. and y^e.

The following abbreviations are used for individual plays:

AC	*Antony and Cleopatra*
AW	*All's Well that Ends Well*
AYL	*As You Like It*
CE	*The Comedy of Errors*
Cor	*Coriolanus*
Cym	*Cymbeline*
Ham	*Hamlet*
1H4	*King Henry IV, Part 1*
2H4	*King Henry IV, Part 2*
H5	*King Henry V*
1H6	*King Henry VI, Part 1*
2H6	*King Henry VI, Part 2*
3H6	*King Henry VI, Part 3*
H8	*King Henry VIII*
JC	*Julius Caesar*
KJ	*King John*
KL	*King Lear*
LLL	*Love's Labour's Lost*
MA	*Much Ado About Nothing*

Mac	*Macbeth*
MM	*Measure for Measure*
MND	*A Midsummer Night's Dream*
MV	*The Merchant of Venice*
MW	*The Merry Wives of Windsor*
Oth	*Othello*
Per	*Pericles*
R2	*King Richard II*
R3	*King Richard III*
RJ	*Romeo and Juliet*
Son	*Shakespeare's Sonnets*
TC	*Troilus and Cressida*
Tem	*The Tempest*
TGV	*The Two Gentlemen of Verona*
Tim	*Timon of Athens*
Tit	*Titus Andronicus*
TN	*Twelfth Night*
TNK	*The Two Noble Kinsmen*
TS	*The Taming of the Shrew*
WT	*The Winter's Tale*

LIST OF ILLUSTRATIONS

Cover: Musical company, by Simon van de Passe (1612). Kunst-sammlungen der Veste Coburg.

Frontispiece: 'Poorly rewarded musicians', woodcut, by Jost Amman. Erlangen, Graphische Sammlung der Universitat, Jost Amman (AH41).

INTRODUCTION

Enter FERDINAND, *and* ARIEL *invisible, playing and singing.*

SONG

ARIEL	Come unto these yellow sands,
	And then take hands.
	Curtsied when you have, and kissed,
	The wild waves whist.
	Foot it featly here and there,
	And sweet sprites the burden bear.

> Hark, hark
>> The watch-dogs bark
>> Bow wow, bow wow.

[*Spirits dispersedly echo the refrain 'Bow wow'*]

> Hark, hark! I hear
> The strain of strutting Chanticleer,
>> Cry cock-a-diddle-dow.

[*Spirits dispersedly echo the refrain 'cock-a-diddle-dow'*]

FERDINAND	Where should this music be? I'th air, or th' earth?
	It sounds no more; and sure it waits upon
	Some god o'th' island. Sitting on a bank,
	Weeping again the king my father's wrack,
	This music crept by me upon the waters,
	Allaying both their fury and my passion

With its sweet air. Thence I have followed it –
Or it hath drawn me rather; but 'tis gone.
No, it begins again.[1]

Towards the end of the very long second scene in *The Tempest*, Ferdinand, Prince of Naples, enters, accompanied with music played and sung by Prospero's spirit-servant, Ariel. He believes that his father has perished in the storm which wrecked their ship in the play's opening scene, and for Prospero's purposes it is essential that his delusion is sustained. It is important, too, that he arrives at Prospero's cell not too distracted by grief, since another part of Prospero's plan is that he shall see and fall in love with his daughter, Miranda. At the simplest level, then, the song serves necessary narrative and dramatic functions: by drawing Ferdinand to Prospero's cell it prevents him from stumbling across his father and his retinue, themselves wandering about the island; by calming him it makes plausible his immediate attraction to Miranda. At the same time the introduction of song and music acts as a kind of theatrical punctuation, generating for the audience a shift of mood from the angry exchanges between Prospero and Caliban which immediately precede it, and also enabling them more readily to accept the romantic convention of love-at-first-sight in what follows. From this perspective there is nothing obviously problematic in this episode, and a modern audience, familiar with dramatic genres that mix music and speech, and habituated to the 'incidental' music of screen and stage, readily accepts both the introduction of song, and the way in which it establishes a particular emotional colouring for the action. But as soon as one attends closely to what is being said and done in this brief passage, then many questions are raised, questions that form the basis of the enquiry to be conducted in the later chapters of this book.

To begin with practicalities: Ariel, the stage direction informs us, enters 'playing and singing', but there is no indication of what instrument he plays. The most obvious, and most likely possibility is that he accompanied himself on the lute.[2] The wording of the stage direction, however, might well not be Shakespeare's, but that supplied by the scribe, Ralph Crane, who prepared the manuscript for the printers;[3] and it is perfectly possible that Ariel, dressed as a water-nymph, did not himself play, but was accompanied by off-stage music. The indeterminacy of instruction extends to the spirits who sing the 'burden' (or 'refrain') to Ariel's song. We do not know how many there were, whether they were boys' treble voices, or included the tenor and bass of adult males, whether they were visible to the audience or not, and whether additional instruments were employed in the accompaniment. There are, then, a number of immediate questions to be asked about the musical personnel of the Shakespearean theatre: who they were, what instruments and expertise they had, whether they performed on- or off-stage. Answering such questions is further complicated by the fact that by the time that *The Tempest* was written, in 1610/11, Shakespeare's company, the King's Men, played in two very different theatres – outdoors at the Globe and indoors at Blackfriars – and the musical provision had been, in the past, very different in each of them. It might, indeed, be argued that the acquisition of Blackfriars – where music had traditionally been much more extensive in the plays performed by its previous tenants, the children's companies – was one of the stimuli that prompted Shakespeare to call explicitly for more music in this play than he had ever done before.

If we do not know what instruments were being played, we also do not know what music Ariel sang. Although settings by Robert Johnson survive for two songs ('Full fathom five' and 'Where the bee sucks'), which probably were employed in the play's first production, there is no extant music for 'Come unto these yellow sands'. This is, disappointingly, true for the majority of the songs in Shakespeare's plays. There are many reasons for the dearth of contemporaneous scores – music publishing was relatively limited in early modern England, and then, as now, no doubt, musical scores provided for plays remained the property of the theatrical company, who would have little incentive to make them more widely available or even carefully to preserve them once a play slipped from the repertoire. (It is still true that theatrical organizations, even the most important, are notably careless about preserving musical records – the massive *Shakespeare Music Catalogue*[4] lists thousands of settings of songs and music composed for performances over the centuries that have simply disappeared.) But there are a number of consequences of this lack.

In the case of 'Come unto these yellow sands', the absence of any setting means that we cannot even be sure of the text of the song itself. The version printed at the head of this chapter is not identical with that in the Folio of 1623, the only source for Shakespeare's play. There it reads:

Enter Ferdinand & Ariel, inuisible playing & singing.
Ariel Song.   *Come vnto thcse yellow sands,*
                and then take hands :
          Curt sied when you haue, and kist
                the wilde waues whist :
Foote it featly heere, and there, and sweete Sprights beare
                the burthen.   Burthen disperse dly.
Harke, harke, bowgh wawgh : the watch-Dogges barke,
                bowgh-wawgh.
Ar. Hark, hark, I heare, the straine of strutting Chanticlere
                cry cockadidle-dowe.

As it stands, this makes little sense – the form of the verse is confused, what words constitute the 'burthen' is not clear, and it is not obvious why there should be the additional speech prefix 'Ar.' before the penultimate line.[5] Different editors have tried to make sense of the confusion in different ways: Arden 3, for example, prints the end of the lyric thus:

> Foot it featly here and there
> And sweet sprites bear
>   The burden.
>
> *(burden dispersedly)*

SPIRITS   Hark, hark! Bow-wow
              The watch dogs bark, bow-wow.
ARIEL   Hark hark, I hear
              The strain of strutting chanticleer
              Cry cock a diddle dow. (1.2.380–7)

Here the word 'burden' floats unintegrated into the verse structure, the whole of the next two lines are given to the spirits, and there is no suggestion that the strains of the cock to which Ariel instructs us to 'hark' are provided by the spirit-refrain. There is no right answer to the problems posed by the original printing of the lyric, and this might seem merely a rather abstruse editorial debate – for, after all, composers are not neces-sarily bound to the detail of the lyric they set and may choose to realize it in any number of ways – but the important general point is that the printed texts of the plays do not necessarily give us a clear guide as to how song lyrics might have been translated into a musical event. Indeed, on some occasions the printed texts of early modern plays do not give us the words of a song at all. Among the Shakespearean examples of such 'blank' songs are the song sung by a Welsh lady in *Henry IV, Part 1*, 3.1.238, Marina's song in *Pericles* 5.1.72 and (possibly) an air that Brutus's page sings to his lute in *Julius Caesar*, 4.3.263.

The absence of any surviving musical setting for most of the songs also makes it much more difficult to comment on the ways in which they func-tioned in the plays, since the musical language of a song is intrinsically part of its theatrical meaning. Fanfares, marches, and other musical cues, as well as songs, can only be fully comprehended if one attempts to locate these specific musical moments in a much wider cultural conception of music itself. It is often casually assumed that music is, somehow, a 'uni-versal' language, transcending geography and history; or else that the lan-guage which it speaks is governed entirely by its own internal rules. But, of course, as with any other cultural product, music's 'meaning' is gen-erated in significant measure by the assumptions that its audience brings to its listening, and it is located within historically specific contexts and practices that condition the ways in which it is received and understood. In *The Tempest*, for example, a clear distinction seems to be offered between the accompanied songs of Ariel on the one hand and the unaccompanied 'popular' songs of Stephano, Trinculo and Caliban in 3.3. How these dif-ferences might have been signalled to an audience in terms of musical 'codes', by instrumentation or vocal style, and what ideological freight those codes carried, is an important issue, and one to which we will repeat-edly return.

One immediate question about the assumptions we bring to music in Shakespeare's plays is raised by Ferdinand himself, when he asks: 'Where should this music be?' (1.2.388). In this specific context he simply reminds us of the fact that Ariel is invisible to him, but the implication of his uncertainty about the origin of the music extends much further than this. We are now entirely habituated to the idea that much of the music we hear in the theatre, the cinema, or on television, is 'incidental music', and not necessarily heard by the characters on stage or screen. It has become an independent strand in the theatrical experience, creating mood and influencing our response. So familiar are we with this convention that we take it for granted, and expect that in a modern theatrical performance of Shakespeare we will not just hear music which is specifically called for in the text, but other sounds and snatches of music that will persuade us to respond in particular ways to the action. The example with which this Introduction opens is the first musical cue in *The Tempest*, but in many modern productions we will already have heard music accompanying, for example, Prospero's charming of Miranda to sleep (1.2.185), or underlining parts of his long narrative of usurpation.[6] Music used in this way becomes part of the *mise-en-scène*, and a function of the directorial reading of the play as a whole. It is by no means clear that this was the case in the Elizabethan and Jacobean theatres, where the overwhelming evidence is that music was assumed to be heard by the characters on stage, and is therefore integral to the action, not a commentary upon it.[7] To explore this question is of considerable importance in attempting to define as precisely as possible the way in which music spoke to an Elizabethan or Jacobean audience, and the ways, therefore, that Shakespeare and his contemporaries might choose to deploy it in their plays.

The Elizabethan or Jacobean audience, however, did not just entertain different assumptions about the way music functioned in the theatre; they understood its workings more generally in a very different fashion. Once again, this musical moment from *The Tempest* provides some clues to that understanding. In the first place, Ferdinand qualifies his statement that he had 'followed' the music with the phrase 'or it has drawn me rather' (1.2.395). He thereby suggests that it is not simply his curiosity to identify the source of the music which has led him on his way, but something inherent in the power of the music itself that has compelled his journey. He suggests, furthermore, that this music not only had the ability to ameliorate his grief – something we would readily accept that music can do – but also had the power to quieten the waves of the sea – a control over nature that we would certainly not now attribute to musical sound.[8] These might, of course, be taken simply as conventional poetic conceits – as indeed they are – but at the very least they raise questions about what, exactly, the Early Modern period thought music could effect. Once one concedes the possibility that Ferdinand means what he says, and that the Globe or Blackfriars audience might have believed him at some literal level, then music becomes altogether more powerful, or, rather, powerful in a different way from that we now customarily perceive. In *The Tempest* music's manipulation of Ferdinand is but the first of several similar episodes: it puts the lords to sleep in 2.1, and leads Trinculo, Stephano and Caliban off-stage into a stinking pond in 3.2, for example. In other plays it seems imbued with even stronger influence – curing Lear's madness, raising Thaisa from the dead in *Pericles*, and awakening the 'statue' of Hermione in *The Winter's Tale*.

Underpinning such dramatic moments as these is the belief that human music reflected the harmony of the heavens and derived its compelling force from that parallel, a view which stretches back to the Greeks, and one which informed both the academic study of music and its representation in literature. It is part of a complex set of interrelated philosophical, mathematical and religious ideas which will be further explored in Chapter 1. These ideas were part of the mental furniture of the age, but, although they are frequently and casually invoked, their connection with the composition and performance of music was not necessarily very direct. As Thomas Morley explained in his *A Plain and Easy Introduction to Practical Music*:

> Music is either speculative or practical. Speculative is that kind of music which, by mathematical helps, seeketh out the causes, properties, and natures of sounds, by themselves and compared with others, proceeding no further, but content with the only contemplation of the art. Practical is that which teacheth all that may be known in songs, either for the understanding of other men's, or making of one's own.[9]

Morley's book (though neither as plain nor as easy as its title implies) was one of a number published in the period which appealed directly to an audience wishing to be instructed in basic musical skills, and betokens a rapid increase in musical literacy, at least among the 'better sort', during the Elizabethan period. Since this study is primarily concerned with the ways in which an audience might have responded to the music in Shakespeare's plays in the theatre, the level of musical sophistication in those who attended the Globe or Blackfriars is a matter of some importance, and Chapter 2 will consider the nature and extent of musical education in the period.

One of the important distinctions that prevailed in the period needs to be registered immediately in relation to this dramatic episode. That is the differentiation between the cultivation of musical expertise in a domestic environment for private relaxation, and the manifestation of musical skill in public performance. For although the middle classes (for want of a better term) and above might become skilled executants on the lute or virginals, be capable of reading their part in a madrigal, and practise music for their own recreation, they did not conceive it as socially appropriate to perform in public. This has some significant consequences for the representation of singers on Shakespeare's stage. Here Ariel, Prospero's spirit-servant, performs in order to assuage Ferdinand's grief – Ferdinand does not himself sing to express his feelings. We are accustomed to the notion that a theatrical character who sings is, in some way or another, giving voice to their own emotions; yet in Shakespearean drama almost all performed songs are rendered by professionals or servants who do not articulate their own feelings so much as sing to, or on behalf of, others. Those who sing directly 'for themselves' are generally drunk, mad, in their dotage, or socially subversive.

This distinction is a useful reminder that despite the privileging of music as an image of cosmic harmony, in its practical manifestations it was embroiled in controversy. Post-Reformation religious opposition to music in church services, in the social world of the alehouse, in popular festivity, and in the theatre itself, generated fierce debate. The suspicion of music, indeed, had a history as long, and as authoritative, as that which underlay its more positive representation, as Chapter 1 demonstrates. The belief in music's capacity to bring order to disordered passions coexists in the period with fear of its potential to stimulate lascivious desire. The obverse of its association with order and hierarchy was its characterization as either effeminate or subversive. This is the complex and conflicted environment in which the music of Shakespeare's plays is situated, and it is the relationships between that environment and the presentation of music and song on stage which this study attempts to explore.

Shakespeare actually says nothing particularly original about music (even if he says it better than most); in general he does not use music as frequently as the dramatists who wrote for the children's companies, or playwrights like Fletcher who wrote later for the indoor, or 'hall', theatre audiences. It is the ways in which he puts perfectly conventional ideas in complex play and thereby opens them up to dynamic investigation and critique which marks him out. Part 2 of the book offers a detailed examination of those plays in which Shakespeare explores and exploits music's dramatic and thematic potential, in ways which test out many of the tensions and contradictions implicit in his culture's view of music. In order to make that exploration possible, both the theoretical and social contexts that informed his practice need to be explored more fully.

PART ONE

MUSIC IN SHAKESPEARE'S TIME

Chapter One

MUSICAL THEORY

Here will we sit, and let the sounds of music
Creep in our ears – soft stillness and the night
Become the touches of sweet harmony:
Sit Jessica, – look how the floor of heaven
Is thick inlaid with patens of bright gold,
There's not the smallest orb which thou behold'st
But in his motion like an angel sings,
Still quiring to the young-ey'd cherubins;
Such harmony is in immortal souls,
But whilst this muddy vesture of decay
Doth grossly close it in, we cannot hear it:

[*Enter Musicians*]

Come ho! and wake Diana with a hymn,
With sweetest touches pierce your mistress' ear,
And draw her home with music.
Jes. I am never merry when I hear sweet music.   [*Music*]
Lor. The reason is your spirits are attentive:
For do but note a wild and wanton herd
Or race of youthful and unhandled colts
Fetching mad bounds, bellowing and neighing loud,
Which is the hot condition of their blood, –
If they but hear perchance a trumpet sound,
Or any air of music touch their ears,

You shall perceive them make a mutual stand,
Their savage eyes turn'd to a modest gaze,
By the sweet power of music: therefore the poet
Did feign that Orpheus drew trees, stones, and floods,
Since naught so stockish, hard, and full of rage,
But music for the time doth change his nature, –
The man that hath no music in himself,
Nor is not moved with concord of sweet sounds,
Is fit for treasons, stratagems, and spoils,
The motions of his spirit are dull as night,
And his affections dark as Erebus:
Let no such man be trusted. (*MV*, 5.1.55–88)

This is Shakespeare's best-known expression of his period's conventional theories about the nature and power of music. Familiar though it may be, the passage is worth quoting at length as the starting-point for this chapter because Lorenzo's exquisite amplification of the commonplaces of musical theory both locates the source of music's harmony in cosmic myth, and at the same time gestures towards an explanation of the capacity of music to affect human behaviour.[1] Arcane though the theories entertained about music in the Renaissance might seem to be, and distant though they appear to us from the realities of performed music, throughout their evolving history from classical Greece to the Renaissance these hypotheses represented a serious attempt to describe what music is, and to understand why it generates so powerful a human response.

Lorenzo's exposition begins with a version of the myth of the music of the spheres. Like all the ideas he articulates in this passage, this notion has its roots in Greek philosophy, in the thinking of Pythagoras, Plato, and their followers, mediated by late classical writers, especially Boethius and Macrobius, and given new impetus in the Renaissance by neoplatonic philosophers such as Marsilio Ficino, Pontus de Tyard, and many others. This history has been traced in detail by a number of scholars,[2] and the ensuing summary of some of its most important features necessarily simplifies the sequence in which concepts developed, and is highly selective in detailing the complexity of their elaboration. But then, there is little evidence that Shakespeare was much interested in validating his deployment of musical conceits by anchoring them in precise scholarship – unlike his contemporary Ben Jonson, who encrusted some of his masque texts with learned marginalia. It is more important to have a general sense of the constellation of ideas and assumptions that Shakespeare drew upon than to trace each element accurately back to its source.

There are two fundamental concepts that underpin the first part of Lorenzo's speech. The first is the belief that the universe is essentially harmonious, and that the source of that concord lies in mathematical proportions which can be directly related to musical harmonies. Pythagoras, in an oft-repeated legend, was said to have meditated on the sound of smiths beating hammers upon anvils, and to have argued that a hammer half as heavy produced a note an octave above its full-sized fellow.[3] More important were the experiments with a single string, or monochord, attributed to him by his successors. If a stretched string is divided exactly into two it produces a sound an octave higher than the fundamental pitch (the ratio 2:1), the intervals of the fourth and fifth can similarly be expressed as the ratios 4:3 and 3:2 respectively, and all other intervals can be described in mathematical terms.[4] These numerical proportions were then extended to describe the relationships of the planetary spheres, both in their relative distance one from another, and in the speed of their movement. The ideas were given influential (if obscure) expression in Plato's *Timaeus*, and endlessly elaborated in succeeding centuries up to the Renaissance. One of the final manifestations of this understanding is provided in the illustration of cosmic harmony from Robert Fludd's *Utriusque cosmi … historia 1* (1617; Figure 1). Even after the Copernican revolution displaced the earth from the centre of the cosmos – which might seem to have rendered such hypotheses untenable – Kepler's *Harmonices Mundi* (1619) attempted to map the new heavens using the same principles of mathematical harmony. (Indeed, although it lies outside the scope of this study, it is important to recognize how important the numerical basis of musical theory was to the development of the natural sciences, as Penelope Gouk amply demonstrates.)[5]

The other fundamental concept was also articulated by Plato, in the Myth of Er at the end of the *Republic*, as part of an account of the good

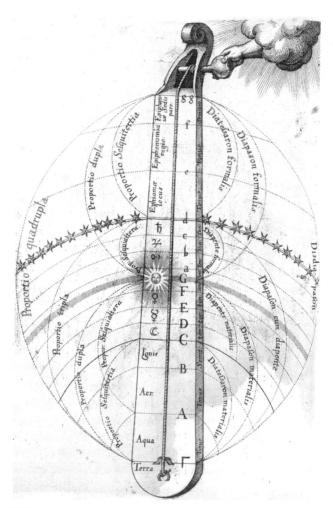

FIGURE 1   The divine monochord, from Robert Fludd, *Utriusque cosmi ...
historia*, 1 (1617), p. 90. Earth is at the base of the scale which leads up from the
four regions of earth, water, air and fire, through the spheres of the planets to
the regions of the heavens, all described in terms of musical intervals.

man's reward in the life after death. Taken up into the heavens, Er sees the universe turning on a spindle fixed in the lap of Necessity, and on each of the spheres 'stands a siren, which is carried round with it and utters a note of constant pitch, and the eight notes together make up a single scale'.[6] This myth (though challenged by Aristotle, who considered that the spheres moved in silence)[7] was given further impetus by Cicero's *Somnium Scipionis*, and, especially, by the fifth-century commentary on it by Macrobius, a work which had profound influence in transmitting Pythagorean and Platonic ideas through the Middle Ages and into the Renaissance.[8] It became a poetical commonplace, and reference to the music of the spheres as an image of and for celestial harmony is pervasive in the poetry and drama of Shakespeare's period.

In fact Lorenzo's representation is less than rigorously scholarly. He is traditional enough in Christianizing the myth, for Plato's sirens were later identified with the Muses, and then became angels (as, for example, in the highly influential concluding cantos of Dante's *Paradiso*). But Shakespeare does not follow either the tradition that one of the nine orders of angels sat on each of the heavenly spheres, or alternatively, that all the angels gathered on the outermost crystalline sphere singing God's praises. By making the music of the heavens an explicit simile – the orbs sing *like* angels – he seems to be recalling the pictorial tradition of the representation of the angels which became increasingly independent of the doctrine of the harmony of the spheres during the later Middle Ages and Renaissance, rather than the versions offered in neoclassical treatments of heavenly music.[9] Furthermore, the reason he gives for human inability to hear the celestial music is somewhat unconventional. 'Neither of the traditional reasons (acclimatization, or the physical thresholds of perception) is given. Instead the unheard music is related to immortality, and by extension to a prelapsarian condition.'[10] Here it would seem that Shakespeare has deployed other central strands of neoplatonic thinking – that humankind's descent from the divine renders us incapable of perceiving absolute reality, but only its shadow, so that although human music gets its power through its reflection of celestial harmony, and we respond to it because of our faint memory of its original, we have no direct access to the heavenly music itself.[11] Milton, when he uses the same reason for our inability to hear the music of the spheres in *Arcades*, 62–73 (perhaps influenced directly by *The Merchant of Venice*)[12] is, as one might expect, much more exact in his description of the Platonic universe. It would, however, not merely be pedantic, but positively wrongheaded to object to Shakespeare's somewhat cavalier way with his material – and it is important to stress this now.

One of the dangers of any study which attempts to locate Shakespeare's plays in their historical, literary, and cultural contexts – and a malady most incident to scholars and editors alike – is the tendency either to dissolve his text into the contexts of which it then becomes simply an exemplification, or, on the other hand, to claim that all variation from the sources is of itself intrinsically significant. To pursue the first line flattens the individuality of a text, while the danger of the second is to assume that an audience is capable of recognizing citation in the rapid movement of theatrical action. What matters is the particular dramatic moment. Here Shakespeare creates an opportunity to move into a rhetorical set-piece, one which connects significantly with the play's wider dramatic and thematic concerns, especially the opposition of the mercantile world of Venice to the golden world of Belmont. Few, if any, of his audience could have noticed his eclectic and compressed way with neoplatonic material. Even if they did, they would not have objected to it precisely because the basic ideas he invokes were so familiar that they could be allusively and elliptically handled; instead, they would have admired the eloquence of this recasting of poetical and philosophical commonplaces. Because we are now unfamiliar with these conventional ideas our ears cannot fully hear what his contemporaries could, and we therefore have effortfully to reconstruct the frames of reference which they possessed, but always in order to try to respond more fully to what is actually there on the page or in the theatre.

And so, before turning to the second part of Lorenzo's speech, it is necessary briefly to explore further some of the ramifications of the theories of consonance between music and the structures of the universe which resonate in Shakespeare's work. One of the principal intermediaries between the classical authors and the Middle Ages and Renaissance was Boethius, whose *De Institutione Musica*, derived from a lost work by

Nichomacus, and written in the early part of the sixth century AD, became a standard textbook in universities and schools throughout the whole period.[13] He included music with arithmetic, geometry, and astronomy in the 'quadrivium' of mathematical sciences which, together with the 'trivium' of grammar, rhetoric, and logic, made up the seven liberal arts of the university undergraduate curriculum. (These were the arts for which Prospero boasts that he had an unparalleled reputation in *Tempest*, 1.2.73–4.) Music was therefore firmly associated with mathematics – as is comically evidenced when Petruchio introduces the disguised Hortensio to Baptista as a potential tutor for his daughter Bianca: 'a man of mine / Cunning in music and the mathematics' (*TS*, 2.1.55–6). On a more elevated level, Dr John Bull, the first lecturer at Sir Thomas Gresham's college in 1596, was expected to give 'the solemn music lecture ... the theorique part for half an hour, or thereabouts; and the practique by concent of voice or instruments, for the rest of the hour'.[14]

The relationship between practical and theoretical music was established by Boethius in his division of the subject into three parts, *musica mundana*, *musica humana*, and *musica instrumentalis*. The first of these, 'the music of the universe', includes the mathematical harmony of the heavens and the music of the spheres which we have already discussed, but extends further. Boethius writes that it 'is especially to be studied in the combining of the elements and the variety of the seasons which are observed in the heavens', and continues:

> Unless a certain harmony united the differences and contrary powers of the four elements, how could they form a single body and mechanism? But all this diversity produces the variety of seasons and fruits, yet thereby makes the year a unity.[15]

For Christian writers neoplatonic theory could easily be accommodated, since to uncover the harmonies of the universe was to demonstrate the truth of the Book of Wisdom's assertion that God 'ordered all things in measure and number and weight' (11.20). Thomas Campion spoke of God as 'Author of number that hath all the world in / Harmonie framed'.[16] The French poet Du Bartas, in his enormously influential *Semaines*, translated into English by Joshua Sylvester as *The Divine Weeks and Works*

(1592–1608), described God's 'numbrie Law' and amplified Boethius' analogies to encompass humours, elements, seasons and the parts of a musical composition:

> Even so th'all-quickning spirit of God above
> The heav'ns harmonious whirling wheeles doth move,
> So that, re-treading their eternall trace,
> Th'one beares the Treble, th'other beares the Base.
>
> But, brimmer farre then in the Heav'ns, heere
> All these sweet-charming Counter-Tunes we heare:
> For *Melancholie*, *Winter*, *Earth* below
> Beare aye the *Base*; deepe, hollow, sad, and slow:
> Pale *Phlegme*, moist *Autumne*, *Water* moistly-cold,
> The Plommet-like-smooth-sliding *Tennor* hold:
> Hot-humide *Blood*, the *Spring*, transparant *Aire*,
> The Maze-like *Meane*, that turnes and wends so faire:
> Curst *Choler*, *Sommer*, and hot-thirsty *Fire*,
> Th'high-warbling *Treble*, loudest in the Quire.[17]

Such musical correspondences could be, and often were, extended with enthusiasm, especially in the works of those influenced by the occult philosophies of the period. One extension of particular importance is that which saw the ideal human society as hierarchically reproducing the harmony of the heavens. It receives its classic Shakespearean statement in the speech of Ulysses on degree in *Troilus and Cressida*, 1.3.75–137. There, after describing the order of 'The heavens themselves, the planets and this centre' (85) Ulysses turns to social organization, concluding:

> Take but degree away, untune that string,
> And hark what discord follows. Each thing meets
> In mere oppugnancy. (109–11)

Here, as in Lorenzo's speech, Shakespeare is articulating a commonplace. Thomas Elyot believed that instruction in music was valuable precisely because the tutor could:

> commende the perfecte understandinge of musike, declaringe howe necessary it is for the better attaynynge the knowledge of a publike

weale: whiche, as I before have saide, is made of an ordre of astates [*estates*] and degrees, and, by reason thereof, conteineth in it a perfect harmony.[18]

It is, however, important to note that music here functions primarily as a persuasive analogy. Though Ulysses' invocation of the 'string' suggests the monochord which binds the universe together in Fludd's depiction of celestial harmony, the musical image is not essential to the validation of the comparison between orderly heavens and a hierarchical society. This is clear if one considers the passage from the *Exhortacion, concerning good order and obedience* often cited as a parallel to Ulysses' speech:

Almighty god hath created and appointed all thinges, in heaven, earth, and waters, in a most excellente and perfect ordre. In heaven, he hath appointed distinct or severall orders and states of Archangels and Angels. In earth he hath assigned and appoynted kinges, princes, with other governours under them, in all good and necessary order.[19]

Music is not here invoked, but the argument is similarly analogical, and to argue by such similitudes was endemic in the mental world of the time. The ideological force of images such as these should certainly not be underestimated, but in the last analysis they are doing something significantly different from the quasi-scientific pursuit of mathematical and musical correspondence as a means of describing the actual nature of the world. John Hollander's important study, *The Untuning of the Sky*, tracks the process by which scientific statements about music and world harmony turned ineluctably into metaphor during the later sixteenth and seventeenth centuries. It is often impossible to be certain when Shakespeare or his fellow poets and dramatists are invoking musical analogy as decorative image, when they expect an audience to treat such references as myth, or when they are to be accepted as a statement of fact. It is out of these uncertainties, indeed, that some of the subtlest of dramatic effects are generated.

But this is to jump ahead. For the moment it is enough to note that Boethius' *musica mundana*, both as belief and as image, has considerable power and currency in the period. And the same is true for his second category of *musica humana*. He speaks of it in these terms:

> What human music is, anyone may understand by examining his own nature. For what is that which unites the incorporeal activity of the reason with the body, unless it be a certain mutual adaptation and as it were a tempering of low and high sound into a single consonance? What else joins together the parts of the soul itself, which in the opinion of Aristotle is a union of the rational and the irrational? What causes the blending of the body's elements or holds its parts together in established adaptation?[20]

Ornithoparchus, in his *Musice active micrologus* (1518), a work translated by the foremost English lutenist, John Dowland, in 1609, elaborated:

> *Humane Musick*, is the Concordance of divers elements in one compound, by which the spirituall nature is joyned with the body, and the reasonable part is coupled in concord with the unreasonable, which proceedes from the uniting of the body and the soule. For that amitie, by which the body is joyned unto the soule, is not tyed with bodily bands, but vertuall, caused by the proportion of humors. For what (saith *Caelius*) makes the powers of the soul so sundry and disagreeing to conspire oftentimes each with other? who reconciles the Elements of the body? what other power doth soder [*solder*] and glue that spirituall strength, which is indued with an intellect to a mortall and earthly frame, than that Musicke which every man that descends into himselfe finds in himselfe? Hence is it, that we loath and abhorre discords, and are delighted when we heare harmonicall concords, because we know there is in our selves the like concord.[21]

At the simplest level this is a variation on the commonplace that the individual human being reflects in miniature the whole universe – he or she is the 'microcosm' or 'little world' corresponding to the 'macrocosm' or 'greater world'. Combining all four elements, and at the same time poised between brute creation and the angels, endowed with soul as well as body, as Herbert put it:

> Man is all symmetrie,
> Full of proportions, one limbe to another,
> And all to all the world besides:
> Each part may call the furthest, brother:
> For head with foot hath private amitie,
> And both with moons and tides.
>
> Nothing hath got so farre,
> But Man hath caught and kept it, as his prey.
> His eyes dismount the highest starre:
> He is in little all the sphere.[22]

Donne, in his *Holy Sonnets* (7.1) put it pithily: 'I am a little world made cunningly', and Du Bartas considered that:

> Thear is no Theame more plentifull to scanne,
> Then is the glorious goodly frame of MAN:
> For in Man's self is Fire, Aire, Earth, and Sea,
> Man's (in a word) the World's Epitome,
> Or little Map.[23]

Writers of all kinds enthusiastically accepted the invitation to 'scan' this little world, and to elaborate its analogical potential. As with the music of the spheres, the precise status of the image is often in doubt. Sir Thomas Browne interestingly recorded that 'to call ourselves a Microcosme, or little world, I thought it onely a pleasant trope of Rhetorick, till my nearer judgement and second thoughts told me there was a reall truth therein'.[24] Whether gesturally, as in Hamlet's outburst, 'What piece of work is a man' (2.2.305), explicitly in the Gentleman's description of Lear, who 'Strives in his little world of man to outscorn / The to and fro conflicting wind and rain' (3.1.10–11),[25] or comically in Toby Belch's dispute with Andrew Aguecheek about which astrological sign governs which bodily part (*TN*, 1.3.133–6), Shakespeare readily takes advantage of the belief to fashion his rhetorical tropes.

The analogy between heavenly music and the concord of the human body is, then, a variation on, or a subset of, a familiar and pervasive theme. Robert Fludd elaborated the idea in an image where the human

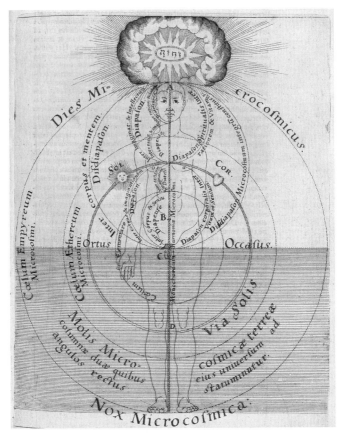

FIGURE 2   Man the microcosm, from Robert Fludd, *Utriusque cosmi ... historia*,
2 (1619), pp. 274–5. A string extends from God to Earth, and the three realms
of the empyrean, ethereal, and elemental correspond respectively to the head,
the thorax, and the abdomen.

body is divided into three regions, each manifesting the same harmonic
relationships of fourth, fifth, and octave as was evidenced in the musical
relationships of the heavens (Figure 2). Fludd was writing in the occult
tradition where:

Together sympathy and antipathy ... sustained the magical cosmos. They constituted a world of likeness and its opposite that was differentiated but unified. They maintained the universe, thus, in the image of *discordia concors*, of harmony created from dissimilarity (or of dissimilarity in harmony). So it is no accident that Renaissance writers ... repeatedly framed this world in metaphors of harmony – metaphors that were not mere tropes of imagined relationships where none existed in reality ... but that instead discovered in their creation truths about the structure itself of the world.[26]

For writers such as Marsilio Ficino or Cornelius Agrippa the analogy between the music of the cosmos, human music, and actual musical sounds was central to their magical philosophies. The most immediately significant consequence of such beliefs was that the understanding of human physiology in musical terms enabled connections to be drawn between the three Boethian divisions of music. Ficino's belief in the possibility of composing and performing music which had a magical power is significant precisely because he

is not content to point out possible analogies between macrocosm and microcosm, between musical and celestial harmonies, but gives practical, if somewhat vague, directions for making music which may usefully exploit these analogies.[27]

This observation returns us to the text of Lorenzo's speech. After his invocation of the music of the spheres he calls for some actual, performed music, and then takes the opportunity to instruct Jessica in the standard notions of music's capability to affect mood and behaviour in the real world. Just as the mathematical harmonies of speculative music were founded in empirical observation of the properties of the monochord, so the discussion of music's effects also began with naturalistic consideration of the ways music functioned in the real world. St John Chrysostom, in the fourth century AD, for example, noted that:

To such an extent, indeed, is our nature delighted by chants and songs that even infants at the breast, if they be weeping or afflicted, are by reason of it lulled to slumber. Nurses, carrying them in their arms, walking to and fro and singing certain childish songs to them, cause their eyelids to close in sleep. For this reason travelers also sing as they drive their yoked animals at midday, thus lightening the hardships of the journey by their chants. And not only travelers, but peasants are accustomed to sing as they tread the grapes in the winepress, gather the vintage, tend the vine, and perform their other tasks. Sailors do likewise, pulling at the oars. Women, too, weaving and parting the tangled threads with the shuttle, often sing a particular melody, sometimes individually and to themselves, sometimes all together in concert. This they do – the women, travelers, peasants, and sailors – striving to lighten with a chant the labor endured in working, for the mind suffers hardships and difficulties more easily when it hears songs and chants.[28]

His examples were endlessly repeated and elaborated in succeeding centuries – finding an echo, for example, in Orsino's recommendation of 'the song we had last night' to Viola:

> Mark it; Cesario, it is old and plain;
> The spinsters and the knitters in the sun,
> And the free maids that weave their thread with bones
> Do use to chant it. (*TN*, 2.4.42–5)

To these examples of music's comforting presence in the ordinary working world were added many legends of music's power to alter human and non-human behaviour alike. Among the most frequently cited were those of Timotheus, who with his music at a banquet was able first to raise Alexander to martial fury, and then to calm his passions; Arion, who charmed dolphins in order to escape from his enemies; and Amphion, who summoned with his music the stones that built Thebes.[29] The most often invoked of the classical legends were those which surrounded the figure of Orpheus, who not only charmed the god of the underworld to release Eurydice, but, as Lorenzo remarks, was feigned to command all of nature with his lyre (*MV*, 5.1.79–81; see Figure 3).[30] The Biblical figures of David and Jubal were similarly celebrated as exponents of a wonder-working,

FIGURE 3 Orpheus charms the animals. This woodcut by Virgil Selis turns up
in a number of different texts in the period, here taken from a German
translation of Ovid's *Metamorphoses* of 1581, p. 128.

divinely inspired harmony. As we will see shortly, the resonance of the
stories of music's power were important and influential in the changing
musical practice of the later sixteenth century; but they raised the fundamental problem – which is still contentious in our contemporary musical aesthetics – of how to explain the simple and observable fact that music
elicits a powerful emotional response.

Classical writers did develop theories to account for musical effect. Plato,
in the *Republic* (398c–403c) considered that it derived from the proper
combination of words, rhythm and musical mode, and influentially attributed a specific character to each of the modes, reserving only the Dorian
and Phrygian as acceptable, the former as inspiring military bravery, the
latter as appropriate to the 'ordinary voluntary occupations of peace-time',
both of them expressing 'courage and moderation in good times and in
bad'. The other modes were dismissed as provoking lust and effeminacy.[31]
Variations on Plato were replayed throughout the Middle Ages and the
Renaissance, but, as Tomlinson crucially observes, 'conceptions of musical

ethos and celestial harmony intersect ... rarely and inconsequentially in ancient writings'.[32]

Renaissance writers, however, did begin to speculate rather more fully on the nature of that intersection. Thomas Wright in 1604 offered a fascinating meditation on precisely these problems, summing up his period's thinking on the subject. Music, he avers, is miraculous because:

> it moveth a man to mirth and pleasure, and affecteth him with sorrow and sadnesse; it inciteth to devotion, and inciteth to dissolution: it stirreth up souldiers to warre, and allureth citizens to peace ... musicke in like maner elevateth the mind to devotion and pietie, and abaseth the soule with effusion and levity.[33]

He instances many of the familiar classical and Biblical examples of music's power, but unlike many writers faces squarely

> a question to be answered, as difficult as any whatsoever in all naturall or morall Phylosophy, *viz*. How musicke stirreth up these passions, and moveth so mightily these affections? What hath the shaking or artificiall crispling [*sic*] of the ayre (which is in effect the substance of musicke) to doe with rousing up choller, afflicting with melancholy, jubilating the heart with pleasure, elevating the soule with devotion, alluring to lust ... ?[34]

Tentatively, he offers four possible reasons: the first, following Ficino and the neoplatonists, suggests 'a certaine sympathie, correspondence, or proportion betwixt our soules and musick'. The second notes that some 'assigne and ascribe [it] to Gods general providence, who when these sounds affect the eare, produceth a certaine spiritual quality in the soule' (a notion reflected in many of the defences of music against Puritan attack). His third suggestion is that the musical disturbance of the air

> passeth thorow the eares, and by them unto the heart, and there beateth and tickleth it in such sort, as it is moved with semblable passions ... musick in those cels plaieth with the vital and animate spirits, the only instruments and spurs of the passions.

This is the idea that Viola picks up when praising the music of 'Come away, death', that it 'gives a very echo to the seat / Where love is throned' (*TN*, 2.4.21–2).

His final explanation, his 'last and best', however, is one which decisively leaves behind the arguments by analogy, divine providence, or physiology, to suggest a much more relativist position:

> as all other senses have an admirable multiplicity of objects which delight them, so hath the eare: and as it is impossible to expound the variety of delights, or disgusts, which we perceive by them, and receive in them ... so in musicke, divers consorts stirre up in the heart, divers sorts of joyes, and divers sorts of sadness or paine: the which as men are affected, may be diversely applyed: Let a good and a godly man heare musicke, and he will lift up his heart to heaven: let a bad man heare the same, and hee will convert it to lust ... True it is, that one kinde of musicke may be more apt to one passion then another ... Wherefore the naturall disposition of a man, his custome or exercise, his vertue or vice, for most part at these sounds diversificate passions: for I cannot imagine, that if a man never had heard a Trumpet or a Drum in his life, that he would at the first hearing bee moved to warres.[35]

This final argument that it is the nature of the hearer, not the nature of the music, which is fundamental to the differentiation of music's effects is strongly articulated. Wright leaves it to the reader to choose between his alternatives, but his conspectus conveniently enables a fuller gloss of Lorenzo's speech.

In its first part, Lorenzo's suggestion that celestial harmony is 'in immortal souls' would accord with Wright's first explanation, and the analogy between *musica mundana* and *musica humana* that we have already discussed. Hooker, similarly, if tentatively, noted that music's force and effects were such, 'even in that verie parte of man which is most divine, that some have bene thereby induced to thinke that the soule itselfe by nature is, or hath in it harmonie'.[36] But in the second part of the speech, Lorenzo deploys a physiological account of music's power. Jessica is moved by music, he tells her, because her 'spirits' are attentive. 'Spirit' is a word which sustained many meanings in the period, and is notoriously elusive of definition; but in this context, and in its plural form, it refers primarily to the three 'spirits' which, in Galenic physiology, mediated between the bodily humours and the reason or soul. As Burton explains:

> Spirit is a most subtle vapour, which is expressed from the blood, and the instrument of the soul, to perform all his actions ... Of these spirits there be three kinds, according to the three principal parts, brain, heart, liver; natural, vital, animal. The natural are begotten in the liver, and thence dispersed through the veins, to perform those natural actions. The vital spirits are made in the heart of the natural, which by the arteries are transported to all the other parts ... The animal spirits, formed of the vital, brought up to the brain, and diffused by the nerves to the subordinate members, give sense and motion to them all.[37]

The spirits were also, crucially in this context, the conduits which took sense impressions to the brain, where they were processed in the imagination. It is because of this mediating function that music can be said to 'pierce', as Lorenzo suggests it will; air moved by music penetrates the ear, and thence, through the spirits, the brain, and heart.[38] (It is the same physiological understanding which underlies the idea that love arises as a consequence of a 'piercing' through the eye by the beauty of the loved object.) Music then, as Wright suggests, animates the spirits, and through them affects both the higher faculties of the mind and soul and also the four humours whose balance was essential to bodily and mental harmony.

It is important here to note that Lorenzo's mention of the spirits comes in answer to Jessica's statement: 'I am never merry when I hear sweet music' (5.1.69). This is a line which has been taken, especially in some recent productions, to hint at Jessica's unhappiness or uncertainty in her marriage to Lorenzo.[39] But such a reading misconstrues – or at least perhaps reads too naturalistically – what she is saying. Lorenzo had earlier anticipated 'touches of sweet harmony', and he asks the musicians for a 'hymn' to Diana. The music, therefore, is solemn, 'still' music, and Jessica is responding appropriately to its affect. To feel 'merry' would be the proper response to something like a lively dance-tune, rather than to the 'sweet' music she actually hears. Part of the dramatic point of the opening of Act 5 is its rapid transitions of mood, which are here underlined.

Music can confirm a state of mind or modify it. But since, in Renaissance physiology, the mind and body were interconnected, music could be employed as a cure for disease, and especially for diseases of the mind. Timothy Bright, for example, specifies how music might cure melancholy when he writes:

> So not onely cheerfull musicke in a generalitie, but such of that kinde as most rejoyseth, is to be sounded in melancholicke eares ... That contrarilie, which is solemne, and still: as dumpes, and fancies and sett musicke, are hurtfull in this case, and serve rather for a disordered rage, and intemperate mirth, to reclaime with mediocritie, then to allure the spirits, to stirre the bloud, and to attenuate the humours, which is (if the harmonie be wisely applied) effectuallie wrought by musicke.[40]

The concept is one of rebalancing the humours, to arrive at the 'mediocrity' or temperance which is the state of health. It is the application of the appropriate kind of music that enables it to function in a context of healing. How often physicians actually employed musical therapy in their medical practice in the sixteenth century is open to debate, but its efficacy in harmonizing the disordered mind is a staple image in both poetry and drama.[41]

'Melancholy' is a general term covering a number of different mental ailments; but included in its compass was the specific disease of love melancholy, for which music was thought to be a particularly suitable remedy. Music's capacity to 'pierce' the mind, and to raise affections, meant that it could be employed as a means of inspiring love in another (the serenades of Proteus to Sylvia, in *Two Gentlemen of Verona*, and Cloten to Innogen[42] in *Cymbeline*, are inspired by this hope, and will both be discussed more fully later). Equally, the 'moody food of us that trade in love' as Cleopatra calls it (*AC*, 2.5.1–2) could be applied to quieten the disordered mind of the unrequited lover. As Linda Austern observes: 'In matters of lovesickness, music was thus understood to be the flame to light the fire or to ignite the hope of reciprocal passion, as well as the cooling draught of purgation and distraction.'[43] At the opening of *Twelfth Night* Orsino seems to be rather unsure which of these effects he wishes to command:

> If music be the food of love, play on,
> Give me excess of it, that surfeiting,
> The appetite may sicken, and so die. (1.1.1–3)

The failure of the remedy – as he commands the music to stop – might suggest both that his spirits are insufficiently attentive, and that he has not respected Bright's prescription that the harmony be wisely applied. Rather than soliciting the 'dying fall' of a doleful air, he should perhaps – if he really wanted to escape his enslavement to love – have called for something much more lively.[44] Music's effects on the lover, however, are not entirely predictable; as Burton notes, it might ease his melancholy, but equally it might be 'most pernitious, as a spurre to a free horse, will make him runne himselfe blind, or break his winde ... for musicke enchants, as *Menander* holdes, it will make such melancholy persons mad'.[45] Nonetheless, the similarity of music and love – both of which work upon the passions by mysterious means, and both of which stimulate the spirits and therefore are capable of raising the mind to divine ecstasy or of abasing it to bestial disorder – will be a significant theme for later consideration.

Before leaving the question of 'spirits', it is appropriate briefly to consider the extension of Platonic and Plotinian notions in the work of Marsilio Ficino, who 'proffered an essentially new explanation for the affective powers of music which not only took into account the similarity between air moved by music and the motion of the human spirit, but also linked these to the *spiritus mundi* which served as a channel of influence between the heavenly bodies and the sublunary world'.[46] Ficino argued that 'between the tangible and partly transient body of the world and its very soul, whose nature is very far from its body, there exists everywhere a spirit, just as there is between the soul and body in us'; and he suggests that humankind is 'permitted to absorb [the world-] spirit. This is absorbed by man in particular through his own spirit which is by its own nature similar to it, especially if it is made more akin to it by art'.[47] Music, above all, was the art which put the human spirits in contact with the world-spirit, and in Ficino's magical thinking this made it theoretically possible to use actual performed music to summon the celestial influences of the planets. It is impossible to convey in brief compass the complexity of Ficino's abstruse meditations; what is significant is the way in which they represent perhaps the most extreme attempt to bring together the three realms of Boethius's musical worlds, so that the analogical relationship of cosmos and human body could be mediated and exploited through *musica instrumentalis*. It must be extremely doubtful whether Shakespeare knew Ficino at first-hand – in asking the musicians to 'wake Diana with a hymn' Lorenzo was not requiring them to perform a Ficinian incantation – but Ficino's ideas were filtered and transmitted through a number of sources, so that, in attenuated form, they figured as part of the network of ideas about music on which Shakespeare drew.

In his account of music's effects in the second part of Lorenzo's speech, however, as in his description of the harmony of the spheres, Shakespeare does not take a straightforwardly conventional line. Having commended Jessica for her sensitivity to musical mood, Lorenzo continues, not by invoking examples of music's power over human spirits – and there were plenty of conventional examples he could have chosen – but by turning exclusively to equally familiar examples of music's power over animal and inanimate nature.[48] Just as the first part of his speech ended on the negative fact that we cannot hear the harmony of the spheres, the second is designed less to celebrate music's effects than to point up the limits of its command over any fundamentally inharmonious soul. In this respect the speech seems to anticipate the meditation on the limits of the powers of art, including music, in *The Tempest*, where, in 2.1, Antonio and Sebastian's irreducible villainy is symbolized by their total inability to hear the sounds of Prospero and Ariel's music. It would seem that, in certain respects at least, Shakespeare might have endorsed the last of Wright's explanations – that the nature of music's effects is ultimately dictated by the individual who listens, rather than by something instinct within the music itself. Indeed, as this scene proceeds beyond Lorenzo's formal praise of music there is a further undercutting of too mystical or magical a view of music's power, as the returning Portia, hearing the music from the house, comments:

> The crow doth sing as sweetly as the lark
> When neither is attended; and I think
> The nightingale if she should sing by day
> When every goose is cackling, would be thought
> No better a musician than the wren!
> How many things by season, season'd are
> To their right praise, and true perfection! (5.1.102–108)

This provisional stance, and its questioning of the solidity of the philosophical concepts Lorenzo so eloquently utters, is characteristically Shakespearean.

There were many other artists in the period, however, who took the classical narratives of music's effects entirely seriously, and they must now be considered in order to provide a full sense of the contexts within which Shakespeare offered, and his audience might interpret, musical events. A classically inspired humanism led musicians and musical theorists, especially in France and Italy, to wonder why it was that the music of their own time failed to reproduce the startling transformations of mood that were reported in the oft-repeated classical myths. In both countries this perception fuelled attacks on current musical styles, and prompted efforts to recreate what they imagined was a version of the music of the Greeks and Romans.

Vincenzo Galilei (father of the astronomer), for example, ridiculed the imitation of individual words in madrigalian style, concluding:

> And yet they wonder that the music of their times produces none of the notable effects that ancient music produced, when, quite the other way, they would have more cause for amazement if it were to produce any of them, seeing that their music is so remote from the ancient music and so unlike it as actually to be its contrary and its mortal enemy ... and seeing that it has no means enabling it even to think of producing such effects, let alone to obtain them. For its sole aim is to delight the ear, while that of ancient music is to induce in another the same passion that one feels oneself.[49]

The problem, of course, was to identify precisely what qualities in ancient music had enabled these effects. Scholars considered arcane matters of scales and tuning, and turned back to the idea of the moral characters of the modes as defined by Plato and his successors, but, as Frances Yates observes: 'In these attempts of which there were no examples and the theory of which it was not possible to reconstruct with certainty – even on this essential question of the modes – the humanist musicians were on shifting and unstable grounds.'[50]

But on one thing the humanists of France and Italy were agreed – that it was necessary to revise the relationship between words and music. They felt that the music of the more recent past had privileged musical form over the words, and that classical effects would only be possible if the balance of power was reversed, so that the unstable signifiers of musical language could be commanded and directed by the rational sense of the words. Different routes were taken to achieve this control. In France, in Baïf's *Académie de poésie et de musique*, established by Charles IX in 1570, the effort focused first on recreating in poetry the metres of classical verse, and then in setting these words to rhythms that exactly imitated their metres (a style called *musique mesurée à l'antique*). These settings were usually in four vocal parts, where every part followed the same rhythm, enunciating the words at the same time, and ensuring therefore that they would be heard – an effect quite different from the polyphony of the madrigal, where overlapping musical lines frequently make it difficult to distinguish the text. They wished to re-establish a poetry and music in which 'number' and 'measure' were central, thus embodying in musical composition the numerical harmonies of *musica mundana*.

In Italy, in the Camerata of Giovanni de' Bardi, a rather more informal group established in Florence also in the 1570s, a similar effort was being made through rather different means. A letter written by Bardi's son Pietro in 1634 to the antiquarian Doni, looking back at his father's academy, described its ambitions:

> besides restoring ancient music insofar as so obscure a subject permitted, one of the chief aims of the academy was to improve modern music and to raise it in some degree from the wretched state to which it had been reduced, chiefly by the Goths, after the loss of

the ancient music and the other liberal arts and sciences. Thus he [Galilei] was the first to let us hear singing in *stilo rappresentativo*.[51]

As the name for this new music suggests, the emphasis was upon the forcible representation of the emotions of the words in solo song, or monody, accompanied by a relatively slow-moving bass line. In the sternest application of these theories the madrigalian habit of illustrating individual words was rejected absolutely; instead 'the business of making the music representational is left almost entirely to the executant, who is to give a vivid and dramatic impersonation of someone influenced by the passion or ethos with which it is desired to affect the listener'.[52]

Underlying these developments was a long-standing belief that music could directly imitate feeling and emotion. Ficino wrote that 'song is a most powerful imitator of all things. It imitates the intentions and passions of the soul as well as words'.[53] Hooker articulates the same idea in accounting for music's force:

The reason hereof is an admirable facilitie which musique hath to expresse and represent to the minde more inwardlie then any other sensible meane the verie standinge risinge and fallinge, the verie steppes and inflections everie way, the turnes and varieties of all passions wherunto the minde is subject: yea so to imitate them that whether it resemble unto us the same state wherein our mindes alreadie are or a cleane contrarie, wee are not more contentedlie by the one confirmed then changed and led away by thother.[54]

In fact the pure application of neoclassical theory, whether in the measured songs of the French or the recitative of the Italians, had but a brief life; composers were not about to surrender the musical expressiveness of polyphony, nor the representation of single words or ideas through harmonic or melodic illustration.[55] Nonetheless, the self-conscious classicism of humanist scholars was an important ingredient in the transformation of musical styles in the late sixteenth century.

This brief and necessarily very over-simplified sketch of neoclassical humanism in practical music during the sixteenth century may seem to be taking us some considerable way from the subject of music in

Shakespeare. After all, and not for the last time, continental theory was slow to arrive in England, and never in the period, it would seem, was it taken up with the same purist and scholarly zeal. Though there had been a brief vogue for attempting to recreate classical quantitative metres in English poetry,[56] only Byrd in two settings, and Thomas Campion – who was influenced directly by the experiments of the French Académie – essayed a musical translation of the poetic metre. Declamatory song, deriving from Italian practice, was only beginning to have much impact in England at the very end of Shakespeare's career, and then principally in the world of the court masque rather than the popular theatre (though some of Robert Johnson's theatrical songs, including 'Care-charming sleep' from Beaumont and Fletcher's *Valentinian* (c. 1614), and 'Oh, let us howl' from Webster's *Duchess of Malfi* (c. 1613) are powerful theatrical examples of expressive declamatory style). The principal importance of humanist thinking in the context of this book is, however, the way it is symptomatic of a significant cultural transformation in the underlying premises for the explanation of music's power.

The emphasis on recreating the effects of ancient music shifts the focus from the cosmic harmony which human music dimly reflects, towards music as a species of rhetoric, a kind of persuasion. It is notable, for example, that when Henry Peacham writes of music in *The Complete Gentleman* he notes the 'sweet variety that the theoric of music exerciseth the mind withal' yet does not even allude to the music of the spheres or the cosmic harmony so central to earlier musical theory. Like Lorenzo, he is contemptuous of those who are 'of such disproportioned spirits that they avoid [Music's] company', averring that such men 'are by nature very ill-disposed and of such a brutish stupidity that scarce anything else that is good and favourable to virtue is to be found in them'. His knowledgeable survey of the contemporary musical scene, however, concludes with the assertion 'in my opinion, no rhetoric more persuadeth or hath greater power over the mind. Nay, hath not music her figures, the same which rhetoric? What is a revert but her antistrophe? her reports but sweet anaphoras? her counterchange of points, antimetaboles? her passionate airs but prosopopoeias?'[57] As Brian Vickers points out,[58] the theorists whom Peacham is following here (he had received some musical training in Italy) were not original in identifying music's command over the passions as fundamentally rhetorical; they drew on a tradition extending back to Quintilian and beyond, and a terminology deployed throughout the sixteenth century. But the experiments in Paris and Florence with new musical styles, and their focus upon the effects of music, gave renewed emphasis to the old parallel; and its centrality to the evolving understanding of music's power usefully raises issues that are central to the exploration of the use of music in Shakespeare's drama.

In the first place – and obviously enough – to concentrate on music's effects requires a focus upon its relationship to an audience. The membership of Baïf's academy was made up of poets, musicians, and other practitioners of the liberal arts, on the one hand, and 'Auditeurs' on the other. (Indeed it was these listeners who were expected to provide the funds to enable the academy to function.) Its statutes required the regular performance of public concerts (and enforced on its audience properly attentive behaviour, with no talking during the music). Among its most significant contributions to the court life of France was the participation of its members in the composition of fêtes and masquerades, of which the *Balet comique de la reyne* of 1581 is the most fully recorded and best known, for it was precisely in such a public forum that the theoretical revival of classical musical effects could be put to the test. The Florentine, Giovanni de' Bardi, and members of his academy, were similarly involved in a number of court celebrations, and he supervised the most elaborate of all the *intermedi*, those of 1589 honouring the marriage of Ferdinando de' Medici and Christine of Lorraine. Music had, of course, always been part of State celebration, but what was new was the self-conscious application of neoplatonic programmes to the devices, and the centrality of music not merely as accompaniment of, but as agent in, and subject of, the fictions of these entertainments. The plot of the *Balet comique* concerned 'the establishment of the rule of reason, harmony, and of order in the soul, and the taming of the beasts of the passions', and built to a climax:

> when the eye and the ear together might drink in the whole of the
> musical philosophy. The eye saw the moral and intellectual virtues
> ... The ear heard the chorus of poetry sung to the *musique mesurée*,

and the verses spoke of the world music of the elemental laws of Nature combined with the human music which, amidst the constant flux, strife, and tension to which man is subject through his association with the natural world yet strikes another, an eternal note.[59]

The six 1589 *intermedi* 'were unified by the theme of the power of music to influence both the human soul and the gods ... . Three of the series, nos. 1, 4, and 5, illustrated aspects of *musica mundana*, ... while the other three represented *musica humana*.'[60] Both French and Italian celebrations were crucial inspirations for the transformation of English court entertainment in the hands of Ben Jonson, Inigo Jones, Thomas Campion, George Chapman, and their successors in the series of masques performed at the Stuart court from 1604 onwards.

In the Stuart masque, as in other European festivals, neoplatonic concepts were central to the uniting of music, design and words. The first of the Florentine *intermedi* depicted the Harmony of the Spheres, and included the Platonic figure of Necessity, together with the eight sirens who controlled the celestial spheres.[61] In Jonson's *Masque of Beauty* (1608) the central device was a Throne of Beauty.

> This *Throne*, (as the whole *Iland* mov'd forward, on the water,) had a circular motion of it owne, imitating that which wee call *Motum mundi* ['movement of the world'], from the *East* to the *West* ... The steps, whereon the *Cupids* sate, had a motion contrary, with *Analogy ad motum planetarum* ['to the movement of the planets'], from the *West* to the *East*; both which turned with their severall lights. And with these three varied *Motions* at once, the whole *Scene* shot it selfe to the land.[62]

Presiding over this physical imitation of the movements of the heavens was the figure of Harmonia, summing up the correspondences between physical beauty, celestial harmony, and music. Three years earlier, the central scenic device of *Hymenaei* was a huge globe, described as a 'Microcosm', on which the countries of the world were depicted. This globe turned, and revealed within itself the eight masquers who represented the

Humours and Affections, presided over by Reason. This device dramatically figured the correspondence of the human body and the world. The initial threat the disordered masquers offered to the nuptial rites was dissipated by the 'sacred concords' of the music which surrounded the subsequent entrance of Juno, and harmony was restored in the dances which followed. In masques such as these, then, cosmic harmony and the relationships between the heavenly and the human were rendered in visual images, and the power of music to command disorderly faculties was dramatically enacted.

It is important to note that in the court masque dance itself was accorded many of the powers and properties that were associated with music. The patterns of dance steps were perceived as analogous to the cosmic dance of the heavens, as John Davies put it:

> *Dauncing* ... then began to be,
> When the first seedes whereof the world did spring,
> The Fire, Ayre, Earth, and Water did agree,
> By Loves perswasion, Natures mighty King,
> To leave their first disordred combating;
>> And in a daunce such measure to observe,
>> As all the world their motion should preserve.[63]

Thomas Elyot recommended dancing in the same way that he commended musical instruction, as honest recreation but, more important, as figuring social harmony, as in his most frequently quoted assertion that 'in every daunse, of a moste auncient custome, there daunseth together a man and a woman, holding eche other by the hande or the arme, whiche betokeneth concorde'.[64] He goes on to argue that dance may figure the virtue of prudence, and concludes that dance is 'as well a necessary studie as a noble and vertuouse pastyme'.[65]

For Elyot, the instruction that dance can offer is one which affects the beholder as well as the dancer, as he wrote:

> Wherfore all they that have their courage stered [*steered*] towarde
> very honour or perfecte nobilitie, let them approche to this passe
> tyme, and either them selfes prepare them to daunse, or els at the

leste way beholde with watching eien other that can daunse truely, kepynge juste measure and tyme.[66]

It is precisely upon this foundation that masque writers claimed that
dances, as spectacles of order and harmony, functioned to instruct and
move the audience. In Jonson's *Pleasure Reconciled to Virtue* (1618) the
character of Daedalus introduced the 'curious knots' of the dances with
the words:

> Then, as all actions of mankind
> > are but a Laborinth, or maze,
> > so let your Daunces be entwin'd
> > yet not perplex men, unto gaze;
> But measur'd, and so numerous too,
> > as men may read each act you doo.
> And when they see the Graces meet,
> > admire the wisdom of your feet.
> For Dauncing is an exercise
> > not only shews the movers wit
> but maketh the beholder wise,
> > As he hath powre to rise to it.[67]

The last three lines are crucial in declaring Jonson's belief that the harmonies of music and dance could directly affect the beholders – even if
they also (and characteristically) suggest that not all the audience have
the capacity fully to understand what they see and hear. Nonetheless, in
this vision the power of music and dance is inherent within them, not con-
ferred upon them by the auditor. And this is the underpinning of the claim
that when Claude LeJeune's music for the celebrations of the marriage of
the Duc de Joyeuse in 1581 was rehearsed at a private concert before the
event, it

> caused a gentleman who was present to put his hand to his arms,
> loudly swearing the while that he could not refrain himself from
> fighting someone, and that when they began to sing another air in
> the Sub-Phrygian mode he grew tranquil as before.[68]

One might well doubt whether this story has any substance, so close is it to the legend of Timotheus and Alexander, but it cannot be denied that the court entertainments of Europe were founded on the belief that the harmony of music and dance, united with spectacle, and based, as Jonson puts it, on 'solid learnings', were capable of affecting the minds and hearts of those who watched them.[69]

The preoccupation with these effects in the context of courtly entertainment has a further important consequence, since the deployment of music and spectacle was firmly tied to the good ordering of the state. The Letters Patent setting up Baïf's academy note that it is

> the opinion of many great personages, both ancient legislators and philosophers ... that it is of great importance for the morals of the citizens of a town that the music current and used in the country should be retained under certain laws, for the minds of most men are formed and their behaviour influenced by its character, so that where music is disordered, their morals are also depraved, and where it is well ordered, there men are well disciplined morally.

It is of no little significance that the academy was established by the sovereign, Charles IX, who 'is anxious to encourage the revival of "ancient" poetry and music because he desires to see in his kingdom the good moral effects which should flow from such a revival'.[70]

The analogy of the cosmos and the State here takes on a rather more active force than in Ulysses' speech discussed earlier. Music becomes not merely an image of the hierarchically ordered State, but the persuasive agent which will sustain it. In all the European entertainments stage images were devised in significant part to celebrate the ruler under whose aegis they were composed, and in whose praise they were offered. One frequently therefore finds the analogical correspondence focused specifically on the ruler as a kind of divine musician. Three examples will serve for many that could be invoked. Campion's *The Lords' Masque* (1613) is built upon a very explicit neoplatonic programme, of the four 'furies',[71] and includes the figure of Orpheus, who is called upon to curb the excesses of the frantics who make up the antimasque. They first enter to 'a strange music', and then 'by vertue of a new change in the musicke' fall 'into a madde measure', finally to be calmed by 'a very solemne ayre'. This exhibition of music's effects is entirely in line with those that the humanists wished to recreate. But before he begins, Orpheus says:

> *Jove* into our musick will inspire
> The power of passion, that their thoughts shall bend
> To any forme or motion we intend.[72]

In this masque Jove is a figure for James, and so Orpheus explicitly attributes the power of his music to the power of the monarch who commands him. In Jonson's *Pan's Anniversary* the audience is informed that the figure of James/Pan 'From his loud Musicke, all your manners wraught, / And made your Common-wealth a harmonie'.[73] Even more remarkably, the climax of *The Irish Masque* (1614) comes as the Irish bard is summoned to view the monarch sitting in the audience, and is told:

> This is that IAMES of which long since thou sung'st
> Should end our countreyes most unnaturall broyles;
> And if her ear, then deafned with the drum,
> Would stoupe but to the musique of his peace,
> She need not with the spheares change harmony.[74]

Here the monarch's music is equivalent to, or even more powerful than, the harmony of the spheres themselves.[75] European court entertainments were directly engaged in yoking traditional understanding of musical harmony to the defence and promulgation of increasingly absolutist monarchy.

Since Shakespeare wrote no court entertainments, it might seem that these elite and learned celebrations have little direct relevance to his plays. The point, however, is precisely that the masque's dramatic vocabulary, and its intimate association with the machinery of the state, provided an image that playwrights could employ as a kind of synecdoche or shorthand to conjure up the world of the court, and one which could be ironically turned back upon it. Middleton, for example, ends both *The Revenger's Tragedy* and *Women Beware Women* with masques that are the cover for chaotic scenes of blood-letting, where 'Destruction plays her triumph, and great mischiefs / Mask in expected pleasures'.[76] Shakespeare deploys the masque as an image of and for the court-world rather less extremely, but with considerable subtlety, throughout his career, from *Love's Labour's Lost* to the late romances. His most developed imitation of the genre occurs in the fourth act of *The Tempest*, where it contributes significantly to the play's testing of the conventional correspondence of the power of the monarch and the power of music. Shakespeare in this play exploits perhaps the most important single consequence of the rhetorical characterization of music's power to command human behaviour: that it opens the exercise of musical influence to the same radical uncertainty that always hovers about the use of rhetoric – it matters who is using it, and to what ends. Music is no longer the impersonal echo of a divine order, nor a repertory of modes whose effects are predictable because they are a consequence of qualities inherent in their musical character, but a mobile, unpredictable agent, vulnerable in its effects not only, as both Lorenzo and Portia recognize, to the nature of the listener, but also to the purposes of the person who commands or performs it.

It is not only the changing direction of music theory which accounts for its instability as a signifier in dramatic contexts. As we have seen, throughout history even the most celebratory invocations of music's harmonizing power have been haunted by the recognition that mere human music is capable of soliciting less desirable emotional responses. In the court masque this dangerous potential is articulated in the disordered figures of the antimasque, often accompanied with 'wild' music. There it is invoked in order that it can be contained, policed, and redirected by the celestial order of the masque itself. In the public playhouse such overt control is absent, and it was fear of the provocation music might supply to disorderly feeling that contributed significantly to anti-theatrical propaganda. Indeed, even an ardent defender of the art, the author of *The Praise of Musicke*, confessed that 'I dare not speake of dauncing or theatrall spectacles, least I pull whole swarmes of enemies upon me'.[77]

If the capacity of Orpheus's music to charm brute creation is a symbol of its effective force, it is easily possible to turn the image on its head, and fear the brutishness of the human behaviour which music can also inspire. The sirens whom Plato fixes upon the whirling spheres have their malign double in the half-women, half-birds whose seductive song led sailors onto

FIGURE 4   The three sirens play and sing to lure the ship onto the rocks. Behind them lurk the harpies who prey on their victims. Cartari, *Le Imagine dei Dei degli Antichi* (1608 edition, p. 231)

the rocks (Figure 4). Plato's praise of the Dorian and Phrygian modes is framed by the rejection of Lydian, Ionian, and others which prompt to 'drunkenness, softness or idleness'.[78] The dangerous doubleness of music which Plato attempts to regulate is observed by the Duke in *Measure for Measure*: 'music oft hath such a charm / To make bad good, and good provoke to harm' (4.1.14–15).[79] These associations of music with idleness, lust, and effeminacy rendered problematic any easy mapping of *musica instrumentalis* on to *musica mundana*.

St John Chrysostom follows his earlier-quoted account of music's place in everyday human existence with stern injunctions about the kind of music that might be permitted in religious service. This controversy was, throughout the sixteenth century, one of the fiercest arenas of debate about music and its effects. Many reformers, if they were prepared to allow music any place at all in worship, confined it to the simplest unison singing of the psalms, and saw Elizabeth's refusal to banish anthems and choral singing as a sign of the imperfection of the Anglican reformation. Hooker's comments on music are part of a defence of the Elizabethan settlement, and the author of *The Praise of Musick* devotes by far the longest part of his treatise to the defence of music in church services.[80] This debate does not figure directly in Shakespeare's plays, but the terms in which it was conducted are of considerable significance as indications of the ways in which 'good' music was divided from 'bad'. Curiously, the Puritan reformers objected to the traditional music of the church on grounds very similar to the objections raised by the humanists – that elaborate polyphony obscured the words, substituting the sensuous allure of sound for the rational delight of verbal meaning. William Prynne, for example, argued:

> Modest and chaste harmonies are to be admitted by removing as far as may be all soft effeminate music from our strong and valiant cogitation, which using a dishonest art of warbling the voice, do lead to a delicate and slothful kind of life. Therefore, chromatical harmonies are to be left to impudent malapertness, to whorish music crowned with flowers.[81]

In characterizing elaborate singing as 'effeminate', Prynne echoed the way in which the opposition between masculine strength and feminine weakness lay at the centre of Plato's prescription of suitable and unsuitable modes, and this gendered distinction permeates early modern writing about music.

Lodowick Lloyd, for example, writes that:

> Mars claymeth Musicke in the fielde, and Venus occupieth Musicke in chambers. That kind of gentle and soft Musick, the *Egyptians*

forbade the youth to be taught therein, least from men, they would become againe women.[82]

On this theme many Puritan writers descanted throughout the sixteenth and seventeenth centuries. Gosson, attacking music in the theatre, drew on classical authority, observing that:

Plutarch complayneth that ignorant men, not knowing the majestie of auncient musike, abuse both the eares of the people, and the arte it selfe, with bringing sweet comfortes in Theaters, which rather effeminate the minde as prickes unto vice, then procure amendement of maners as spurres to virtue.[83]

Philip Stubbes similarly fulminated against the effect of music on both women and men, writing: 'And if you would have your daughter whoorish, bawdie, and uncleane, and a filthie speaker, and such like, bring her up in musicke and dauncing, and my life for yours, you have wun the goale', and topping it with:

If you wold have your sonne softe, womanish, uncleane, smoth mouthed, affected to bawdrie, scurrilitie, filthie rimes, and unsemely talking, brifly, if you wold have him, as it weare, transnatured into a woman, or worse, and inclyned to all kinds of whordome and abhomination, set him to dauncing school, and to learn musicke, and than shall you not faile of your purpose.[84]

The opposition between the manly world of war and the effeminized world of the court is not infrequently characterized in the drama as an opposition of musics. Benedick comments ironically on Claudio: 'I have known when there was no music with him but the drum and the fife, and now had he rather hear the tabor and the pipe' (*MA*, 2.3.13–15). Melantius, in Beaumont and Fletcher's *The Maid's Tragedy*, distances himself from the courtly world of masques with the words:

These soft and silken wars are not for me:
The music must be shrill and all confused
That stirs my blood, and then I dance with arms.[85]

The characterization of music as an effeminizing art has its roots in the way in which the attractions of feminine beauty and of music could readily be mapped one onto the other. As Linda Austern has persuasively argued, its basis lay in the fact that: 'like the love of a woman, the love of harmony and rhythm frequently led not to spiritual fulfillment but to the deceptive delights of the sensual world'.[86] The close correlation of the force of love to affect the passions and bypass rational control with music's direct effect on the spirits, and the projection of both on to the stimulus and lure of female beauty, is of considerable significance in the deployment of music in the plays.

The Praise of Musicke confronted the issue directly:

> those which are glad to take any occasion to speak against musicke, will ... affirme that it maketh men effeminate, and too much subject unto pleasure. But whom, I praie you, doth it make effeminate? Surely none but such as without it would bee wanton: ... the same musicke which mollifieth some men, moveth some other nothing at all: so that the fault is not in musicke, which of it selfe is good: but in the corrupt nature, and evill disposition of light persons, which of themselves are prone to wantonnes.[87]

His rebuttal of the charge turns, as did Thomas Wright's final account of music's power, on the centrality of the listener's moral qualities to music's effect. Thus, from a different direction, we have ended at the point that concludes Lorenzo's speech. In returning for the last time to the text which opened this chapter, it may be recognized that all too often critical commentary on it as an invocation of the divine power of music occludes the ways in which it also reflects some of the tensions that inhere in the commonplaces it so eloquently articulates.

The problematic relationship between speculative and practical music is actually embodied in the abrupt transition in Lorenzo's speech between the music of the spheres, and the effects of music on human ears. Cornelius Agrippa ridiculed those who attempted to link the two:

> The Musicians take occasion to extol themselves far above the Rhetoricians, for that their Art has a greater power to move the

passions and affections: and to such height of madness they are carry'd as to *affirm* that the Heavens themselves do sing; not that they were ever heard to do so, but only as their drunken Dreams and Imaginations prompt them to believe.[88]

Lorenzo does not go as far as this, though he actually offers no link between the two parts of his speech and the two musics he invokes – except the mournful recognition that we cannot hear one, and may not respond to the other.

It is possible, then, to see this speech as actually marking the retreat of *musica mundana* into metaphor; still potent, but increasingly detached from the workings of music in the real human world. Stephen Gosson directed his readers:

If you will bee good scholers, and profite well in the arte of musike, shut your fidels in their cases and looke uppe to Heaven: the order of the spheres, the unfallible motion of the planets, the juste course of the yeere, the varietie of the seasons, the concorde of the elementes and their qualities, fyre, water, ayre, earth, heate, colde, moisture and drought concurring togeather to the constitution of earthly bodies, and sustenaunce of every creature. The politike lawes in wel governed common wealthes that treade downe the proude and upholde the meeke; the love of the kinge and his subjectes, the father and his chylde ... are excellent maisters to shew you that this is right musicke, this perfecte harmony.[89]

The familiar analogies are paraded, but as rhetorical weapons to diminish and belabour the music and musicians of his own time.

Shakespeare's preoccupation, however, is precisely with the diversity and complexity of performed music's effects in the human narratives he constructs in his plays. It is the possibility of testing the speculative against the practical, the ideal against the humanly actual, that continuously excites him. In properly refusing Gosson's invitation to turn one's attention only to celestial harmonies, the dramatist focuses upon the dynamic relationship of listener and performer. And it is to the performers and listeners in Shakespeare's playhouses that we now turn.

Chapter Two

MUSIC IN PRACTICE

PETER Musicians, O musicians, 'Heart's ease', 'Heart's ease'! O, and
    you will have me live, play 'Heart's ease'.
1 MUSICIAN Why 'Heart's ease'?
PETER O musicians, because my heart itself plays 'My heart is full'.
    O play me some merry dump to comfort me.
1 MUSICIAN Not a dump, we! 'Tis no time to play now.
PETER You will not then?
1 MUSICIAN No.
PETER I will then give it you soundly.
1 MUSICIAN What will you give us?
PETER No money, on my faith, but the gleek! I will give you the
    minstrel. (*RJ*, 4.5.100–112)

In this passage from *Romeo and Juliet* the three musicians summoned
to perform at the anticipated wedding of Juliet and Paris pack up their
instruments and prepare to go after Juliet's death is revealed. They
exchange some comic banter with the Capulet's serving-man, Peter (probably played at the first performances by the company's clown, Will Kemp),
and emerge from the anonymity which shrouds most Shakespearean
instrumentalists as Simon Catling, Hugh Rebec, and James Soundpost,
soubriquets obviously alluding to their trade – suggesting that they were
players of stringed instruments (see Figure 5). Their appearance raises
some of the questions central to this chapter. We want to know how typical
they are of the instrumental ensembles that Shakespeare's audience might
have encountered in the world outside the theatre. We need to ask whether

FIGURE 5 A duet team playing outside a tavern, in a woodcut used in a number of English seventeenth-century broadside ballads.

the actors who appear and speak are those who played off-stage in the previous scene (and accompanied the dances in 1.4). The tunes Peter asks for are popular dances, and again, one wants to know how characteristic a repertoire this might be. To these questions we will return.

The nature of the band and their repertory might tell us something of the Capulets who hire them, and there are certainly questions to ask about the curious dramatic effect of this comic scene coming hard upon the tragic discovery. But what makes this moment particularly useful as a starting-point for consideration of the kinds of public music-making in Shakespeare's society is Peter's final comment in this extract. The 'gleek', or gibe, he threatens is to insult them by calling them 'minstrel'. The question why this label might be construed as a demeaning one opens up the larger issue of the place of musicians in early modern England.

'Minstrel' was originally the term used without disapprobation to describe any wandering musician, who might also be an actor, acrobat, or juggler; and it was, indeed, the nomenclature deployed in court contexts for servants retained by the Crown,[1] but it had by the end of the sixteenth century become contaminated by its association with vagabondage and vagrancy. The masterless man was particularly an object of concern in the period, and legislation in 1572, tightened up further in 1597, placed severe curbs on unattached travellers of all kinds, with the threat of whipping, branding, and even the death penalty for persistent offenders.[2] The insult Peter threatens, therefore, is one aimed as much at the social status of the three-man band as it is addressed to their musical competence.[3]

A revealing gloss on the attitudes that underlie Peter's gibe is offered in the autobiography of the composer Thomas Whythorne (1528–86). He notes that 'Ever since that music came to any perfection and was accounted one of the seven liberal sciences ... there have been degrees thereof, as there be of divines, lawyers and physicians.' At the top of his hierarchy he places composers, and then continues:

> Then is there organists in churches; then be there teachers of music, and also to sing pricksong [*i.e. to sing from musical notation*] and to sound on musical instruments, which be named schoolmasters; then there be singers in churches, of the which there be of children or boys, as well as of men; then out of the Church there be that do teach and serve privately, as some in noblemen's houses and men of worship's houses, and some in their own houses.
>
> Lastly there be those do use to go with their instruments about the countries to cities, towns, and villages, where also they do go to private houses, to such as will hear them, either publicly or privately; or else to markets, fairs, marriages, assemblies, taverns, alehouses and suchlike places and there, to those that will hear them, they will sell the sounds of their voices and instruments ... These in ancient time were named minstrels; and as the foresaid *Marcus Aurelius* did banish this sort of people for their misused life, so have they been of late in this our realm restrained somewhat from their vagabond life, which some of them used.

He later calls those at the bottom of the hierarchy 'the rascal and off-scum of that profession who be, or ought to be, called minstrels (although nowadays many do name them musicians)'.[4] Whythorne's contempt explains and underscores the forcefulness of the gibe that Peter threatens to throw at the musicians in *Romeo and Juliet*.

Whythorne's list, however, simplifies a complicated picture. As Walter Woodfill notes:

> The independent minstrels and musicians of the provinces formed a homogenous group only by definition: all lacked permanent municipal or private patrons and all resorted to music for at least part of their livelihood. Some were skilled and respected freemen of their town, others vagabonds using music as a cloak for lives of petty crime and idleness. No sharp line divided the men of these extremes.[5]

The problem was not simply that minstrels/musicians ran foul of the increasingly severe laws against vagrancy, nor, necessarily, that they were incompetent performers. More generally, musicians struggled to find a place within the regulatory systems of their society. There were attempts in a number of places to establish minstrel fraternities which might protect their interests, by regulating the number of apprentices, setting minimum requirements for the size of bands recruited to play for weddings and feasts, attempting to bar outsiders from musical employment, and so on; but the York company 'was probably unsuccessful', and in London the competition from royal musicians, musicians attendant on noble visitors, as well as the continuous press of incomers living outside the city's jurisdiction, rendered the company 'one of the city's smallest and poorest'.[6]

Nonetheless:

> London had no rival as the focus of musical life in Britain. The city afforded the richest opportunities to hear music in all its varieties. For those who practised the art London offered the best, the most lucrative and the greatest number of positions. The city remained the centre of the music business, the site of the music-printing trade – such as it was – and a home to most foreign musicians, music teachers and instrument makers. Most important, London was the seat of the court and the monarch, whose essential role in the patronage of music can scarcely be overstressed ... A place in the musical institutions of the royal household remained the ultimate goal, however remote, of any aspiring musician.[7]

Craig Monson rightly places the royal court and chapel at the top of the pyramid, but does not here mention the group of players who occupied the premier position amongst the freemen of the company of musicians – the city waits. Originally a domestic wait was a watchman, and his instrument the loud and piercing shawm (Figure 6).[8] The town waits,

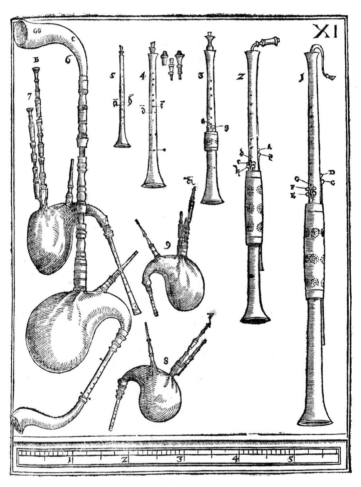

FIGURE 6   Praetorius (*De Organographia*, 1618); the family of shawms, from the bass 'bombard' to the higher shawms (1–5), together with bagpipes.

however, were never watchmen, and their marching round the town at night between Michaelmas and Epiphany was not, as is often supposed, a remnant of this security function.[9] During the second half of the sixteenth century, if not before, the waits' function expanded to be the providers of music for the city on all kinds of ceremonial and festival occasions.[10] During this period the London waits increased in number (from about six plus one apprentice each in 1475 to about eleven men and twenty apprentices in 1620); and they added to their original consort of shawms and sackbuts a set of viols in 1561, recorders and cornetts in 1568, together with other unspecified instruments, and, later, singers. Though they retained their practice of marching round the city at night for three months of the year, their ceremonial functions at civic occasions such as the annual lord mayor's pageants, the requirement that they played at festivals before the mayor and sheriffs' houses, and, from 1571, their regular public performances on Sundays at the Royal Exchange (perhaps the first public concerts in England, but also paralleled in a number of other cities) became much more important. The waits, unlike their fellow company members, received a guaranteed annual salary and livery, and their privileged position and musical expertise meant that they were best placed to be recruited for private functions, and by the theatres – for all of which they would get extra reward.

Their non-civic opportunities, and the expectation that, as in *Romeo and Juliet*, waits will provide music to accompany marriage feasts, are represented dramatically in many plays. In Robert Armin's *The Two Maids of More-Clacke* (1609), for example, it is the waits of London who are said to perform at the ill-fated marriage with which the play opens; and in Shirley's *The Wittie Faire One* (1633), 4.1, the foolish Sir Nicholas plans that for his wedding in Croydon 'we'll ha' the City Waits down with us'. In the first scene of Heywood's *A Woman Killed with Kindness* Sir Francis somewhat contemptuously characterizes the wedding celebrations for Anne and Frankford in these terms:

> the town musicians
> Finger their frets within, and the mad lads
> And country lasses, every mother's child

With nosegays and bride-laces in their hats
Dance all their country measures, rounds and jigs.[11]

In the following scene we see the servants and 'country wenches' arguing over the tunes that the 'two or three musicians' are to play – finally
settling on Sellenger's Round.

The musical excellence of the London waits was explicitly recognized
in the dedication of Thomas Morley's *The First Booke of Consort Lessons*
(1599) to the mayor and aldermen of the city, in which he comments:

> But as the ancient custome is of this most honorable and
> renowned Cittie hath been ever, to retaine and maintane excellent
> and expert Musitians, to adorne your Honors favors, Feasts and
> solemne meetings: to those your Lordships Waits, after the com-
> mending these my labors to your Honorable patronage: I recom-
> mend the same to your servants carefull and skilfull handling ...
> purposing hereafter to give them more testimonie of my love
> towards them.[12]

This tribute, from one of the most important of Elizabethan composers,
himself a member of the Chapel Royal, is much more than conventional
hyperbole. This publication was for the standard mixed consort of three
plucked stringed instruments, the lute, bandora, and cittern, two bowed
instruments, the treble and bass viol, together with the flute, depicted in
the famous picture of Sir Henry Unton, and closely paralleled in an
illustration by Simon van der Passe (Figure 7). Its instrumental variety
indicates clearly how far the waits had developed their musical expertise
during the later sixteenth century. Membership of the waits was eagerly
sought after, and amongst their company were distinguished musicians,
including composers, some of whom later went on to obtain positions in
the royal music.

The London waits was the foremost ensemble of its kind in the country, but most towns and cities appointed waits. Some places probably had
no more than one or two instrumentalists, but many employed three to
five musicians, plus apprentices.[13] As with the London waits, there is some
evidence in the larger towns, such as Norwich, Chester, Oxford, or York,

FIGURE 7   This engraving of 1612 by Simon van de Passe, entitled 'Musical Company', depicts a consort, from the left, of cittern, violin, bandora, and viol. The man entering at the back carries what might be a flute or a recorder. There is no lute – which would have completed the typical English 'mixed consort'.

that the range of the waits' musical expertise increased over time, even though the shawm continued to be indelibly associated with them as their primary instrument (as it is by the Citizen in Beaumont and Fletcher's *Knight of the Burning Pestle*, who evinces his lack of familiarity with the musical sophistication of the indoor Blackfriars theatre by offering two shillings to bring over the waits of Southwark to play the shawms he deems necessary for Rafe's 'stately part').[14] Many of the provincial waits, protected by their civic livery, still travelled widely across the country, securing occasional employment in towns and in noble households. The earls of Cumberland, for example, employed at least nineteen different bands of waits in the period 1595–1613, on over seventy different occasions (sometimes for periods of several weeks) – and they came to the earl's Londesborough estate from up to 140 miles away.[15] Though the vagrancy laws probably made musicians who were unprotected by either civic licence or noble patronage less likely to travel far from home, nonetheless in some larger towns, and in London, small bands of unattached musicians could still make a living performing at weddings and other feasts, for special occasions at a noble or gentleman's residence, or in taverns and ale-houses.

Whether we are to imagine the Verona musicians as 'waits' or simply as an independent band, Capulet's employment of them to celebrate his daughter's marriage is entirely typical of upper-class patronage in the period. The Skipton waits, for example, were hired for no less than twelve weeks by the fourth Earl of Cumberland to celebrate the visit and wedding of Viscount Dungarvon.[16] The frostiness of the Veronese musicians' response to Peter's insult is a mark of the fact that they, like musicians in England, aspired to musical expertise, and to the respectability and status to which they felt it should entitle them. For many of Shakespeare's audience it was these civic musicians, the waits and other independent members of the company of musicians, who provided one major part of their experience of public music. They would have been heard in musical activity ranging from ceremonial fanfares and flourishes to the mixed repertory of dance tunes, some traditional, some newly composed, that Peter assumes the Verona musicians will be able to play on demand.

Direct experience of the most prestigious musical provision in London, that of the royal court, must, for most, have been a rather less frequent occurrence. They would, however, have been familiar with the trumpets that heralded state occasions and royal progresses (see Figure 8), and with the other music that might accompany them. Shakespeare may have been versifying North's Plutarch when Enobarbus says of Cleopatra's barge that 'the oars were silver, / Which to the tune of flutes kept stroke' (AC, 2.2.204–5), but Londoners might themselves have seen their queen making her progress up the Thames in a barge 'towed by a long galley rowed by 40 men in their shirts, with a band of music, as usual when the Queen goes by water'.[17] The more privileged, of course, might have attended at court, where music of all kinds punctuated the day, preceding the queen, accompanying meals, and supporting the dancing which was the queen's favourite activity and a virtually daily practice. As Peter Holman records:

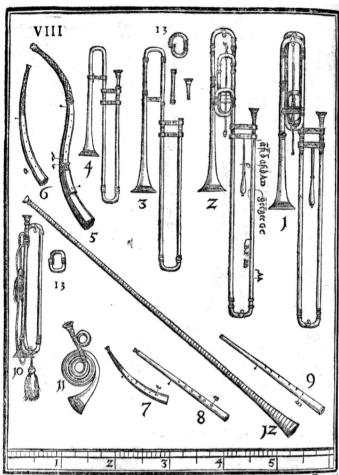

1, 2. Quart-Posaunen. 3. Rechte gemeine Posaun. 4. Alt-Posaun. 5. Corno/
Groß Tenor-Cornet. 6. Recht Chor Zinck. 7. Klein Discant Zinck / so ein Quint höher.
8. Gerader Zinck mit ein Mundstück. 9. Still Zinck. 10. Trommet. 11. Jäger Trommet.
12. Hölgern Trommet. 13. Krumbbügel auff ein gantz Thon.

FIGURE 8 Praetorius (*De Organographia*, 1618) depicts the family of sackbuts (nos. 1–4) various sizes and styles of cornett (5–9), trumpet (10) and hunting horn (11).

In June 1559 a Venetian diplomat wrote that 'the Queen's daily arrangements are musical performances and other entertainments (*feste*), and she takes marvellous pleasure in seeing people dance; in 1589 it was said that 'VI or VII gallyards in a mornynge, besydes musycke & syngynge, is her ordynary exercyse' ... In 1599 a diplomat reported in disgust to the Spanish court that 'on the day of Epiphany the Queen held a great feast, in which the head of the Church of England and Ireland was to be seen in her old age dancing three or four galliards'.[18]

Robert Sidney describes the queen's presence almost every night over the Christmas holiday season of 1599/1600 'to see the ladies dawnce the old and new cowuntry dances with the taber and pipe'.[19] This comment makes it clear that court dancing might be accompanied exactly as the most rural of festivities were by the humblest of instrumental combinations of three-hole pipe and drum (see Figure 9). It is one of many instances which demonstrate that the gap between the 'courtly' and the 'popular' musics was neither as wide, nor as readily perceived, as a modern readership might anticipate.

A detailed account of the royal music lies outside the scope of this study, but a few observations may be made of matters which will intersect with the later discussion of Shakespeare's plays. First, the organization of the musicians was into distinct consorts – of strings (viols and violins), plucked instruments, flutes and recorders, shawms and sackbuts, trumpets and drums, together with keyboard players, and, at times, harpists.[20] (The dependent households of Queen Anne, Prince Henry, and then Prince Charles, however, were, it seems less rigidly organized, more readily espousing the music of mixed consorts.) It is noteworthy that throughout most of the Tudor and Stuart periods the number of trumpeters always exceeded that of any other group – reflecting the centrality of the instrument to the announcement of the royal presence, indoors as well as out.[21] The various consorts were expected to be in daily attendance on the monarch, to provide music to accompany meals, for dancing, and for the sovereign's private recreation. The royal musicians were the best rewarded in the land, and had ample opportunity to supplement their income through other gifts and benefits of place not necessarily connected

FIGURE 9 Jost Amman 'Outdoor amusements'. The courtly dancing couples are accompanied by a violin and a pipe and tabor; a bass viol leans against a tree in the background.

to music. But they might also 'moonlight' as advisers, teachers, and musicians for noble families, or be recruited by them for their own entertaining. Robert Johnson, although a court lutenist and musician to Prince Henry, was also closely connected with the theatre, composing some of the finest of surviving theatrical songs.

One of the most visible traces of the royal musicians at work, however, is to be found in the published texts of the court masques of the Jacobean and Caroline court – though even here detail is often deficient.[22] The full resources of the royal music, including singers from the Chapel Royal, might be called upon to accompany the various stages of the entertainment. Trumpeters or shawms announced the arrival of the monarch; the grotesque or comic dances of the antimasque, part of the fixed form of the genre after 1609, might be accompanied by various and strange instruments (often called the 'wild music'); songs were sung to lutes and cornetts; and the dances with which the entertainment ended were sustained by the strings. In Campion's *Lord Hay's Masque* of 1607 three consorts of musicians were arranged around the masquing stage, two of mixed strings and plucked instruments, the third of six cornetts and six 'chapel voices'; some of the characters in the masque also played lutes to which others sang, and at the masque's climax the chorus in praise of the King 'was in manner of an Eccho seconded by the Cornets, then by the consort of ten, then by the consort of twelve, and by a double Chorus of voices ... bearing five voices a peece'.[23] It is perhaps not surprising that Campion, himself a musician, should have left such a detailed record of the musical arrangements; which in their mixing of different consorts may not have been entirely typical of normal practice, but which clearly made a major contribution to the work's effect, to its symbolic structure, and to its demonstration of the magnificence of the royal court.

Jonson, who provided the majority of the masques in James's reign, was much more reticent about musical detail; but the records of payments for *Love Freed from Ignorance and Folly* are unusually complete,[24] and, in addition to recording the rewards of the writer, designer, dancing masters and composers, list payments to twelve 'lutes that suplied and with fluits', a total of fourteen violins, thirteen 'hoboyes and sackbutts', twelve 'Musitions that were preestes that songe and played' (perhaps they might have been divided as in Campion's masque into six voices and six cornetts), and then, gnomically, '15 Musitions that played to the Pages and fooles'. This amounts to some sixty-three musicians in all, very nearly exhausting the instrumental resources of the royal music. We do not know, of course, whether some musicians were 'bought in' for this specific occasion; and, crucially, we are left in the dark about what instruments played to accompany the antimasque dance of fools. But it would seem that, unlike the mixing of consorts in Campion's masque, here each was separate; emphasizing that 'the modern practice of using large numbers of all types of instruments together in one orchestra had not yet developed: the King's Musick was not one band, not a symphony orchestra'.[25]

Not many of the public theatre audience could have witnessed court masques themselves, or experienced their musical richness directly, but the genre was sufficiently identifiable (and identified with the court environment) for it to be imitated in the drama of the period, whether in the celebratory masque of *The Tempest*, or in its bitterly ironic perversion in Middleton's *Women Beware Women*. On the public stage it is very unlikely that any attempt could be made to imitate the musical richness of the court original; although the indoor hall theatres, as we shall see later, might have been able more closely to approximate to the variety of the masque's musics.

If the full magnificence of the court's music was not part of the experience of the majority of the Globe's audience, all of them would have encountered public music in the church. But where the story of the secular musicians is one of widening musical horizons, the history of the music of the Church after the Reformation was, in many ways, one of contraction. As Whythorne lamented:

> In time past music was chiefly maintained by cathedral churches, abbeys, colleges, parish churches, chauntries, guilds, fraternities, etc. But when the abbeys and colleges without the universities, with guilds and fraternities, etc., were suppressed, then went music to decay.[26]

The decline was a consequence of a number of different pressures. The Reformation engendered a loss both of liturgical occasion for, and of the endowments to support, choral provision, and it was combined with a doctrinal mistrust of chant and elaborate polyphonic music, regarded as relics of popery, to result in the stripping out of organs and the disappearance of choirs from most, if not all, parish churches.[27] That music did not disappear even more completely from the Church was, in part at least, due to the personal convictions and tastes of Queen Elizabeth. In the Injunctions of 1559 a long clause was inserted allowing the continued performance of 'an Hymn or such like song ... in the best sort of melody and music that may be conveniently devised'.[28] Her predilections certainly helped to ensure the continuance of the choir of the Chapel Royal, together with choirs at St Paul's, Westminster Abbey, and St George's

Chapel, Windsor, as centres of highly wrought music, to which most of the distinguished church musicians of the period were attached, and where the music of Tallis, Byrd, Gibbons, and many other composers, whose work still forms part of the choral and cathedral repertoire, could be heard. Distinguished foreign visitors were taken to hear services, on which they commented with approval – and some surprise. Thomas Platter, for example, went to the chapel at Windsor, where: 'we heard some glorious music in the church at English vespers, choir with organ, cornett and fife accompaniment, for as stated above, in outward ceremonies they much resemble the papists'.[29]

Cathedrals outside London and a very few parish churches maintained their choirs – though there is conflicting evidence as to their success in preserving standards of performance.[30] Certainly the funds were no longer available in many places to pay the singers at a rate which would maintain a decent standard of living, and the pattern was established which still obtains in Anglican cathedrals, of lay clerks for whom church employment was but an adjunct to other activity, ranging from teaching music to pursuing a trade.[31] By the side of Platter's compliments needs to be set Morley's complaint that:

> the matter is now come to that state that though a song be never so well made and never so aptly applied to the words yet shall you hardly find singers to express it as it ought to be, for most of our churchmen, so they can cry louder in their choir than their fellows, care for no more, whereas by the contrary they ought to study how to vowel and sing clean, expressing their words with devotion and passion whereby to draw the hearer, as it were, in chains of gold by the ears to the consideration of holy things.[32]

Nonetheless, it was from the choirs of the Chapel Royal and of St Paul's Cathedral that there emerged during Elizabeth's reign the choirboys' companies which developed their traditional roles of presenting entertainments before the monarch into the creation of full-blown theatrical troupes which for a time were sufficiently threatening to the dominance of the adult companies to lead to the so-called 'War of the Theatres' in 1601, and for them to be famously put down by Shakespeare himself in the passage about the 'little eyases' in the Folio text of *Hamlet* (2.2.335–58).[33] Their story becomes significant for our purposes when we turn later to consider the musical resources of the playhouses.

Some of Shakespeare's audience might have attended choral services at St Paul's – indeed Robert Greene suggests that pickpockets found that 'their chiefest time is at divine service, when men devoutly given do go up to hear either a sermon, or else the harmony of the choir and the organs'.[34] But the majority were perhaps less familiar with the elaborate polyphony accompanied by organs, and sometimes by cornetts and sackbuts, which they might have heard at St Paul's, than with the metrical psalms that were sung at their local parish churches, since all but the most determined of Puritan ministers admitted the possibility of (unaccompanied) congregational singing of psalm texts as part of the service.

The Sternhold and Hopkins psalter, first issued in complete form in 1562 and running through countless editions over the next two hundred years, offered metrical versions of all the psalms, together with a few other scriptural and non-scriptural hymns. It was provided with a selection of tunes, most of which in the original publication are curiously aimless and musically unshapely. It would seem that the majority of these tunes were quickly abandoned, and new ones were provided in a succession of publications during the later sixteenth and early seventeenth centuries. Nicholas Temperley traces the evolution of the psalm-tunes in fascinating detail, and concludes that:

> The psalms were at first probably sung to well-known popular tunes in which all could join. The Puritan leaders then tried to introduce the tunes that had been used by the exiles on the Continent, and which had originated probably in accompanied songs known only to a small circle. They printed them in the psalm books, but were only partially successful in spreading a knowledge of them over the country. The main reason, no doubt, was that these tunes, deprived of instrumental accompaniment, were not very suitable for popular singing ... the better-known kind of tune, also originating in court or theatre songs but simpler, more up to date in style, more obviously rhythmical, and shorter by half, overtook most of

the official tunes in popularity, and gradually found its way into the psalm books.[35]

This account has interesting implications for the nature of 'popular' music, to which we will return shortly. But it certainly helps to explain why the singing of psalms was enthusiastically adopted. In an often-quoted letter to Peter Martyr, Bishop John Jewel claimed as early as 1560 that:

> Religion is somewhat more established now than it was. The people are everywhere exceedingly inclined to the better part. Church music for the people has very much conduced to this. For as soon as they had once commenced singing publicly in only one little church in London, immediately not only the churches in the neighbourhood, but even distant towns, began to vie with each other in the same practice. You may now sometimes see at Paul's Cross, after the service, six thousand persons, old and young, of both sexes, all singing together and praising God.[36]

Psalm-singing was not only a matter of public religious rites. Many of the publications of metrical psalms anticipated domestic use, and there is plenty of evidence that pious households sang psalms as part of their domestic religious observance, or for private recreation. Margaret Hoby, for example, in her diary, mentions that she 'talked and song psalmes with divers that was with me', and 'sung a psalme with some of the sarvants'.[37] Lady Grace Mildmay was instructed in her youth in the singing of psalms to the lute, and later, during her husband's absences, 'practised [her] voyce in the singing of psalms'.[38] In the 1563 edition of *The Whole Booke of Psalms*, which contained an introduction to elementary musical theory, a man is pictured teaching the singing of psalms to his family (Figure 10). The importance of the revolution in parish church music to popular musical activity and awareness should not be understated. Kümin is surely right to assert that:

> the Reformation brought enormous losses in terms of intercessory endowments and qualified performers, but its overall effect was not so much a complete breakdown of parochial music as a notable shift

FIGURE 10 A father teaches his family to sing the psalms, indicating the pitches by pointing to his hand (the 'Guidonian hand'). From *The Whole Book of Psalms* (1563).

of emphasis. Within the churches, parishioners moved from being patrons and consumers to performers of music.[39]

If the religiously minded were happy to encourage the singing of psalms, their attitude to public music of other kinds was much more less positive. Puritans[40] were not, as they insistently declared, antagonistic to music itself, when used for the praise of God or for recreation in a strictly domestic environment. Stubbes, for example, wrote: 'I graunt Musicke is a good gift of God, and that it delighteth both man and beast, reviveth the spirits, comforteth the hart and maketh it apter to serve God ... and being used to that end, for mans private recreation, Musicke is very laudable'.[41] The highly religiously observant Margaret Hoby records that on at least one occasion 'to refreshe my selfe being dull, I plaied and sunge to the Alpherion [orpharion]',[42] and Percy Scholes has demonstrated the widespread use of music in households.[43] The sting comes in Stubbes' continuation:

But being used in publike assemblies, and privat conventicles, as a Directorie to filthy dauncing, through the sweet harmony and smooth melody thereof, it estrangeth the minde, stirreth up filthy lust, wommanisheth the mind, ravisheth the heart, inflameth concupiscence, and bringeth in uncleannes. But if Musick were used openly (as I have said) to the praise and glory of God ... it would comfort man woonderfully ... but being used as it is, it corrupteth good minds, maketh them wommanish, and inclined to all kinds of whordome and uncleannes.[44]

Public music is indelibly associated in his fevered mind with dancing, and on that subject he, and many others, become incandescent with rage:

For what clipping, what culling, what kissing and bussing, what smouching and slabbering one of another: what filthy groping and unclean handling is not practised every where in these dauncings? Yea the very deed and action it selfe, which I will not name for offending chaste eares, shall bee purtrayed and shadowed foorth in their bawdy gestures of one to another.[45]

A significant additional spur to Stubbes' objection was that such dancing frequently took place on Sundays. Thomas Lovell fulminated that 'wheras many Minstrels live idlye moste parte of the week when they should woork, doo not they by wicked abuse of their instruments provoke the people to unhallow the Lords holy day, by develish dauncing the Nurce of much naughtiness'.[46] Worse still, much popular festivity was sponsored by the Church itself. 'Church-ales' were a significant source of revenue; beer was brewed and sold, and dancing sponsored specifically for Church funds.

In the minds of men such as these it was the association of music and musicians with dance in particular which rendered them suspect; yet it was precisely upon popular festivity and dancing that musicians relied for their income, and the decline in the traditional occasions for such musical provision must have hurt many a local and itinerant musician in the pocket as well as reputation.[47] The contest rumbled on throughout the late sixteenth and early seventeenth centuries, and in due course James I became directly involved when, in 1618, he issued the declaration known as the *Book of Sports*, saying:

And as for Our good peoples lawfull Recreation, Our pleasure likewise is, That after the end of Divine Seruice, Our good people be not disturbed, letted, or discouraged from any lawfull recreation, Such as dancing, either men or women ... nor from having of May-Games, Whitson Ales, and Morris-dances, and the setting up of Maypoles & other sports therewith used, so as the same be had in due & convenient time, without impediment or neglect of divine service.[48]

He had been prompted initially to issue the declaration in Lancashire in 1617, where the forbidding of popular festivity was seen as playing into the hands of the significant number of Roman Catholics in the county who thereby could 'breed a great discontentment in our peoples hearts' and prevent their conversion. This political and religious motivation takes precedence in the declaration over what might seem the simple and humane question 'when shall the common people have leave to exercise, if not upon the Sundayes & holydaies, seeing they must apply their labour, & win their living in all working daies?'[49] Nonetheless, the battle continued, the *Book of Sports* being reissued by Charles I in 1633 only to face in 1643 'An ordinance for burning a book of sports by the hand of the common hangman'. This is sign enough that the contest over feasts and dancing was highly politicized, and, of course, the theatres were implicated in the same struggle.

Stubbes and his like wanted to banish 'all leud, wanton and lascivious daunsing in publique assemblies and conventicles without respect, either of sex, kind, time, place, person, or anything else'.[50] Malvolio echoes his phraseology when accusing Sir Toby and his fellows: 'Is there no respect of place, persons, nor time in you' (*TN*, 2.3.90–91), but their misdemeanour is not that they dance, but that they 'make an alehouse of my lady's house'. Travelling minstrels had long plied their trade in the tavern – the fourteenth-century poet Langland mentions labourers sitting and singing in the alehouse[51] – and it is equally part of the standard characterization especially of the lower class of musicians that they are likely to be 'drunken sockets'.[52] The anonymous author of *Pasquils Palinodia* makes the same assertion, though rather more benignly:

> *Musitions,*
>
> And red-faced *Trumpetters*, with many others
> Which haue with Crochets stuft their *pericranions*,
> Are still reputed to be good Companions,
> And for this reason which is here presented,
> My Muse to see the Taverne was contented.[53]

In John Earle's *Micro-cosmographie* 'A Trumpeter' is similarly described: 'The Sea of Drinke, and much wind make a storme perpetually in his Cheeks'.[54] The 'common singing men' are also characterized as 'a company of good Fellowes, that roare deepe in the Quire, deeper in the Tauerne [...] Their pastime or recreation is praiers, their exercise drinking'.[55] In *The Puritan* Master Edmond is asked to 'liquor' the arriving musicians, and promises that he will 'make ech of them as drunck as a common fiddeler',[56] conforming to Earle's representation of the 'poor Fiddler' as a drunkard who 'hates naturally the Puritan, as an enemie to this mirth'.[57]

Whether or not musicians entirely deserved this alcoholic reputation, the alehouse was another significant arena where music might be performed. Drinking establishments in the period were hierarchically characterized as inns, taverns, and alehouses, and Malvolio's complaint is intensified by associating the knights, Sir Toby Belch and Sir Andrew Aguecheek, with the lowest category.[58] As Peter Clark comments: 'there is plentiful evidence to suggest that in the aftermath of the attack on church-oriented games, rituals and the like, the alehouse progressively developed as a rival centre for communal and neighbourhood activities'.[59] He also notes that 'Just as games and entertainments took on new shapes and guises in their translation to the alehouse, so communal music may also have experienced some reorientation in that different environment ... Minstrels may have lost ground to ballad-singers.'[60]

'Ballads' are of central importance to the music of the theatre, as we will see, and formed a significant part of the musical experience of the period for a wide range of people. The label, however, includes such diversity of material that some categorization needs to be attempted. The ballad as genre includes the orally transmitted traditional narrative, which Puttenham describes rather contemptuously as:

stories of old time, as the tale of Sir *Topas*, the reportes of *Bevis* of *Southampton*, *Guy* of *Warwicke* ... and such other old Romances or historicall rimes, made purposely for recreation of the common people at Christmasse diners and brideales, and in tavernes and alehouses and such other places of base resort.[61]

Such stories, however, might move even the highly sophisticated Sir Philip Sidney, as he reported in *The Defence of Poesy*:

Certainly, I must confess my own barbarousness, I never heard the old song of Percy and Douglas that I found not my heart moved more than with a trumpet; and yet is it sung but by some blind crowder [*harpist*], with no rougher voice than rude style.[62]

The genre might include, too, traditional seasonal or work-songs. The singing of songs to lighten tedious labour is, as we have seen, a commonplace in defences of music's utility. *The Praise of Musick* suggests:

And hence it is, that manual labourers, and Mechanicall artificers of all sorts, keepe such a chaunting and singing in their shoppes, the Tailor on his bulk, the Shomaker at his last, the Mason at his wal, the shipboy at his oare, the Tinker at his pan, and the Tylor on the house top. And therefore wel saith *Quintilian*, that every troublesom and laborious occupation, useth Musick for a solace and a recreation.[63]

It is precisely in this way that Thomas Deloney chooses to characterize Jack of Newbury's workers. His weavers and spinners sing ballads as they labour, when they are presented to the visiting King and Queen.[64] The second of their songs, a narrative ballad sung by the women, beginning 'It was a knight in Scotland born', whether it began with Deloney or not, survived in oral tradition.[65]

Miles Coverdale, however, in printing the first English metrical version of some of the psalms with music, his *Goostly psalmes and spirituall songes* (?1539), hoped that it might mean that 'our mynstrels had none other thynge to playe upon, neither oure carters and plowmen other thynge to whistle upon, save Psalmes, hymns, and soch godly songes as David is occupied withal'.[66] It was, similarly, the aspiration of Day's psalter of 1563 to supplant 'vayne and trifling ballads'[67] with psalms. That they might have met with occasional success is suggested by the difficulty of the Clown in *The Winter's Tale* in finding performers for his three-man song, for there is 'one puritan amongst them, and he sings psalms to hornpipes' (*WT*, 4.3.43–4).

But the most frequent target of Puritan objection was the circulation of ballads in printed form – the 'broadside' ballads issued in huge quantity in the latter half of the sixteenth century.[68] Tessa Watt has calculated that at least 3000 were published in this period, so that between 600,000 and three million copies may have been in circulation.[69] Nicholas Bownd in 1595 lamented that the psalms were being pushed to one side, even in the houses of great persons, by what he saw as a new spate of ballads, and complained:

> For as when the light of the Gospell came first in, the singing of ballades (that was rife in Poperie) began to cease, and in time was cleane banished away in many places: so now the sudden renewing of them, and hastie receiving of them every where, maketh me to suspect, least they should *drive away the singing of Psalmes againe.*[70]

The content of this published repertoire was enormously varied, including love-songs of varying degrees of ribaldry, versified historical narrative, 'news' and current events (including very popular accounts of the confessions and execution of criminals, which Quicksilver imitates in *Eastward Ho* as a device to persuade others of his repentance),[71] versions of the plots of successful plays,[72] satires, and, in the earlier part of the period especially, 'godly ballads' aimed at reinforcing Protestant belief.

Though these are printed texts, they occupied a liminal space between oral and print culture. The ballad of 'Chevy Chase', for example, which so moved Sidney, probably started life as a manuscript poem in the fifteenth century, before moving into oral culture. It seems then to have returned to print in a now lost edition, from which it was retranscribed, in 1557 and 1565, finally to be entered into the Stationers' Register in 1624.[73] Throughout the period printed texts might simply set down pre-existing oral material, or they might adapt and transform traditional 'originals' into new versions which then took on an independent life in oral culture. As Bruce Smith remarks: 'The movement of ballads into and out of print in the sixteenth and seventeenth centuries stands as a signal illustration of Michel de Certeau's point that orality and literacy, far from being polar opposites, exist only in terms of each other – and in terms that are constantly changing.'[74]

The same mobility characterizes the music. It was seldom printed with the text of a broadside ballad, which characteristically indicated that it should be sung 'to the tune of ... ' Something like 1000 tunes are referred to (of which about 400 survive),[75] but, far from being the timeless music of the folk, many clearly derive from 'art-music', both from that of the earlier court of Henry VIII, and from contemporary musical publication. In turn, many popular tunes were taken up by composers as the subjects for sets of variations or published later as gentrified dance tunes.[76] Indeed it is precisely from these 'high-art' versions, in print or in manuscript, that Simpson derived the tunes for the sixteenth-century ballads he exhaustively surveys, and from which, as we shall see, the possible tune for Shakespeare's 'O mistress mine' has been extrapolated. An example of the mobility of ballad and tune is that:

> the Nottingham version of 'Bonny Nell' for example, was hammered out in the streets to the rough music of candlesticks, tongs, and basins, but was also played in taverns by professional pipers, and 'prickt in 4 parts to the vyalls' in gentlemen's houses, demonstrating the way in which such material could simultaneously circulate in many forms and operate on many social levels.[77]

The traditional, oral ballad and the printed broadside do not exhaust the possibilities of the genre, for new ballads might originate from specific local circumstances, particularly in satirizing or libelling individuals. Some of them might be written and pinned up in the locality; some of them were never written down at all, and survive only through their being mentioned in court records. Such extempore ballads were no doubt fitted to a known tune, and on occasion musicians would be hired to perform and circulate them, as in the case of George Thomson, Vicar of Aberford, who 'made use of various minstrels, "profesing of pipeinge and fidling, running and ranginge upp and downe the countrie from place to place ... " to perform the many songs he had conceived in derogation of Thomas Shillito, the high constable of Barkston'.[78]

Audiences in the sixteenth and seventeenth centuries, then, might have come into contact with many kinds of 'ballad' in many different contexts, and would have experienced many kinds of performance of them. The printed broadside was distributed by travelling salesmen (or 'chapmen') who moved up and down the country offering ballads as part of their stock-in-trade – a profession represented on the Jacobean stage most memorably by Nightingale in Jonson's *Bartholomew Fair* and Autolycus in *The Winter's Tale*, and depicted in Inigo Jones's costume design for *Britannia Triumphans* (1633, Figure 11).[79] Such chapmen were not necessarily particularly musical, using their 'vocal performance primarily as a sales pitch for the printed text'.[80] This is endorsed by the representation of Simplicity, a ballad-seller in Robert Wilson's *The pleasant and stately morall, of the three lordes and three ladies of London*, who offers his wares to three pages, Wit, Wealth, and Will, and bursts into a rendition of 'Peggy and Willy' which prompts Wit to respond 'It is a dolefull discourse, and sung as dolefully.'[81]

Simplicity is of mature years, but ballad-sellers were stigmatized by Henry Chettle in *Kind-hart's Dreame* as youngsters:

> I am given to understand, that there be a company of idle youths, loathing honest labour and dispising lawfull trades, betake them to a vagrant and vicious life, in every corner of Cities and market Townes of the Realme singing and selling of ballads and pamphletes full of ribaudrie, and all scurrilous vanity, to the prophanation of Gods name, and with-drawing people from christian exercises, especially at faires markets and such publike meetings.[82]

Despite such disapproval, their wares, according to frequent testimony, were bought and put up in people's homes and in public places, becoming 'lasting-pasted monuments upon the insides of Country Ale-houses'.[83] Cokes, in Jonson's *Bartholomew Fair*, asks his sister 'doe you remember the ballads over the Nursery-chimney at home o'my owne pasting up?'

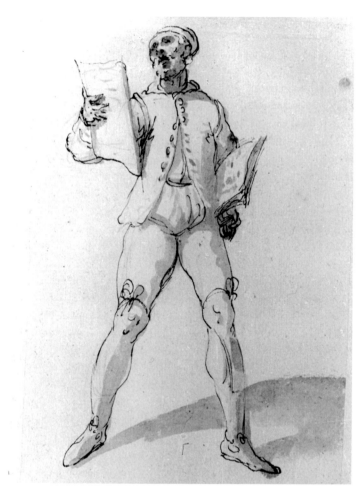

FIGURE 11   Inigo Jones's costume design for a ballad singer in an antimasque entry in *Britannia Triumphans* (1637).

(3.5.49–50).[84] Wye Salstonstall's characterization of 'A Petty Countrey Faire' asserts of a ballad-singer that: 'If his Ballet bee of love, the countrey wenches buy it, to get by heart at home, and after sing it over their milkepayles.'[85]

It is important to stress the way this last comment indicates that ballads impressed themselves upon the folk memory. Evanescent though they may seem to us, and fragmentary though their survival has been, it is precisely their common currency which enables them to form a very significant part of the musical fabric of the drama of the period. But yet, despite Sidney's approval, and their evidently widespread popularity, it was not only Puritans who disapproved of them. The objection was, no doubt, partly occasioned by the ribaldry or the satire to which they gave voice (a reason, perhaps, why the music, freed from its contaminating text, could move more readily across social strata than the words) but disapproval also stemmed from contempt for the artistic standards of their composition (and most are indeed woeful verse), from class-conscious condemnation of those who wrote and performed them, from condescension towards the alehouses in which they circulated, and from the frequent association in the literature of roguery between the ballad-seller and crime. Brathwaite, for example, asserts that 'ballad monger' 'is the ignominious *nickname* of a penurious poet of whom he partakes in nothing but in pover-tie. His straine (in my opinion) would sort best with a funerall Elegie, for hee writes most pitifully.' He continues: 'the Quintessence of his Genius [is] extracted from the muddie spirit of Bottle-Ale and froth'.[86] The pick-pocketing of Autolycus dramatizes the association of ballad-seller and petty criminal which is elaborated in *Bartholomew Fair* 3.5 as Nightingale, with comic irony, sings a ballad warning against cutpurses while his associate Edgeworth picks the pocket of the complacent Cokes.

Thus far we have surveyed the various kinds of music and the differ-ent sorts of performers who might have been part of communal musical experience – from the itinerant ballad-seller, through the bands of musi-cians who entertained at feasts, in alehouses and taverns, or the waits who walked the streets of larger towns and performed on civic occasions, to the elite of the royal music. But, of course, as Whythorne's catalogue of musicians makes clear, there was music and employment for musicians in more domestic environments.

The anonymous author of a plaintive treatise on the decay of church music argues:

But objection will be made that musick is in as great request and as much esteemed as ever it was, which objection may be answered, that it is true indeed for noble men and Gentlemens private service and delight in their houses, that such either men or children are esteemed which have any extraordinarye skill upon instruments, together with their singinge, who have had the same instruction in the Kinges Chappelle, or in *Paules* or *Westminster*; which objection is so true, as thereby those which have any skill or government of their voices are, as it were, pluckt away violently from those Churches, which in their youth were bred Choristers.[87]

The writer has an axe to grind (his treatise is, in effect, an extended and learned pay-claim), but there is no doubt that throughout the period some household musicians had previously been cathedral choristers.[88] So too, the research of scholars such as Woodfill, Price, Wainwright,[89] and Hulse have demonstrated the considerable extent of the patronage of musicians by gentry and noble families. Patronage, of course, may imply many different relationships ranging from occasional reward to full-time employment, but it is clear that musicians, like writers, depended upon the support of the well-off. There is no reason to doubt that many dedications of published work paying tribute to a patron are indications of more than perfunctory help. When John Daniel (or Danyel) told Mrs Anne Grene of Milton that his songs were 'onely privately compos'd / For your delight',[90] or Thomas Campion spoke to Thomas Monson of 'These youth-borne Ayres, then, prison'd in this Booke, / Which in your Bowres much of their beeing tooke',[91] or Orlando Gibbons dedicated his *First set of madrigals and motets* to Sir Christopher Hatton, claiming that they were 'most of them composed in your own house'[92] they were recording significant debts. The three composers were of different backgrounds: Daniel, the brother of the poet Samuel Daniel, worked as a tutor in various households, acquired a position amongst the royal musicians, and was later connected with dramatic activity in Bristol and at the Blackfriars; he published, however, only one collection of songs. Gibbons, the son of a Cambridge town wait, and chorister at King's College, rose to be one of the most eminent of royal musicians, holding appointments in the Chapel

Royal and as court virginalist, and associated with the company of musicians created for Prince Charles. By contrast, where both of these composers took music degrees, Campion was an amateur; though he published five books of songs (an output only exceeded by John Dowland and Robert Jones) he made his living as a doctor. For many musicians, however, for some of their career at least, domestic service in a noble household may have been their principal source of income. Lynn Hulse has questioned Woodfill's oft-quoted assertion that 'of well-known composers John Wilbye (1574–1638) is perhaps the only one who was without question a professional musician and in domestic service most of his life',[93] arguing that about 50 per cent of the servants she identifies in noble households as contributing to musical activities were employed primarily in a musical capacity.[94]

For present purposes, however, it is more important to enquire how far the patronage of musicians extended to the maintenance on a more or less permanent basis of instrumentalists and singers who might function as a slimmed-down version of the royal establishment. Here the evidence is much less easy to gather and interpret. Some lords gave their names and liveries to bands of itinerant musicians, in the same way as they might to groups of strolling players, helping them thereby to avoid the charge of vagrancy but requiring in return no more than the occasional visit and performance. Many more, especially during the sixteenth century, might accept and reward visits from such itinerant bands or from the local waits to entertain them on specific occasions. But it is clear that some, even if not many, households went much further in maintaining musicians on a permanent or semi-permanent basis, whose role might involve teaching the family or taking on the training of young servants in music, and might extend to the provision of musical entertainment for (and with) the family itself. The Earl of Salisbury, for example, maintained a group of two boys and three to five men, and retained others, including members of the royal music, on a part-time or occasional basis. The Earl of Dorset was even more expansive, maintaining eleven musicians.[95] Such men sustained precisely the kind of ensemble that we are to imagine provides the music for Duke Orsino's entertainment at the opening of *Twelfth Night*. They were perhaps exceptional, though 'a number of patrons could assemble a consort of singers and/or instrumentalists, but some of its members were either competent amateurs gathered from within the household or professional musicians borrowed temporarily from relatives and friends or from the court'.[96] More widespread was the appointment of a music teacher for the family's children. This is how Thomas Whythorne made his living for most of his career – and his autobiography shows how chancy such employment might be, his contracts at various times being terminated because of lack of funds, or because of undue amatory entanglement with either his pupil or the mistress of the household. (Shakespeare's portrait of Hortensio posing as a music teacher to gain access to Bianca is perhaps rather more realistically founded than one might expect.) If Whythorne's career is the best documented, it is certainly not untypical.

At this point we turn from considering the nature and organization of the musical profession, and discussion of the kinds of music that Shakespeare's audience might have experienced, to the related but rather different question of the extent of the musical expertise and knowledge that his audience might themselves have brought to the performances they witnessed. The channels by which many professional musicians learned their craft, through apprenticeship, training at choir schools, or simply by being born into a family of musicians, are obvious enough. But the later sixteenth century also saw, under the influence of humanist educational ideals and courtly aspiration, the beginnings of the requirement that any child of a gentry family should acquire some musical proficiency. The careers of Whythorne and his fellows testify to the emergence of that social pressure which still today sees middle-class parents send their children off to lessons on the piano, flute, or clarinet, determined to see them achieve at least a modest grade in Associated Board examinations.

The place of music as a courtierly accomplishment stretches back into the Middle Ages, when 'Music had an undisputed, though lowly, place in courtly and chivalric theory', and 'the sixteenth-century idea of a courtier – or rather the confused and contradictory bundle of ideas – is directly descended from [the] medieval idea of a perfect knight'.[97] Castiglione's *Book of the Courtier*, first published in 1528, and translated into English by Thomas Hoby in 1561, influentially transmitted the idea of music as a necessary part of the training of the ideal courtier. The Count remarks:

I am not pleased with the Courtier, if he be not also a Musition, and beside his understanding and cunning upon the booke, have skil in like manner on sundry instruments. For if wee weigh it well, ther is no ease of the labors, and medicines of feeble mindes to be found more honest and more praise worthie in time of leisure than it. And principally in Courtes, where (beside the refreshing of vexations that musike bringeth unto eche man) many things are taken in hand to please women withall, whose tender and soft breastes are soone pierced with melodie, and filled with sweetnesse.[98]

A century after Castigilione's work was first published in Italy, the English gentleman is urged by Henry Peacham to acquire musical ability because 'the physicians will tell you that the exercise of music is a great lengthener of the life by stirring and reviving of the spirits, holding a secret sympathy with them. Besides, the exercise of singing openeth the breast and pipes. It is an enemy to melancholy and dejection of the mind.'[99] This utilitarian recommendation of music is repeatedly to be found. William Byrd dedicated his *Psalmes, Sonets, and songs of sadnes and pietie* (1599) to Sir Christopher Hatton hoping that 'these poore songs of mine might happely yeeld some sweetnesse, repose, and recreation unto your Lordships mind, after your dayly paines and care taken in the high affaires of the Comon Wealth', but among the eight 'reasons ... to perswade every one to learne to sing' several are much more functional:

2. The exercise of singing is delightfull to Nature, and good to preserve the health of Man.

3. It doth strengthen all parts of the brest, and doth open the pipes.

4. It is a singular good remedie for a stuttering and stamering in the speech.

5. It is the best meanes to procure a perfect pronounciation, and to make a good Orator. (sig. A3v)

The invocation of such practical motivations for learning to sing suggests a society – not unlike our own – where utility was a measure of the value of acquiring accomplishments (or 'skills'). But to it was added a social pressure that is evidenced in an often-quoted passage in Morley's

A Plaine and Easie Introduction, where the character Philomathes is represented as seeking out a teacher in music because, he reports, he had been at a banquet where 'all the propose [*subject*] which then was discoursed upon was music'. He confesses that he could not participate in abstract conversation about music, and worse, 'supper being ended and music books (according to the custom) being brought to the table, the mistress of the house presented me with a part earnestly requesting me to sing; but when, after many excuses, I protested unfeignedly that I could not, every one began to wonder; yea, some whispered to others demanding how I was brought up'.[100] How realistic a picture of middle-class social life Morley presents is precisely the question we must address; but the important point for the moment is the obvious way in which his sales pitch incites the kind of social anxiety that motivated parents to ensure that their offspring had some kind of musical education.

How might they have acquired their musical expertise? One route remained the choir school; another, as we have seen, would have been the hiring of a private tutor. In addition to Whythorne's autobiography, the evidence from the accounts of many noble households recognizes the presence of a music teacher. The Cavendishes of Chatsworth and Hardwick, for example, paid one Thomas Baines, probably a local musician, for eight years from 1598 to 1606 to teach both of the children of William, first Earl of Devonshire, to sing.[101] Rather earlier, in 1560, Sir William Petre paid 10s 'to Persey for teaching the gentlewoman to play on the virginals' (she was the family's senior female servant).[102] Indeed, for girls, domestic teaching was the only route by which they could learn music. But for those boys who went to grammar school an opportunity to learn music might, if they were lucky, be provided. The evidence for music in the school curriculum is patchy. It was, for example, on the curriculum of Bedford School,[103] at Winchester, and for a time at Christ's Hospital,[104] but the testimony of one of the most important of writers on education in the period, Richard Mulcaster, whose *Positions*, and *The First Part of the Elementarie* enthusiastically espouse the benefits of teaching music, needs to be set beside other leading educationists – Kempe and Brinsley, for example – who mention it not at all.[105] No doubt, then as now, the possibility of music forming a significant element in a school depended on the availability of a teacher competent to deliver instruction, and on the pressures of a curriculum which had other principal preoccupations.

Mulcaster's defence of music is couched as a response to those who 'thinke it to be too too sweete, and that it may be ... quite forborne', and though he calls upon the traditional accounts of music's power to affect the mind and spirits, his justification for including it in the elementary curriculum is that '*Musick* will proue a double principle both for the soule, by the name of learning, and for the body, by the waye of exercise'.[106] Mulcaster was headmaster first of the Merchant Taylors' School, and then St Paul's, and one of his pupils, Sir James Whitlocke, testified that 'His care was my skill in musique in which I was brought up by daily exercise in it, as in singing and playing upon instruments'.[107] How typical his experience was of the average schoolboy in the period must be doubted, but if he went on to the universities or Inns of Court, then there would have been considerable opportunity to acquire or to improve his practical expertise.

Lord Edward Herbert rather primly recorded in his autobiography that during his time at Oxford:

> I attained also to sing my part at first sight in music, and to play on
> the lute with very little or almost no teaching ... and my learning
> of music was for this end, that I might entertain myself at home,
> and together refresh my mind after my studies, to which I was
> exceedingly inclined, and that I might not need the company of
> young men, in whom I obserbed [*sic*] in those times much ill exam-
> ple and debauchery.[108]

Perhaps he used for his own self-instruction in singing William Bathe's *A briefe introduction to the skill of song*, which boasted that 'by these rules, a good skill may be had in a moneth: and the wayes learned in four or five dayes: none commeth too late to learne',[109] or else Morley's treatise, published the following year. He might have turned for his lute-playing to one of two translations of Adrien Le Roy's instruction book,[110] or to William Barley's *A new Booke of Tabliture*, which was specifically designed to meet the needs of those who did not live near London 'where expert Tutors are to be had', and promised, like Bathe, that by observing his rules 'thou maist in a short time learne by thy selfe with very small help of a teacher'.[111]

Although the instructions translated by Robert Dowland as a preface to his *Varietie of lute-lessons* state that they are not 'set forth to the end to draw thee away from the lively teaching of thy Maister (whose speach doth farre exceede all writing)', he offers his work 'to young beginners, and such as oftentimes want a Teacher'.[112] The very existence of books of instruction of this kind testifies to some serious interest in acquiring musical skills amongst those with time and income to spare.

Not all students were autodidacts as Herbert claimed to be. Others, like Whythorne's pupil, the son of a merchant, took their music tutor with them to university, where many of the college fellows were also capable musicians who might offer instruction.[113] Hulse gives a number of instances of members of the nobility, from the Earl of Northampton to Robert Sidney, who were taught music outside the formal curriculum.[114] The presence in college statutes throughout the sixteenth century of prohibitions against music being played at times of study or rest is evidence that even in an age before electronic amplification, students were habitually capable of disturbing the peace of others. And not only students, for the Caius College *Articles against the Master* of 1581 complained that Dr Caius 'hath used continuall and expressive loud singings and noyse of organs, to the great disturbance of our studyes'.[115] Students at the universities and the Inns had ample opportunity for participating in musical and dramatic activity, and although the students in the *Parnassus Plays* who actually take up employment as musicians do so only as a desperate last resort,[116] these opportunities for social musical activity must have been significant for the development of a musical interest and some real proficiency across a fairly wide social range.

In teaching himself to sing and to play the lute Herbert was following the dominant practice of musical instruction in the period. Children would normally be instructed on the lute, or else on the keyboard instrument, the virginals. They might also, from later in the sixteenth century at least, have learnt to play viols, but, as Hulse notes, 'perhaps of all musical accomplishments singing was the most attractive to the nobility, principally because it was possible to sing in consort from an early age and with little training'.[117] The repertoire they played and sang is rather more difficult to determine. Much music must have been composed or transcribed by the music teachers themselves, and, in the nature of things, a very high percentage of this music is now lost. (As a result of the discovery of a single set of partbooks in Kassel 'the known repertory [of ensemble music] increased by over 5 per cent, but that of known polyphonic dance music expanded by over 25 per cent'.)[118] Diana Poulton comments that 'owing to the scarcity of texts both MS and printed, the character and extent of the repertoire of early songs with lute accompaniment remain uncertain'.[119] Music publishing began later, and was more fitful, in England than on the Continent. Nonetheless, the success of John Dowland's *The First Booke of Songs or Ayres*, published in 1597, and reprinted five times up to 1613, is testimony to a significant appetite for musical scores.[120] It is important, too, that the format of the publication itself suggests that it was designed for domestic use.

> Dowland used a single folio book intended to be placed flat on a small table, to be read by the performers grouped around it. The table layout brilliantly solved the problems of combining lute tablature with staff notation in a printed collection, and allowed for many different types of domestic performance: all the songs in *The First Booke* can be performed by a single person singing the cantus part and playing the underlaid tablature on the left-hand page. Alternatively, they can be sung as partsongs using some or all the lower parts on the right-hand page, or with viols replacing or doubling some or all of the voices [see Figure 12].[121]

It was precisely this environment which Morley imagines in his exactly contemporaneous treatise, and that Nicholas Yonge recorded almost a decade earlier in the dedication of his publication of madrigals, *Musica Transalpina*:

> since I first began to keepe house in this Citie, it hath been no small comfort unto mee that a great number of Gentlemen and Merchants of good accompt (as well of this realme as of forreine nations) have taken in good part such entertainment of pleasure, as my poore abilitie was able to afford them, both by the exercise of Musicke daily used in my house, and by furnishing them with Bookes of that kinde yeerly sent me out of Italy and other places ...[122]

FIGURE 12 A song from Thomas Campion's *Second Booke of Ayres* (c. 1613). The melody with lute accompaniment is at the bottom of the page; above it the optional bass and alto parts are arranged so that all can be read simultaneously from the single copy by singers standing round a table.

Yonge himself was a singing man at St Paul's, but those who shared his 'pleasure' were not, it seems, professional musicians. What is particularly important about this preface, and his collection of 57 pieces, however, is that it indicates that the deficiencies of native printing of music were being rectified by the importation of foreign scores. Yonge published a second set of madrigals in 1597, and that his enthusiasm for Italian music was shared is evidenced by the fact that both his books were purchased early in 1599 by the Cavendish family.[123] In the music library of Sir Charles Somerset, by 1622, Yonge's two books were accompanied with an impressive range of madrigals by native English composers, together with the work of many Italians, including Marenzio and Monteverdi.[124] There were a significant number of noble collectors of music, and by the early seventeenth century even 'patrons living in the more remote parts of England had little difficulty in obtaining recent publications from home and abroad'.[125] If the fashion once was to exaggerate the general musical literacy of Elizabethan and Jacobean society, the mid-twentieth-century reaction against that view may itself have been somewhat overstated.

Henry Peacham addressed his 'complete gentleman' with the words 'I desire no more in you than to sing your part sure and at the first sight withal to play the same upon your viol or the exercise of the lute, privately, to yourself.'[126] It might be that 'Peacham's fondness, perhaps immoderate, for music, shown by the chapter itself, makes it somewhat suspect as a mirror for the effective standards of the day',[127] yet Edward Herbert put himself to learn exactly these skills, and the evidence must surely suggest that a significant part of the upper social levels of the Globe or Blackfriars audience were not unknowledgeable of, or even unskilled in the performance of music of some considerable sophistication.

There are, however, important caveats. The first is suggested by the final clause of the quotation from Peacham. He, like Castiglione, thinks of the performance of music as, for a gentleman, a private activity. And this is the anxiety registered by the characters of Amiens in *As You Like It*, and Balthazar in *Much Ado About Nothing*. The former self-deprecatingly responds to Jaques's request to sing again with the remark: 'My voice is ragged, I know I cannot please you', and continues reluctantly, 'More at your request than to please myself' (*AYL*, 2.5.14, 21). The latter answers Don Pedro's request for a song with the response 'O good my lord, tax not so bad a voice / To slander music any more than once' (*MA*, 2.3.43–4).[128] In both cases these characters are men of some social standing, rather than menial servants, and they are modest about the abilities they are called upon to display. Or perhaps one should say that we know they aspire to some social status precisely because they are reluctant to sing.

There is another shadow which perhaps inhibits Amiens and Balthazar. Castiglione argued that the courtier's musical talents were especially 'meete to be practised in the presence of women, because those sights sweeten the mindes of the hearers, and make them the more apt to bee pierced with the pleasantnesse of musicke'.[129] But the Lord Gasper tartly comments: 'I believe musick ... together with many other vanities is meet for women, and peradventure for some also that have the likenesse of men, but not for them that be men in deede: who ought not with such delicacies to womannish their mindes.'[130] The eccentric Tobias Hume began his address to the reader which prefaces *Captaine Humes Poeticall Musick* (1607): 'My Profession beeing, as my Education hath beene, Armes, the onely effeminate part of mee, hath beene Musicke; which in mee hath beene alwaies Generous ['*noble*'], because never Mercenarie.'[131] He diverts the charge of effeminacy not only by his past history as a soldier, but also by his amateur status. As we have seen, the association of music with lovesickness, was a powerful one in the period, and Burton argued that an 'amorous fellow ... must learne to sing and dance, play upon some instrument or other, as without all doubt he will, if he be truely touched with this Loadstone of Love'.[132] Conversely, for a gentlewoman to be able to play or sing was also beginning to be a mark of her social status.

Queen Elizabeth herself was exceptionally well-educated, and was no doubt influenced by the talents of her father – a composer as well as enthusiastic performer – to develop her musical abilities, but her competence must have been a model for aspirant noble women. Of course, as for the male courtier, these abilities were not for public display. Famously, Elizabeth was overheard playing upon the virginals by Lord Hunsdon and Sir James Melville, although, as the latter reported, 'she left off immediately, so soon as she turned her about and saw me'.[133] There is a portrait of her playing the lute,[134] and there can be no doubt about her interest in and patronage of music. Many noble ladies must similarly have acquired a musical education, and by the next century, as Burton somewhat iron-ically suggests, a talent for music was becoming one of the means of a girl's rendering herself attractive to a suitor:

> our young women and wives, they that being maids tooke so much paines to sing, play, and dance, with such cost and charge to their parents, to get those gracefull qualities, now being married will scarce touch an instrument, they care not for it.[135]

Even for the most assiduous female musician, however, the opportunity to perform did not extend beyond this domestic environment. While, as we have seen, a musical female servant might instruct the children of a family such as the Petres, there were few, if any, arenas where women might perform in public. There were, of course, no female actors, with one or two particular brief exceptions,[136] and there was no parallel in England for the employment of female musicians at the Italian courts of Ferrara and Florence. No woman musician appears in the court records or as a singer upon the stage of the court masque until the reign of Charles I. His French queen, Henrietta Maria, herself a keen participant in theatrical activity, numbered among her servants the two women, Mistress Shepherd and Madame Coniack who, in Townshend's *Tempe Restored* (1632), became the first known female performers in a (semi-) public entertainment in England. Neither, however, was retained prima-rily as a musician.[137] Women, though they might be instructed in music, and be important patrons and sponsors of musicians, were doubly debarred from public performance, first by the general prohibition on courtiers, male or female, exhibiting their skills in any but a private envi-ronment, and then, second, by the pervasive association of music with dangerous feminine allure.

Lynn Hulse concludes her survey of music in noble households with the enthusiastic assertion that 'during the late Elizabethan and early Stuart periods music flowered on a scale and with a quality rarely equalled before or after'.[138] This may be overstated: no doubt many of those put to their expensive music lessons were, as Burton implies (and is still the case today) less than enthusiastic in later life; many others of the middling sort would have had little opportunity to acquire musical skills; outside relatively privileged households sophisticated madrigals or consort music for viols must simply have been unknown; a high percentage of the population would never have heard the anthems of Gibbons and his fellows. Nonetheless, the evidence presented in this chapter does suggest that in communal activity at all levels of society the population at large was exposed to a varied diet of musics which might lighten their working lives; be a recreation after work was done, whether in the alehouse or at home; and have been regularly encountered in feasts and celebrations. The evidence suggests, too, that though exposure to the latest fashions in musical styles must have been confined to relatively few, yet the lines of demarcation between 'popular' and 'high-brow' music were always permeable.

The soundscape of this music, however, was distinctly unlike that of more recent times. The instruments were different; some, such as lute, virginals and viol, disappeared almost entirely during the seventeenth century until their revival by the twentieth-century early music movement,[139] and others which do have modern equivalents, such as the trumpet or trombone, were lighter and brighter in their sound than their successors. Above all, perhaps, the volume of the musical sounds with which Shakespeare's contemporaries were familiar was, by modern standards, very modest. Even the mightiest of instruments, the church organ (where it was still to be found) was tiny by comparison with the German organ of the later seventeenth century.[140] Ensembles were small, and even at court, where twenty lutes might be assembled at one time in the court masque, these 'thousand twangling instruments' (*Tem*, 3.2.138) would seem restrained to a modern audience. Above all, of course, there was no amplification, and, as Bruce Smith observes: 'Two inventions – electricity and the internal combustion engine – make it difficult for us even to imagine what life in early modern England would have sounded like'.[141] His fascinating, exploratory mapping of the sound-world of early modern England attempts to recover the auditory environment of which music formed a part. London was noisy – but, apart perhaps from the firing of cannon or the ringing of church bells, the sounds of workmen or the rattle of carts, it had a human scale. The only musical instruments that could begin to dominate the aural environment were trumpet and drum. It is no coincidence that they were the instruments which announced noble or royal presence, nor that it was the sound of trumpet-blasts that signalled the start of performances at Shakespeare's Globe.

And, conveniently, that brings us to the last part of this chapter, to the music that might have been heard on the Shakespearean stage. Trumpets were used by travelling players as a sign of their approach – as is the case in *Hamlet*, 2.2.369, and the Induction of *The Taming of the Shrew*, where the Lord first assumes they are a sign of 'some noble gentleman' (1.74), only to be corrected a couple of lines later. So too, in Theseus's court, in the last act of *A Midsummer Night's Dream*, trumpets are the prelude to the mechanicals' play.[142] In the permanent theatres trumpets conventionally signalled that a performance was about to begin, sounding three times. Dekker, in *The Gull's Hornbook*, satirically advises the fashionable playgoer: 'present not yourself on the stage, especially at a new play, until the quaking Prologue hath by rubbing got colour into his cheeks and is ready to give the trumpets their cue that he's upon point to enter'.[143] In three comedies, *Every Man Out*, *Cynthia's Revels*, and *Poetaster*, Jonson presents his audience with an Induction which begins after the 'second sounding', and only after the 'third sounding' does the Prologue enter and the play proper begin. The first of these plays was performed by the Lord Chamberlain's men at the Globe, the other two by the Children of the Chapel at Blackfriars; Dekker's satire has his gallant go either to the public or to the private playhouse.[144] This suggests that both kinds of theatre observed this convention. But it is essential, before turning to discussion of the music that Shakespeare's audiences might have heard, to recognize that the musical provision in the outdoor amphitheatres and the indoor hall theatres was in many respects fundamentally different.

In the first place, musicians were differently disposed in the theatre. The De Witt drawing of the Swan theatre (Figure 13) shows a trumpeter perched on high in a turret at the side of the stage. This may or may not be an accurate representation of the position taken for sounding the opening blasts signalling that the performance was about to commence. More contentious is the gathering of people in the gallery over the stage. At one time it was suggested that some of these might have been musicians, and

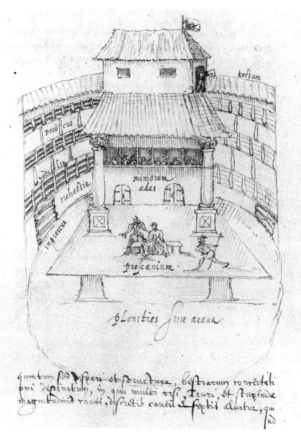

FIGURE 13 Johannes de Witt's sketch of the Swan theatre. A trumpeter is shown on the right at the upper level. The figures over the stage are probably spectators, rather than musicians.

it was generally assumed that this was the normal place occupied by a theatre band throughout the period. But Richard Hosley, analysing stage directions for public theatre plays in the sixteenth and early seventeenth centuries, found no reference to musicians 'above', which might be expected if this was indeed their normal place. Instead, there is repeated reference to music 'within', implying that they played behind the *frons scenae* at stage level.[145] It is only in later plays that we begin to find reference to music 'above' – as, for example, in *The Tempest*, where Ferdinand hears the music 'now above me' (1.2.408), or in Middleton's *A Chaste Maid in Cheapside*, performed at the Swan theatre in 1613, which calls for '*a sad Song in the Musicke-roome*'.[146] The scholarly consensus now is that the use of the central space in the gallery over the stage as a music-room (when required) was probably imported into the open-air theatres some time after about 1608, in imitation of the practice at the indoor theatres, where the evidence for musicians 'above' is earlier and clearer. It also, and importantly, suggests that it was only after this date that there might be a fixed band of musicians needing separate accommodation.

To this question we will return, but the difference in placing of the musicians is one symptom of the fundamental differences between the musical arrangements in the two types of playhouse. The children's companies, from their earliest appearances in plays before the sovereign in the mid-sixteenth century, and throughout their later sporadic emergence into semi-permanent troupes, always had music and musical provision as a key ingredient in their work. It is not simply that on average the children's plays call for more songs in the course of the action, for the preponderance of comedies in the children's repertoire accounts significantly for their higher frequency,[147] but the children's performances were surrounded with more music than the adult companies aspired to. In an often-quoted remark, Frederic Gershow, a German in the train of the Duke of Stettin-Pomerania, described his visit to the Blackfriars in 1602:

> For an entire hour before [a play] one hears an exquisite instrumental concert of organs, lutes, pandoras, mandoras, bowed strings, and woodwind, such as this time when a boy sang so beautifully in a warbling voice to a bass viol, that unless the nuns in Milan may have outdone him, we did not hear the like on our travels.[148]

The practical necessity in the hall theatres of trimming the candles between the acts was also covered by music, known simply as 'The Act' – and in plays such as Marston's *Sophonisba* the movement into and out of the music was integrated into the action of the play itself. The instrumental resources of the children's companies were more extensive than those of the adults, but the confined indoor space meant that trumpets, in particular, were rarely used, and the shawm/hautboy or the softer and more versatile cornett were substituted. (A variant between the Quarto and Folio printings of *Titus Andronicus*, where the stage direction at 5.3.25, originally '*Trumpets sounding*' became in the later edition '*Hoboyes*', may reflect precisely the musical practice of the two types of theatre.) Unambiguous, and again often-quoted, testimony to the difference of musical practice comes in Marston's play, *The Malcontent*, originally a choirboys' play which the adults also acquired. The new Induction (possibly by Webster) speaks of additions made to the play 'Sooth not greatly needefull, only as your sallet [*salad*] to your great feast, to entertaine a little more time, and to abridge the not received custome of musicke in our Theater'.[149] Only after 1608 did the custom become 'received' by the King's Men, and

> the new music consort brought the largest single alteration to the King's Men's practices when they took over the Blackfriars playhouse. The housekeepers immediately altered the Globe's stage-balcony to make a curtained music-room over its stage so the musicians could play there as well as at the Blackfriars … In the next few years, stage-music and song was what differentiated the King's Men at the Globe from the other amphitheatre companies.[150]

It is important to recognize that for most of his career Shakespeare was operating within the resources and practices of the public theatres. Many of the existing studies of theatrical music in the period, and in Shakespeare in particular, conflate amphitheatre and hall theatre customs and conventions, too confidently assuming that evidence derived from one can simply be translated to the other.

In attempting to clarify what the musical practices of the amphitheatres were, some important caveats need to be entered about the nature of the evidence which can be drawn upon. In the first place, the surviving play scripts are customarily laconic in their description of the music. Where, in examples as diverse as *Gorboduc*, performed in 1561 by the Gentlemen of the Inner Temple, or Marston's *Sophonisba*, a choirboy play of 1606, the instrumentation of required music is often precisely specified, the same is not true for the majority of amphitheatre plays. Furthermore, when a play's publication significantly postdates the original production, stage directions may well reflect later performance practice. So, for example, it is an open question whether the cornetts which herald the entrance of the King of France in the opening stage direction of *All's Well*, 1.2, were the instruments that were heard at its first performance, since it is the only public theatre play written before 1609 which calls for them.[151] Although this play is usually assumed to have been set in the Folio from Shakespeare's foul papers, the form of the stage direction suggests a later book-keeper's annotation of that manuscript.[152] And finally, it may well be that music was played at points not indicated by any stage direction. The text of the opening scene of *Twelfth Night*, for example, demands that music play, yet there is no accompanying stage direction or specification of the instruments that 'play that strain again' for Duke Orsino. In 2.4 we do have the direction '*Music plays*' as Orsino requests instrumentalists to play the tune of 'Come away death'. In the intervening scene at Orsino's court, 1.4, there is no obvious call for music in the text, and no direction for it to be played – but Peter Thompson suggests that music 'is one of the things that distinguishes Orsino's court from the other "places" of the play. It is quite likely, despite the absence of a confirming stage direction, that there was music behind the remaining scene set there.'[153] When even necessary exits and entrances are quite frequently omitted from play texts, it is entirely likely that conventional fanfares and flourishes might equally remain unregistered in the stage directions.

The major absentee from the surviving texts' musical indications is, however, any mention of the 'jig' which customarily in the 1580s and 90s was offered as an afterpiece, which might be sung and danced. Thomas Platter's oft-cited account of a performance of *Julius Caesar* on 21 September 1599, where, at the play's end the actors 'danced together admirably and exceedingly gracefully, according to their custom'[154] does not, however, suggest the often bawdy or satirical content of the after-pieces, to which there is plentiful testimony elsewhere.[155] Perhaps some performances were followed with dances that were not necessarily 'jigs'.

The jig was closely connected with popular ballad and dance forms, and identified particularly with the two great clowns of the later sixteenth century, Richard Tarlton (Figure 14) and Will Kempe. It would seem that after Kempe's departure from Shakespeare's company in 1599 stage jigs became increasingly identified with the bottom end of the theatrical market – hence Hamlet's insult to Polonius when he objects to the length of the Player's speech: 'He's for a jig or a tale of bawdry, or else he sleeps' (*Ham*, 2.2.501). Very few texts survive, and the jigs fall outside the compass of this study, except insofar as some of the song and dance endings of Shakespearean texts might be seen as a mutation of a traditional practice;

FIGURE 14 A portrait of the clown, Richard Tarlton (who died in 1588), in rustic clothes, playing the pipe and tabor.

yet their existence is a useful reminder that the texts we now study may often give a very incomplete picture of the theatrical experience of their original audiences – including the music they heard in the course of their afternoon's entertainment.

But despite all these uncertainties, there are some things we do know about the instrumental resources of the amphitheatres during Shakespeare's career. Henslowe in 1599 paid 22 shillings for two trumpets, and had a few months before laid out 40 shillings for a sackbut.[156] There are, indeed, many plays for which no more music than brass flourishes of various kinds were required. But Henslowe also bought 'a basse viall & other enstrementes for the companey' in December 1598 for 40 shillings, and expended a further 30 shillings for 'enstrumentes for the company' in July 1599.[157] The 1598 inventory of the Admiral's Men, listed 'iij trumpettes and a drum, and a trebel viall, a basse viall, a bandore, a sytteren [*cittern*]' and later 'j sack-bute'.[158] The will of Augustine Phillips, sharer in the King's Men, bequeathed to his apprentice a cittern, a bandora and a lute, and to his 'late apprentice' a bass viol.[159]

Brief consideration of the music cues that survive in the plays provides evidence for the use of these and other instruments. The importance of the trumpets is clearly apparent. They not only signalled the start of a play, but were frequently and conventionally employed, with or without the accompaniment of drums, in their dual functions of signalling the entry of kings, emperors, and others of high status, and imitating the sounds of war. Drums alone might sometimes be employed in these contexts, and they were also used for the sound effect of thunder. Equally, drums might be used with the 'fife', a small transverse flute, as emblems of war (Figure 15) – as in Marlowe's *Edward II*, 3.2, and *Timon*, 4.3 where Alcibiades enters 'with drum and fife in warlike manner'. (Falstaff parodies their use when he meets Prince Hal in *2 Henry IV* '*playing upon his truncheon like a fife*' (3.3.87 SD.2).) Although they are not mentioned in the lists of instruments, it is possible that the public theatres also used shawms (or 'hoboys'), which might substitute for or accompany trumpets as the sign of a royal entry, as at the opening of *2 Henry VI*, or in Heywood's *If you know not me, part 2* (1606) where Sir Thomas calls out:

FIGURE 15 A fifer and drummers in a procession during the wedding celebrations for Duke Johann Friedrich von Würtemberg, Stuttgart, 7 November 1609.

> The Queene hath din'd, the trumpets sound already,
> And give note of her comming. Bid the waits
> And Hoboyes to be ready at an instant.[160]

Shawms might also be conventionally associated with feasting, as for example, in *Timon of Athens* where 1.2 opens: '*Hautboys playing loud music. A great banquet serv'd in*'.[161] They are nominated for a particularly striking effect in *Antony and Cleopatra* 4.3.8, where '*Music of the hautboys is under the stage*' signalling that 'the god Hercules, whom Antony loved, / Now leaves him'. It should be noted, however, that in *Hamlet*, 3.2.133 SD, the Quarto prefaces the dumb-show preceding the Mousetrap with the direction '*The trumpets sound*', where the Folio reads '*Hoboyes play*'.[162] Almost all references to hoboys derive from the private theatres, or from texts printed later than 1608/9, and so, like the cornett, it may have been an instrument originally more characteristic of the hall theatres. But the amphitheatres certainly used another instrument of limited capability not listed in the inventories – the horn ('a harsh, stubby little thing like Robin Hood's bugle'),[163] associated either with hunting, or else the arrival of a post.

But, obviously enough, the theatres must have had, in addition to the brass, instruments capable of accompanying dances and songs, and of providing music appropriate to the ducal interior of Orsino's house. Dancing might have been accompanied with the fiddle – presumably the appearance of string players on stage in *Romeo and Juliet* corresponds to the off-stage music that was heard a little earlier in the play – though, again, as Dessen and Thomson note, in their dictionary entry on 'fiddle': 'fiddlers and their music are more common in later plays'.[164] The pipe and tabor, indelibly associated with the clowns Tarlton and Kempe, but, as we have seen, a standard accompaniment for dancing both in court and country, are called for to assist the morris dancers in Dekker's *Shoemaker's Holiday*, scene 11.51, and in Marston's choirboy play, *Jack Drum's Entertainment*. The pipe and tabor are memorably employed by Ariel as he leads Stephano, Trinculo and Caliban to the stinking pond in which they lose their bottles (*Tempest*, 3.2).

Of the plucked strings mentioned in Phillips's will it is the lute that appears most frequently, usually to accompany songs, though it is only in the so called 'bad' Quarto of *Hamlet* that we find the explicit instruction '*Enter Ofelia playing on a lute and singing*', which is omitted in the Second Quarto and the Folio. But there is no ambiguity about Bellafront's singing to the lute in Dekker's *The Honest Whore*, scene 9, nor Franciscina's performance in Marston's *The Dutch Courtesan*. The fact that these last two lute-players are prostitutes suggests the association of music with siren lust to which we have already alluded, an association continued in Dol Common's playing of the cittern – a flat-backed, wire-strung instrument played with a plectrum – in *The Alchemist*, and possibly invoked in the Amazons who dance and play lutes in Timon's masque (*Tim*, 1.2.131 SD).[165] (We will return later to the importance of this association for the understanding of Ophelia's singing.) There are plenty of other lutenists, boys and men, however, scattered through the drama of the period; as we have seen, the lute was the instrument above all that amateurs learnt, and presumably, therefore, an accomplishment many actors acquired. It is often not specified whether or not a singer accompanied himself – if he did, it was likely to be the lute on which he played.

Songs might, however, be accompanied on the bass viol (as was the singing of the anonymous boy at the Blackfriars mentioned by Gershow). Towards the end of the sixteenth century it became fashionable to play solos on the viol, tuned in order to make the playing of chords easier in a manner known as 'lyra-way'. Actors in both arenas appear with a viol. The boy-actor who played Crispinus in Jonson's *Poetaster* accompanies his song on the viol, and the viol-playing Fastidious Brisk appeared in his earlier *Every Man Out of His Humour*, performed by the Lord Chamberlain's Men. Although a distinct and serious repertoire of music was composed for the instrument during the seventeenth century 'every bass viol soloist on the stage – and this implies lyra viol every time – is an affected ass'.[166] The instrument could also, of course, be part of a consort of viols, but, though such a consort is called for in a number of Marston's plays for the choirboy companies, there is no clear evidence that it was ever required in the public theatres. Its sound, indeed, may have been rather too muted to have much effect in an open-air theatre.

A similar difficulty attends the recorder – it could be played on its own, or function as part of a consort. Shakespeare's company certainly possessed at least one, since it is requested by Hamlet as a stage-prop in his taunting of Rosencrantz and Guildenstern (*Ham*, 3.2.324). Earlier in the scene (3.2.275) he had called for 'the recorders' to play some music, which might imply a consort, but, interestingly, where the Folio stage direction reads '*Enter one with a recorder*', the Quarto reads '*Enter the players with recorders*'. Was there one, or many? Did Hamlet himself demonstrate how easy it was to play the instrument? Did they play at any point in the scene? In choirboy plays, and in public theatre plays after about 1610, recorder consorts are specifically mentioned, usually to accompany actions of solemnity, including funeral processions, or to suggest the otherworldly; but I can find no record of their being demanded in earlier amphitheatre plays. Again, their relatively quiet sound, especially that of the lower instruments in the ensemble, might simply have been difficult to hear in the outdoor theatres. Later, in 1611, the King's Men play, *The Second Maiden's Tragedy*, ends with the ambivalent instruction '*recorders or other solempne music*', suggesting that their presence could not be guaranteed.[167]

A single recorder might, however, have been one of the instruments of the mixed consort for which, as we have seen, Thomas Morley composed his *Consort Lessons*. It was long assumed that this was the standard theatre band, which would have supplied most of the instrumental cues that the plays call for. But while most of the required instruments are listed in the inventories quoted above, this view has been challenged. Ian Harwood, for example, finds the evidence for consistent use of the mixed consort in the theatre less than compelling,[168] noting that almost all of the evidence for its employment comes from choirboy plays, or from later printed texts of early plays. There is, in the end, no way of knowing exactly what instruments were employed at every point in the history of Shakespeare's company, and only very intermittent evidence of any kind for instrumental scoring in any of the plays except, significantly, for the plays written after the acquisition of the Blackfriars. Even then, it is entirely probable that the instrumentation would be modified as the company moved between its two homes.

Who actually played these instruments? We tend, perhaps, to assume that Shakespeare's company, like the contemporary RSC (or, indeed, the reconstructed Globe theatre) employed a permanent musical ensemble. The children's companies certainly did. They had the resources to provide extra musicians from amongst the trained choirboys, and since they performed only once a week for the greater part of their history, they were allowed plenty of time for rehearsal and preparation, so that it is possible, even probable, that music might have been composed specifically for individual plays. The adult companies, however, operated an unbelievably punishing schedule, with a different play every afternoon, and they usually repeated a play only at substantial intervals.[169] Since many plays have minimal musical requirements, and since there was no musical performance before the show, or act music during it – which would provide a guaranteed daily need for musicians – it would seem inherently unlikely that the adult theatrical companies would keep a permanent band on call.

Certainly many, if not most, actors would traditionally have acquired some musical expertise, and, as Phillips's will suggests, would have trained their apprentices to play on a variety of instruments. Whether or not Burbage, the King's Men's leading actor, actually demonstrated how easy it is to play the recorder in *Hamlet*, Edward Alleyn, the leading actor at the Rose, and a man who 'first entered the records as a "musician" before he achieved fame as an actor',[170] is very likely to have played the lute when appearing as Barabbas in Marlowe's *Jew of Malta*. It is not clear how far he ever gets beyond attempting to tune the instrument (and the lute was notoriously difficult to keep in tune), since Pilia Borza's comment 'Methinks he fingers very well' (4.4.50) might only allude to the speed with which he pockets his reward, but his comment 'How swift he runs' (4.4.52) does suggest at least a dextrous demonstration of a rapid scale. Many, if not most, of the actors lower down the pecking order must also have been able to perform – and the presence of characters who speak little but do sing or play suggests that some actors were hired in part for their musical competence. As we have seen, actors were likely to accompany their own singing, and individuals might appear playing the pipe and tabor or the fiddle, but this gets us no nearer being certain whether the three actors who appear as musicians in *Romeo and Juliet* were the same people who actually played the music, or whether the (presumably on-stage) musicians of Orsino's court were acting members of the company. Interesting work has been done on the casting of plays in the period,[171] but anonymous musicians are ignored in these accounts, and one would need to include them in order to estimate whether the surviving musical cues could actually be accommodated by the normal-sized acting company.

Though Henslowe bought instruments for the company, there are no payments to musicians recorded in his so-called *Diary*. This absence in itself is not necessarily very significant, since 'it seems clear that it formed only part of Henslowe's accounting records';[172] but it does perhaps suggests that at this time musicians did not feature as a separate category of employed personnel, as they were to do by 1624 where the number of '"musitions and other necessarie attendants" required by the King's Men was twenty-one'.[173] Indeed, if professional musicians had been part of Henslowe's company, they would have possessed their own instruments. Furthermore, his expenditure on this varied collection of instruments suggests that they were in regular use, since they would deteriorate if not played and maintained – strings break, reeds dry out, mouthpieces crack.[174] It is, of course, perfectly possible that a theatrical company might hire musicians for particular performances, and important to remember that Shakespeare's company performed in a number of different arenas beyond the Globe and Blackfriars. On their occasional tours, keeping the company to a minimum size would have been prudent, and this might explain why the Queen's Men, touring in the sixteenth century, apparently paid musicians at Nottingham in 1587, and Canterbury in 1592.[175] Similarly, a court performance might have permitted an expansion of the musical provision, perhaps calling on some of the resources of the royal music. In 1613 the city aldermen complained that they could not get hold of the waits because they were 'then employed at play houses';[176] but how frequent such employment might have been – and whether it was customary earlier in the period – must remain a matter of conjecture. We cannot know whether the 'waits' we have seen called for in Heywood's play were actors or 'real' city waits. We cannot be sure that when Greene's *Alphonsus of Aragon* (1599) calls for a pageant of the nine muses at the beginning and end of the play, all playing upon instruments, it is a demonstration of the musical versatility of the acting company (perhaps the Queen's Men), or whether the four speaking actors were supplemented by musicians bought in for the play. We also do not know whether the trumpets Henslowe provided, and which are so frequently called for in the dramatic literature, were played by actors or by specialists. There is one reference in the accounts of the Queen's Men of payments to trumpeters, but nowhere else are they mentioned. In the royal music trumpeters were men apart, and there is some dispute as to the level of their musical proficiency. It might be that they 'were attendants rather than musicians: they played simple monophonic music and did not belong to the section of musical society that was literate and cultivated polyphonic music'.[177] Christopher Wilson and Michela Calore, however, draw attention to the rising complexity of music for trumpets, and suggest that those who played the highest parts (the *clarini*) must have been considerable technicians.[178] Yet to play basic fanfares and signals on the unvalved trumpet of the period (as on the bugle of more recent marching bands) was not a particularly difficult task, and there is no inherent reason why actors should not have been able to cope with its demands; the only problem is envisaging the practicalities of organizing their presence when the entries and battle scenes they frequently accompanied also required a number of actors on stage to be physically engaged in fighting.

There are, then, as we turn to consider the music in Shakespeare's plays more closely, many uncertainties. But a few generalizations might tentatively be offered. First, and perhaps most important, a clear distinction must be made between the plays written before and after 1608, and some care must be taken to consider the possibility that the texts in the form we now have them represent later rather than earlier practice. But it is obvious that the late romances and the two collaborative works that ended Shakespeare's career not only call for a significant quantity of music, but provide far more specific and varied prescriptions for its scoring than the earlier comedies in which music is required. Second, it seems safest to assume that for the greater part of Shakespeare's career music was provided by the actors themselves, and that, given the lack of back-stage space, ensembles required to play off-stage must have been small. The actors – boys and men – probably had considerable versatility, able, like the city waits, to play a range of wind and stringed instruments. But, equally, there were instruments common in the private theatres that were not employed by the adult companies, and the very absence of particularity in the calls for music suggests that it would be played by whatever and whomever was available at the time. Much has been made of the symbolism of individual instruments and ensembles, but it is perhaps unwise to believe that, before 1608, the King's Men necessarily had the resources to effect such symbolic colouring. Nevertheless, Shakespeare used the resources at his disposal with consummate skill. In doing so he drew on the wide range of associations that music carried in his culture, and on the varied sounds that his audience heard and understood in the world outside the theatre that it has been the business of these first two chapters to sketch.

PART TWO

MUSIC IN SHAKESPEARE'S PLAYS

PRELUDE

The wide area spanned in the opening chapters, from recondite musical theory to the reality of the music heard in the streets and households of Elizabethan and Jacobean England, offered to poets and dramatists alike a deep well of images and ideas which they could draw upon and develop in many contexts. In the *Sonnets*, for example, Sonnet 8 uses the image of 'the true concord of well tuned sounds' (5) and the familiar example of the sympathetic vibration of lute-strings as conceits designed to persuade the young man to marry; while in *The Rape of Lucrece* the heroine's grief is represented in an image derived from accurate observation: 'For sorrow, like a heavy ringing bell, / Once set on ringing with his own weight goes' (1493–4). In the plays, as we have seen, the full weight of musical symbolism can be deployed by Ulysses to characterize political order, an image found also in *Henry V* where Exeter earnestly, if platitudinously, advises:

> For government, though high and low and lower
> Put into parts, doth keep in one concent,
> Congreeing in a full and natural close
> Like music. (*H5*, 1.2.180–3)

Nonetheless, 'the bulk of the references in all the plays is to practical music, which is cited, satirized, and praised in various contexts like any other human activity'.[1] These references can be used powerfully – and two examples from relatively early plays might serve for many. In *Richard II* the banished Mowbray laments:

My native English, now I must forgo,
And now my tongue's use is to me no more
Than an unstringed viol or a harp,
Or like a cunning instrument cas'd up –
Or being open, put into his hands
That knows no touch to tune the harmony. (*R2*, 1.3.160–5).

Even more movingly, the horror and pathos of Lavinia's torture is expressed through the recollection of her capacity for musical performance:

O, had the monster seen those lily hands
Tremble like aspen leaves upon a lute
And make the silken strings delight to kiss them,
He would not then have touched them for his life.
Or had he hear the heavenly harmony
Which that sweet tongue hath made,
He would have dropped his knife and fell asleep,
As Cerberus at the Thracian poet's feet. (*Tit*, 2.3.44–51)

This image can be compared with Sonnet 128, where, in a variation on a conventional topos, the poet describes his mistress playing the virginals, and envies 'those jacks that nimble leap / To kiss the tender inward of thy hand' (5–6).[2] Where the sonnet gives an erotic charge to the kissing jacks, the extended praise of Lavinia's musical accomplishment turns the kiss of the lute-strings into a desolate record of what has been destroyed in her rape and mutilation. In both, the rhetorical figure of personification (*prosopopoeia*) is deployed, but to different effect. Behind both is the social reality of female musical accomplishment, but whereas the first draws on the association of music and sexuality, the second, with its recollection of the Thracian poet Orpheus, invests Lavinia's performance with legendary power.

    The demonstration this last example offers of the way in which music's figurative force is determined by context is a useful prelude to the exploration of performed music in the plays with which I am principally concerned. The underlying question is how and in what ways musical events may be made to 'mean'. Answers to that question are, of course, fraught with problems of various kinds. In the first place, it can be argued that meaning is bestowed on music within and by specific cultural contexts – and it has been the business of the first two chapters to attempt to delineate the most important of them – against which the music in the plays will be read. Not all musicologists would agree that music has no intrinsic 'meaning', although the efforts by figures as diverse as Deryck Cooke, Leonard Meyer, Peter Kivy, and others to explain the ways in which music's language functions have arrived at no consensus.[3] Nonetheless, it is obvious enough that the particular nature of a given tune narrows the range of meanings which might be attributed to it, whether that narrowing is attributed to convention, of melody, harmony, or instrumentation, or to the pressure of the context in which it is performed and heard.

This then raises the issue of the ways in which music is understood in the particular context of the theatre. The semiotician Patrice Pavis baldly states that 'within a performance, music has an utterly unique status ... Whereas signs in setting, actor, or speech refer to given things, music has no object; thus it can mean anything, its value being measured above all in terms of the effect it produces.' He suggests that 'in Western *mise en scènes*, and particularly in productions of classical texts', music's effect is that of accompaniment: 'it is always indirect, "incidental", and thus judged in terms of the degree to which it serves our understanding of the text and the acting'.[4] This definition, however, is most appropriate to more recent theatre, where music is primarily an adjunct to a performance; in Shakespeare's theatre, as we shall see, the assumptions about the place of music are quite different. Nonetheless, an approach which foregrounds the importance of the audience's reception and understanding of the sounds they hear and which demands that they be placed in the context of the total theatrical picture is a useful corrective to the assumption often encountered that: 'the songs in Shakespeare are primarily addressed to the protagonists on the stage ... The playwright does not endeavour to condition his audience by music.'[5] It is a further qualification to this confident dictum that songs themselves are extremely varied not only in the relationships they establish with the audience, but in the ways they are to be construed as expressing the character of their singer, and in the nature of the response they elicit from the onstage audience.

These are some of the major questions which the ensuing discussion explores, and in order to move from the simpler to the more complex, I have chosen to order my account in general by the different kinds of musical resources Shakespeare employs. I begin with the instrumental cues, move on to the allusions to and use of popular song, and thence to the more elaborate performed songs. Chapter 5 brings the threads of the book together in an account of the totality of music's function in two plays, *Twelfth Night* and *The Tempest*.

Chapter Three

INSTRUMENTAL MUSIC
AND DANCE

In the modern theatre instrumental music and synthesized sound are a central part of an audience's experience of most performances of Shakespeare's plays, functioning as vital creators of mood and generators of emotional response. Music frequently makes a significant contribution to a specific directorial perspective on the drama, supplying a consistent 'soundscape' within which the play is enacted, assisting, for example, in the historical relocation of a particular drama as well as reinforcing emotion and feeling in a fashion (more or less) consistent with the particular dramatic embodiment of a scene or action. This has been increasingly the case in the last sixty years or so, when the music for a production has more and more frequently been entrusted to a single composer, working in close co-operation with the director (sometimes, indeed, as with Peter Brook's productions of *Titus Andronicus* and *The Tempest* at Stratford in the 1950s, director and composer might be the same person). This is very different from the practice of the seventeenth and eighteenth centuries, when scores for a production were often assembled from a variety of pre-existing music, only sometimes with new additions. Audiences welcomed the familiar rather than requiring to be surprised by novelty. This practice persisted through the nineteenth and early twentieth centuries so that, for example, Arne's eighteenth-century settings of *Tempest* songs continued to be used at least until the 1930s, as did Mendelssohn's nineteenth-century incidental music for *A Midsummer Night's Dream*. As we shall see, this practice of assembling songs and incidental music from what happens to be available is, in some respects, likely to be closer to the custom of the King's

Men than the uniformity and novelty of the freshly composed music that characterizes more recent production practice. The familiarity of such imported music contributed significantly to the nature of its effect in Shakespeare's theatre, as it did in subsequent centuries.

Music has, of course, been a constituent part of theatrical representation since the Greeks,[1] but it is vital to understand the fundamental differences between its operation in the Shakespearean theatre, and the purposes it serves in modern productions. For while the music for which Shakespeare calls does heighten atmosphere, or gives a particular emotional colouration to speech and action, it is always part of the world of the play itself, heard and responded to by the characters on-stage, and not, as in later theatrical practice, or in film and television, an independent adjunct for the audience's ears only, acting as a commentary or meta-text. It is true that the boys' companies provided additional music both before the play and between the acts, and audiences at the outdoor theatres expected musical entertainment, including songs and dance, to be part of the fare they were offered. It is also undoubtedly the case that more music was heard than the stage directions in surviving texts indicate. Nonetheless, instrumental music – whatever symbolic weight it might carry – is almost always assumed to be audible to the characters on stage.

All instrumental music accompanying the action of a play (or a film) works upon its audience insofar as they recognize its conventional associations. Harmonies, instrumental textures, and melodies bring with them a culturally conditioned implication that establishes mood and atmosphere, or signals the genre of the work we are watching. Some musical meanings and significances, however, are more precise than others, and I want to begin with what might seem the least complex of Shakespeare's musical effects – the use of trumpets and/or drums – where such particularity of meaning is important.

Trumpets and drums are the most widely used of all instrumental resources in the outdoor playhouses, and, as in the real world outside the theatre, they conventionally herald the entrance of royalty or the high-born – Lucius observes in *Titus*: 'The trumpets show the Emperor is at hand' (5.3.16), and Volumnia responds to the sound of off-stage trumpets in *Coriolanus*: 'These are the ushers of Martius' (2.1.158) (see Figure 16). Such signals might be described in the stage directions as a 'flourish', a 'sennet', or a 'tucket',[2] and it is likely that they might have been provided for many entrances where no specific stage direction is given. Dramatically more significant is their use as signs of battle[3] – the to and fro of combatants in *3 Henry VI* is marked by 'alarums' and 'marches',[4] and the closing scenes of *Macbeth* are similarly punctuated and orchestrated by instrumental noise.

At one level, in battle scenes throughout the drama of the period, these musical moments function to generate a sense of conflict which cannot be represented fully on stage by the 'four or five most ragged foils / Right ill-disposed in brawl ridiculous' for which the Chorus apologizes in *Henry V* (4.0.50–1). Such martial music, however, functioned within a commonplace perception of 'war as a harmoniously ordered institution

FIGURE 16 Court trumpeters in the entry procession during wedding festivities in Hechigen for Count von Hohenzollern, 11 October 1598.

in which armies move as in a dance',[5] articulating the paradox that Sidney expressed as 'that ill-agreeing music' of battle.[6] The sense of an aestheticisation of battle is one possible consequence of these musically accompanied dramatic realizations. Frequently, however, the meanings conveyed by trumpets and drums might be much more specific than this. Gervase Markham wrote that:

> The first and last Lesson belonging unto the Horse-troope, is to teach the Souldier the Sounds and Commands of the Trumpet, and to make him both understand the Notes and Language of the Trumpet, as also in due time to performe all those duties and Commands, which are required by the Trumpet.[7]

That trumpets have a 'language' is the crucial term – for these calls have an exact meaning, as do many of the patterns of drum beats. A drummer petitioning for a place in Queen Elizabeth's service, for example, claimed 'I can sownde the englishe, allmaigne, flemishe, frenche, Pyemount, highe Allmaigne, Gascoigne, Spanishe' as well as the 'emperor's' march.[8] This differentiation is reflected in *1 Henry VI*, 3.3.30, 32, where first an 'English march' is called for, followed by a 'French',[9] suggesting that the music itself might have functioned for the audience as an effective and recognizable semiotic code to differentiate the actors on stage.[10]

In the real world of warfare the precise instructions which trumpets and drums give (the former associated more with the cavalry, the latter with the infantry) are more important than any emotional affect, and there are a number of places in the plays where those codes direct an audience's under-standing of the action, whether visible or implied. This is true even of the commonest instruction for 'alarums', which Markham lists as one of the six main signals the horseman needed to know: 'which sounded, every man (like Lightning) flyes upon his enemie, and gives proofe of his valour'.[11] The call is precisely keyed, then, to the 'excursions', or rushes of actors across the stage, with which they are frequently coupled in stage directions, to indicate the onset of battle. Two further calls, the 'parley' and the 'retreat', are signs of ending, and their uses merit special consideration.

The first, a signal for conference under a truce, freezes action in order that speech may be exchanged (a particularly useful device for a dramatist), and is most frequently used by Shakespeare in contexts of siege, summoning, for example, the inhabitants of Angers to the walls in *King John* (2.1.200),[12] or the Senators of Athens to face Alcibiades in *Timon* (5.4). In *Henry V*, 3.3, with more potent dramatic effect, it is the citizens of Harfleur who sound a parley in order to halt the king's advance on the town, making space for Henry's vicious threats of murder and rapine if they do not surrender. It is significant that the stage direction '*A parley*' here *precedes* Gower's explanatory observation that 'The town sounds a parley' (3.2.138). This indicates that the English soldier has certainly learnt, as Markham required, the 'language' of the trumpet, but it also strongly implies that the audience understood the signal.

In a particularly powerful use of the parley, Bolingbroke confronts Richard in *Richard II* and issues the command: 'Go to the rude ribs of that ancient castle; / Through brazen trumpet send the breath of parley / Into his ruined ears' (3.3.32–4). The effect of this signal is only fully to be understood within the series of trumpet and drum sounds that punctuate this scene, and which merit detailed consideration. It opens with Bolingbroke's entry '*with drum and colours*' beating a march, which is itself dramatically juxtaposed with Richard's despairing (and silent) discharge of his followers at the end of the preceding scene.[13] The next Folio stage direction is unusually precise:

> *Parle without, and answere within: then a Flourish. Enter on the Walls,*
> *Richard, Carlisle, Aumerle, Scroop, Salisbury* (3.3.61)[14]

The sequence is interesting. It is the only example of a call to parley being answered – and one wonders whether the second call simply echoes Bolingbroke's parley, or is musically distinct from it, a royal signature as a gesture of defiance from the embattled Richard. Crucially, however, the pair of competing trumpet signals we hear at this tense moment aurally recalls the two opposed trumpet blasts that had signalled the earlier contest between Mowbray and Bolingbroke.[15] It converts the scene, for a moment, into a chivalric challenge of the kind that is memorably deployed in *King Lear* 5.3.113 where Edmund's thrice-issued trumpet call is finally answered by Edgar's off-stage trumpet in reply.[16] The flourish which then follows is the conventional signal of the entry of a royal personage, here given a bitter irony as Richard appears on the walls clutching to himself the empty signifiers of his kingship (a good reason for not adding a trumpet to Bolingbroke's earlier entry). At the very end of the scene, after Richard's capitulation, a final flourish sounds with an effective ambiguity – is it for Richard, or for Bolingbroke, for the old king or the new?[17] This scene suggests how even the most limited of musical resources can be deployed to orchestrate and intensify the drama of Richard's fall, and how the precision of implication in different calls contributes significantly to an audience's understanding of and response to its progress. The Folio stage directions cannot be attributed to Shakespeare himself, but almost certainly derive from the theatrical company who translated his text into performance and the book-keeper who recorded their practice. But, equally, the fact that they do not appear in the Quarto text, generally supposed to be closer to an authorial manuscript, cannot be taken as evidence that Shakespeare was indifferent to musical cues – he no doubt assumed that they would be sorted out in line with convention in the playhouse itself.

The signal for 'retreat' is similarly developed dramatically in a number of plays. In the sequence of short scenes in *King John*, 3.1–3.3, for example, the battle between Philip of France and King John is economically conveyed through music. First King John gives the order: 'to arms let's hie!' (3.1.347); 3.2 begins with '*Alarums, excursions*', signalling that battle has been joined, after which the Bastard enters with Austria's head, and encourages his king: 'But on, my liege, for very little pains / Will bring this labour to an happy end' (3.2.9–10). The next scene (3.3) opens with the direction '*Alarums, excursions, retreat*'. The stage is therefore crossed by fighting soldiers, their forays incited by the conventional 'alarum', before action is terminated by the call for troops to disengage; the whole conduct of a battle is economically foreshortened in this sequence of musical cues. It seems to me highly likely that this signal for battle to cease was one that Shakespeare's audience recognized.[18] In *Troilus*, for example, the retreat sounded in 1.2.173 is followed by Pandarus's comment: 'Hark, they are coming from the field', which would make best sense if the implication of the signal were clear to the audience as well as the on-stage characters.[19] In this play, where the Trojan war rumbles on incessantly in the background, the retreat here suggests no more than temporary cessation of fighting, but elsewhere it generally implies victory for one side or another – as, for example, when Prince Hal hears trumpets off-stage and comments: 'The trumpet sounds retreat; the day is ours' (*1H4*, 5.4.158); or when, immediately after the death of Richard III, the Folio stage direction calls for '*Retreat and flourish*', the first trumpet call signifying the end of the battle, the second the royal salute to the victorious Richmond.[20]

For an audience the sounding of the retreat potentially introduces a moment of anticipation and suspense, giving a special force to the next entry, which will inform us of the battle's outcome. This is exploited to powerful and poignant dramatic effect in *Lear* as Edgar leaves his father, hoping that 'the right may thrive' (5.2.2). An alarum and retreat almost immediately sound 'within' and Edgar re-enters with the news that 'King Lear hath lost' (5.2.6). This play repeatedly taunts its audience with the hope that tragedy might be averted, and as we first hear, as it were with the ears of the blinded Gloucester, the off-stage notice of an outcome in the battle, we might briefly anticipate that 'right' has indeed triumphed. The news that Edgar brings is therefore all the more devastating in its effect. So too, in *Troilus*, whereas the retreat sounded in the play's opening scenes merely signals a pause in the interminable war, the double retreat sounded by both sides in 5.9.15–16 comes poignantly and ironically moments too late to save Hector from Achilles' cowardly victory.

The full effect of many of these musical codes is unrecoverable in modern performance, but the muffled drums that slowly beat the dead march still resonate today. Explicitly called for at the end of *Coriolanus*, *Hamlet*, and *King Lear*, the measured, doleful sound aptly underscores the 'weight of this sad time' (and, more prosaically, ritualizes the practical business of carrying bodies off-stage). The same sound must have been deployed in other tragedies and histories where it is not specified in the texts, though 'dead marches are not employed by Shakespeare or his contemporaries when a character is sullied by crime'.[21] Henry IV's grief at the killing of Richard and the ritual exit of the former king's coffin, for example, would both be reinforced if Henry's command 'March sadly after' (5.6.51) were accompanied by drums, reversing the triumphal flourish which underscored Henry's assumption of the crown at the scene's opening, and at the same time ominously presaging the troubles that will flow from Richard's murder.

One of the most striking uses of this musical motif is not at the end, but the beginning of a play – as *1 Henry VI* opens with a 'dead march' and the funeral of Henry V, a solemn procession which is almost immediately broken off by the entries of messengers bringing bad news from France and by the premonition of the feuds among the nobles that are so quickly to lay waste Henry's achievements. The dead march here is menacingly prophetic. In *Antony and Cleopatra* there is a striking variation on the device, when Enobarbus, having deserted Antony, dies of grief. As the anonymous sentries approach his body there is a cue for '*Drums afar off*', and the sentry remarks 'Hark! The drums / Demurely awake the sleepers' (4.9.36–7). The sound of incipient war becomes, ironically and movingly, Enobarbus's death march.

The semiotic stability of the signals of trumpets and drums readily enables them to be deployed to ironic effect, since there is always the possibility of disjunction between the trumpet's proclamation of dignity and status and the audience's sense of a character's worth. At the beginning of *Antony and Cleopatra*, for example, the 'flourish' that accompanies the entrance of the Roman triumvir and Egyptian queen is undercut by Philo's:

> Look where they come!
> Take but good note, and you shall see in him
> The triple pillar of the world transformed
> Into a strumpet's fool. (*AC*, 1.1.10–13)

At the end of *3 Henry VI* an audience's knowledge of future events (and no Elizabethan would have been ignorant of them) renders heavily ironic Edward IV's command:

> Sound drums and trumpets! Farewell sour annoy!
> For here, I hope, begins our lasting joy. (*3H6*, 5.7.45–6).

It is also important to register the ways in which trumpet calls at the beginning of a scene may achieve some complexity of effect by contrast with what immediately precedes them in the continuous, flowing action of the

Shakespearean stage. Two examples may serve for many. In *2 Henry VI*, at the beginning of 3.2 the 'two or three' who have murdered Humphrey, Duke of Gloucester, enter 'running over the stage' and meet Suffolk, who had set them on to the deed. After a mere fourteen lines they exit, and to the sound of the trumpets King Henry enters, demanding that Gloucester be brought to him for trial. The trumpets therefore stand in ironic contrast to the scene that precedes them, and their royal implication is hollowed out in the juxtaposition.[22] Different, but no less troubling, is the effect at the end of *Troilus and Cressida*, 3.2. After their protracted wooing the lovers finally exit to bed and immediately the Greeks enter, accompanied by a 'flourish', to hear Calchas's request for the exchange of Cressida for Antenor. Whereas in *A Midsummer Night's Dream* the sound of Theseus's hunting horn signals a return from the erotically charged enchantment of the forest to the 'real' world of Athens with striking dramatic effect, but benign consequence, the Greeks' trumpets here interrupt the conclusion of Troilus and Cressida's prolonged foreplay, menacingly portending the events to come.

The collision between the erotic and the martial enacted in this brief moment is, of course, central to the world of this bitterly ironic play, characterized by Thersites as 'wars and lechery' (*TC*, 5.2.201), and it is embodied in contrasting music. It is not until 3.1 that we first see Helen herself, the occasion of the war, on-stage. Her long-awaited entrance is prefaced by a dialogue between Pandarus and a Servant conducted over the sound of music 'within'. It is often difficult to determine for how long music is imagined as continuing underneath speech, but in this scene it is clear that it is sustained throughout the forty-one line dialogue which precedes the entry of Paris and Helen – indeed the punning exchanges in which the servant deliberately misunderstands Pandarus's requests to know on whose orders the music plays seem deliberately contrived to ensure the prolongation of the musical sound. Then, since Pandarus comments at line 48: 'here is good broken music', it is possible that it continues as Paris and Helen appear, though Paris's reply that Pandarus 'has broke it' (49), might equally suggest that it ceases at their entry.[23]

Pandarus's characterization of the sound as 'broken music' indicates that it is played by instruments of more than one family,[24] and Paris's punning insistence on the paradox of a 'broken' harmony connects iron-ically with Ulysses' earlier characterization of the Greek camp as one which has untuned the string of cosmic and political order (1.3.109). What is played is not indicated, although something from the actor-musicians' standard repertoire that the audience might recognize as a tune with erotic associations would be entirely appropriate. Its dramatic effect is a complex one. Following upon the political scheming of the Greeks, it comes to the audience as an aural relief, and, accompanying the long-delayed entrance of Helen, it might seem to assist in building anticipation and contribute to the representation of her mythic beauty.[25] But any positive potential is quickly vitiated by the double entendres of the dialogue which ensues, and by Pandarus's cloying insistence on Helen's 'sweetness'. It is undermined by the claim that Pandarus is 'full of harmony' (51), by the unconscious irony of Helen's statement 'This love will undo us all' (per-haps itself an allusion to an unidentified song or ballad), and above all by the fact that when Pandarus does sing, his lyric, exploiting the conven-tion of love-as-battle, seems grotesquely to embody the confusion of war and lechery of which Thersites bitterly complains.[26]

In this scene Paris confesses that 'I would fain have armed today, but my Nell would not have it so' (130–1), thus suggesting that the music is an expression of the effeminizing enchantment of Helen which inhibits his proper manly exercise; this music is a version of the sirens' alluring and perilous attractiveness (see Figure 4, p. 45). Troilus, when parting from Cressida, fears that she will be tempted by the Greeks, calling his own merit in question because:

> I cannot sing,
> Nor heel the high lavolt, nor sweeten talk,
> Nor play at subtle games – fair virtues all,
> To which the Grecians are most prompt and pregnant. (4.4.84–7)

It is one of the play's many ironies that the only character we actually see singing is not a 'merry Greek', but the Trojan Pandarus. Troilus, how-ever, here articulates the familiar gendered perception of music, and the standard notion that women are particularly susceptible to its influence, attitudes which the music of 3.1. seems to confirm.

The gendered opposition of musics is deployed in rather different circumstances in *1 Henry 4*, when Hotspur responds to Glendower's claim that in his youth he had 'framed to the harp / Many an English ditty lovely well' (3.1.120–1) with the contemptuous: 'I had rather be a kitten and cry "mew" / Than one of these same metre ballad-mongers' (124–5), and later responds to his wife's instruction to 'Lie still ... and hear the lady sing in Welsh' with 'I had rather hear my Lady, my brach [*hunting dog*], howl in Irish' (231–2). The dramatic effect of this music is very different to that in *Troilus*. Although it is threatened both by Hotspur's rejection of its unmanliness, and by his bawdy request to lay his head in his lady's lap while he listens, the song's alienness of language[27] and the suggestion of otherworldly origin (however comic we might consider Glendower's bombastic claims to supernatural powers) means that it offers a glimpse of a harmony, 'charming your blood with pleasing heaviness' as Glendower promises it will (213), for both the characters on-stage and the audience. It therefore briefly and wistfully invokes the possibility of a very different world than that of the rebellion and warfare which surrounds it. Hotspur, shortly before his final battle, cries out: 'Sound all the lofty instruments of war, / And by that music let us all embrace' (5.2.97–8); it is the masculine world of comradeship in battle signalled by trumpet and drum, rather than the feminine attraction of the Welsh song to which he declares his commitment, and by which he dies.

The opposition between 'soft' music and the masculine world of action receives a particularly powerful twist in Richard III's opening soliloquy. He begins with the familiar complaint of the soldier in times of peace:

> Grim-visaged war hath smoothed his wrinkled front,
> And now, instead of mounting barbed steeds
> To fright the souls of fearful adversaries,
> He capers nimbly in a lady's chamber
> To the lascivious pleasing of a lute. (*R 3*, 1.1.9–13)

But, of course, Richard turns his exclusion from the world of love into the motivation for his determination to prove a villain. This is a play which offers no musical relief from the sound of trumpet and drum, no actual embodiment of the 'weak, piping time of peace' (1.1.24); as Wes Folkerth observes, Richard 'prefers to control the soundscape'.[28] It is, then, a sign of the increasing fragility of his control that he responds to the chorus of women accusing him of his crimes with the outburst:

> A flourish, trumpets! Strike alarum, drums!
> Let not the heavens hear these tell-tale women
> Rail on the Lord's anointed. Strike, I say! (4.4.149–51)

His attempt to 'drown their exclamations' (4.4.154) is doomed, and Richmond's victory ensures that 'smooth-faced peace' (5.5.33) replaces the 'clamorous report of war' (4.4.153). The peace which Richard ridiculed at the play's opening is finally triumphant.

Not all musical contrasts in the histories and tragedies play upon this gendered opposition. When, for example, Coriolanus approaches Aufidius's house he hears music playing, and sees servants rushing to serve wine (4.5). How long the music plays is not specified, but its suggestion of sociable conviviality contrasts with the aridity of the Rome Coriolanus has left, and at the same time intensifies the sense of his solitary exclusion from such a world. In *Julius Caesar* Brutus calls for music from his boy, Lucius, in 4.3.255 – though there must be some doubt whether the Folio stage direction '*Music, and a song*' is accurate; since Lucius falls asleep while performing, it is easier to imagine him dropping off 'in mid-strum than mid-warble'.[29] Nonetheless, for him to fall asleep, say, while playing the introduction to a second stanza of a song is not impossible, and for many years theatrical convention introduced the song 'Orpheus with his lute' from *Henry VIII* to fill the gap.[30] The main point, however, is the simple fact of music, rather than its precise content, as Brutus attempts to calm his troubled mind by requiring musical recreation alongside his reading of his book. It is a moment of repose for the audience, coming between the quarrel of Brutus and Cassius and the final battles, but its stillness is quickly undercut as the ghost of Julius Caesar enters, and the doom-laden atmosphere is underlined by the waking Lucius's unintentionally ironic comment: 'The strings, my lord, are false' (4.3.289).

The failure of music here to work its consoling function is more comprehensively addressed in one of the most potent of deployments of non-martial instrumental music in the histories, towards the end of

Richard II. Richard struggles to compare his prison cell to the world, and his anguished meditation is interrupted by the sound of music (5.5.41) which is offered, Richard thinks, as 'a sign of love' (65) by an unidentified off-stage figure.[31] It is not made clear what instrument plays, but since it is to be heard from behind the tiring-house doors it would seem unlikely that it was a solo lute, as is often suggested; a bass viol would perhaps carry more effectively, and its deep tones would certainly be appropriate to the mood.[32] What this music sounds like, and the effect it might have on the audience, is in part dependent on how one reads Richard's first response to it:

> Music do I hear?
> Ha, ha, keep time! How sour sweet music is
> When time is broke and no proportion kept. (5.5.41–3)[33]

On one reading Richard's remarks are to be taken literally, a sign that the musical performance is obviously amateurish and inadequate. If this is the case, then it might prompt one to recognize with pity the good-heartedness of the player(s) doing their best, but it would significantly lessen the affect of the music in intensifying the melancholy of the situation. If, on the other hand, as some have suggested, the comment is to be interpreted as Richard's misperception of the sounds he hears, then the focus upon his disordered mind becomes stronger and contrasts poignantly with the harmoniousness of the music itself. It is likely that some small hesitation prompts Richard's comment, but the music thereafter perhaps should be expertly played, for though in many ways Richard's reflections on the failure of the music of his own life to keep time represent a descant upon familiar ideas about the relationship of musical and human harmony, on time and madness,[34] the scene is given its emotional intensity precisely through the presence of actual music in the ears of the audience. As Richard spins his conceits, moving away from their specifically musical starting-point to more general reflections on Time, the music continues to sound for us, and when Richard turns back to it with the comment: 'For though it have holp madmen to their wits, / In me it seems it will make wise men mad' (62–3), our pain at his suffering is all the more intense if we have ourselves responded positively to the music's affect. The scene plays against what might be an audience's normal expectation, that music should cure the troubled soul, though Richard here represents the alternative possibility, that, as Burton notes, music 'hath diverse effects: and *Theophrastus* right well prophecied that diseases were either procured by Musicke, or mittigated'.[35]

The music outside Richard's cell, however, like Lucius's music for Brutus, turns out to be the presage of disaster, as the murderers, led by Exton, rush in to kill him. In this world it is the loud music of royal power and the 'harsh-resounding trumpet's dreadful bray' as Richard characterizes it (1.3.135), which dominate the aural landscape. This domination is powerfully deployed in *Hamlet*, where even the feasting of the Danish court is marked by the kettledrum and trumpet which, as Hamlet tells Horatio, mark each draught of Rhenish wine the king downs (1.4.10–12). This custom is invoked again with menacing irony in the final scene as drums, trumpets and 'shot' go off when Claudius drinks (5.2.234). At the play's end the militaristic mind of Fortinbras can only conceive of due honour to Hamlet being expressed in 'the soldier's music and the rites of war' (5.2.343). Immediately before his entrance, however, Horatio has saluted the departing Hamlet with the words:

> Good night sweet prince,
> And flights of angels sing thee to thy rest. (5.2.303–4)

It is difficult not to feel that his next line, 'Why does the drum come hither', is spoken with some anger at its martial inappropriateness. The opposition of celestial and military music contributes to the troubling ambiguity of the play's ending.[36]

As we turn to consider instrumental music in the comedies, trumpet and drum may still be heard. They continue to announce the arrival of people of high place – as in the 'flourish' which brings Duke Frederick on-stage to the wrestling match in *As You Like It*, 1.2.134 – and no doubt many other such entrances would have been similarly signalled, though music is not specifically called for in the surviving texts. Such signals are formulaic, and it would probably be wrong to read a great deal into them. So, for example, it is tempting to see the flourishes of cornetts that bring in Morocco and Aragon to the casket-test in *Merchant of Venice*, where no such instruction is given for Bassanio's entrance, as in some way contributing to the self-regarding ostentation of the failed suitors; but such a reading is rendered problematic both by the fact that there is no musical instruction at all in the Quarto text,[37] and by Bassanio's own later arrival at Belmont, signalled by a trumpet (5.1.120).

The 'flourish' which opens *All's Well*, 1.2 is deliberately undercut by the entrance of the sick King of France – presumably carried in on a litter. As the play develops, the military music of the war to which Bertram rushes as masculine escape from the unwished marriage with Helena rings hollowly. He makes explicit his rejection of love in musical terms, when asserting:

> Great Mars, I put myself into this file;
> Make me but like my thoughts and I shall prove
> A lover of thy drum, hater of love. (3.3.9–11)

Bertram places himself in the tradition of masculine refusal of love which we have already seen in Hotspur. But the music of war to which he commits himself is itself rendered problematic in a number of ways. In 3.5 the Widow and Diana, like Pandarus in *Troilus and Cressida*, hear the distant sounds of trumpets as a sign that the soldiers are about to pass by, but the gap between first hearing the signal and the arrival of 'Bertram, Parolles and the whole army' (3.5.74) is filled by the Widow's enjoining of chastity on her daughter and the arrival of Helena, and when Bertram finally appears he is not praised by the onlookers as the Trojans were by Pandarus, but berated for his desertion of his wife. Where the Trojan war carried, for all the scepticism and irony with which it is surrounded, a classical epic resonance, the squabble between Florence and Siena in this play has no such status – the King of France permits his lords to engage on either side indifferently. In this play militarism is represented as youthful masculine vanity, and it is entirely appropriate to its sceptical world that Parolles is humiliated by his failure to live up to his boast that he will recover the soldier's drum, announcing at the climax of his exposure as an empty braggart: 'I'll no more drumming. A plague of all drums' (4.3.292–3). *All's Well* is a notoriously difficult play to place, and it is symptomatic of the problem that, though martial music and the values for which it stands are undermined, there is no contrary harmony to stand against it, no musical celebration of the finally achieved match of Betram and Helena.

The binary opposition of the music of war and that of love continues to haunt the world of the comedies. It forms the basis of Hortensio's wry joke in *The Taming of the Shrew*, when he enters with his head broken by Katherina:

> BAPTISTA   What, will my daughter prove a good musician?
> HORTENSIO I think she'll sooner prove a soldier.
>   Iron may hold with her, but never lutes. (2.1.145–7)

This is, however, more than a transitory joke, and the attitudes it embodies resonate throughout the comedies. Baptista, like many English middle- and upper-class parents of the time, has provided tutors for his daughters since Bianca 'taketh most delight / In music, instruments, and poetry' (1.1.92–3). In this he – and she – are entirely conventional. Katharine's resistance to music lessons, from this perspective, is a further mark of her transgressive nature; although in the event, of course, Bianca and Hortensio use a lute lesson as cover for amatory exchange, and in the end it is she, not her sister, who proves resistant to command. Many women are characterized with reference to their musical abilities. Gower, in *Pericles*, informs us that Marina has been

> by Cleon trained
> In music's letters, who hath gain'd
> Of education all the grace,
> Which makes her both the heart and place
> Of general wonder. (4.0.7–11)[38]

We do actually see Marina singing, but several other heroines are represented as possessing musical skill: Viola, in *Twelfth Night*, claims that she can 'sing / And speak to him [Orsino] in many sorts of music' (1.2.54–5);[39] Perdita's lover, Florizel, in *The Winter's Tale*, wishes she would ever sing and dance (4.4.136–41); and Innogen's epicene quality when disguised as Fidele in *Cymbeline*, is evidenced by Arviragus' comment: 'How angel-like he sings' (4.2.48).[40] The assumption that an ideal woman will be gifted in musical performance, symbolizing her harmonious beauty and her social grace alike, is pithily expressed by Benedick, when he lists the qualities he requires to be combined in a woman before he will consider marriage, and places among them the demand that she should be 'of good discourse, an excellent musician' (*MA*, 2.3.33).

The attribution of excellence in singing to women conforms to the growing emphasis in the period on music as a signal of good breeding and marriageability discussed earlier; but by contrast, and perhaps surprisingly in the light of the prescriptions of Castiglione and others, musical attainment is rarely a matter of moment for male characters. Pericles is the only high-born male figure who is praised as 'music's master' (2.5.28), though we do not hear him perform.[41] More surprising, Polonius includes amongst his instructions to Reynaldo to spy upon Laertes while he is away the command 'Let him ply his music' (2.1.73). No doubt Polonius is thinking in terms of his son's acquiring the courtly accomplishments that were becoming increasingly obligatory for aspiring males in Elizabethan and Jacobean society. Sir John Holles had similarly instructed his son when he set out for France to acquire expertise in dancing as well as riding and fencing 'as so necessarie to a young gentleman, as who cannot expresse himself in them as he ought, shall be disesteemed and neglected of his felloes'.[42] There is, however, no evidence at all in the conspicuously wrathful Laertes that he has so spent his time. But, more than that, there is very little sense in any of the plays that male musical accomplishment is a positive good. Characteristically, men only become musical when they are drunk, or suffering from and for love. Armado instructs Moth to sing because 'my spirit grows heavy in love' (*LLL*, 1.2.118); Orsino commands music to feed his love at the beginning of *Twelfth Night*; Jaques in his 'seven ages' speech characterizes the lover as 'Sighing like a furnace with a woeful ballad / Made to his mistress' eyebrow' (*AYL*, 2.7.148–9); and Speed includes amongst the 'special marks' that indicate that his master is in love that he relishes 'a love-song, like a robin red-breast' (*TGV*, 2.1.19–20). Not far beneath the surface of these and other comic examples of the man reduced to music lies the standard attack on love – that 'it utterly subverts the course of nature in making reason give place to sense, and man to woman' as Sidney's Musidorus sternly puts it.[43]

This commonplace doctrine of love's disempowering force is musically imaged in *Much Ado About Nothing* in the transformation of Benedick. Commenting on the instrumental introduction which precedes the song 'Sigh no more, ladies', he sardonically observes:

> Now, divine air! Now is his soul ravished! Is it not strange that sheep's guts should hale souls out of men's bodies? Well, a horn for my money, when all's done. (2.3.57–60)

Belittling the effect he thinks the music is having on Claudio, Benedick, like Hotspur, declares his preference for the music of the hunt. But soon afterwards he is being ridiculed by the others for having fallen in love, and Claudio taunts him:

> Nay, but his jesting spirit, which is now crept into a lute-string, and now governed by stops. (3.2.54–5)

Love has turned him into an instrument governed by the 'stops' or denials of his beloved. Rosalind similarly chides Silvius because he has allowed Phoebe 'to make thee an instrument and play false strains on thee' (*AYL*, 4.3.67–8). In a man this is a comic abasement.[44]

When applied to a woman, however, such images turn into ones of sexual mastery and command. Pericles, for example, disowns the daughter of Antiochus with the words:

> You are a fair viol, and your sense the strings,
> Who, fingered to make man his lawful music,
> Would draw heaven down and all the gods to hearken. (*Per*, 1.1.82–4)[45]

Thersites caps Ulysses' observation that Cressida 'will sing any man at first sight' with 'And any man may sing her, if he can take her clef. She's noted' (*TC*, 5.2.10–12).

Many of the same issues and questions surround the place of dance and its music. The first two chapters have rehearsed the conflicted attitudes to dance that prevailed in Shakespeare's society, and, like the attitudes to music, they are frequently informed by gendered anxieties. Thomas Elyot, as we have seen, defended dancing as an image of concord between the sexes; but he was also wary of its potential dangers, and so advised:

Nowe it behovethe the daunsers and also the beholders of them to knowe all qualities incident to a man, and also all qualities to a woman lyke wyse appertaynynge.

A man in his naturall perfection is fiers, hardy, stronge in opinion, covaitous of glorie, desirous of knowlege, appetiting [i.e. *desiring*] by generation to brynge forthe his semblable [*likeness*]. The good nature of a woman is to be milde, timerouse, tractable, benigne, of sure remembrance, and shamfast ...

Wherfore, whan we beholde a man and a woman daunsinge to gether, let us suppose there to be a concorde of all the saide qualities, beinge joyned to gether, as I have set them in ordre. And the meuing [*moving*] of the man wolde be more vehement, of the woman more delicate, and with lasse advauncing of the body, signifienge the courage and strenthe that oughte to be in a man, and the pleasant sobrenesse that shulde be in a woman.[46]

According to Elyot, then, dancing should inscribe the 'natural' hierarchy of gender, and be contained in sober civility. Yet a number of the dancing scenes in the plays are more complex in the negotiations they conduct than Elyot suggests.

In *Much Ado about Nothing* Hero is told that the Prince will propose to her in the course of a masked dance. Beatrice comments 'The fault will be in the music, cousin, if you be not wooed in good time' (2.1.63–4), suggesting that it is in part at least the amorous quality of the music and dance itself that will prompt the Prince to make his advances. Immediately afterwards the men enter, masked, with a drum, at line 78; a sequence of conversations between four couples follows; and then, at line 147, the Folio text has the instruction '*Exeunt. Musicke for the Dance*'. There is no specific indication that the preceding dialogues are conducted over music, nor that the couples actually dance forward in turn – though there is no reason why they should not do so, and Alan Brissenden persuasively argues that the sequence of moves and conversations could be fitted to a slow dance such as the pavane 'in duple time and with four or eight figures' (see Figure 17 for a processional dance).[47] But whether or not there is an actual dance at this point, there are a number of interesting features about the episode.

First, male masquers enter with a drum. Allied with the fact that the men are masked, where the women are not, this drum seems to speak an easy assumption of male superiority and aggressive command.[48] It would seem likely to me that they carried not the small tabor which accompanied the pipe (see Figure 14 on p. 95), but something more like the martial drum depicted in Figure 15 (see p. 97). In the event, however, the men are quickly discomfited. Hero rises to a rare moment of self-assertiveness; Margaret makes short work of Balthasar; Beatrice quickly turns the tables on Benedick.

In similar, but more decided fashion, the Princess and her ladies discomfit the King of Navarre and his fellows in *Love's Labour's Lost*. Once the lords find that all have broken their vow of abstinence from love, the King commands them: 'soldiers, to the field', and Berowne encourages his fellows 'Advance your standards and upon them, lords! / Pell-mell, down with them!' (4.3.340–2) and they plot to demonstrate their martially imaged mastery in a masque. The ladies, having notice of their intention, themselves decide to mask and to change favours. When the lords enter, heralded with trumpets and accompanied with music, the ladies quickly put Moth out of his part, refuse the request to unmask, and decline to dance. The masque which began as the confident assault of the soldiers of love is turned to their ridicule and discomfiture.[49] This play, in which 'Jack hath not Jill', confers upon its female characters an unparalleled mastery over their lovers. It is precisely symptomatic of female agency and control that the ladies refuse to participate in a courtly dance which, according to Elyot, would confirm their subordination.

The standard objection to the dancing of the young was that it provoked desire and lecherous behaviour. The whole tragic action of *Romeo and Juliet* is initiated at the dance where Romeo first sees Juliet, in a scene charged with ambiguity. The Montagues only hear of the dance by accident, and Benvolio immediately seizes upon it as an opportunity to drive out Romeo's love for Rosaline. Romeo's companions clearly see the dance as an opportunity for flirtation, to 'measure them a measure and be gone' (1.4.10), which is indeed the perspective Capulet himself offers when recalling that 'I have seen the day / That I have worn a visor and could tell / A whispering tale in a fair lady's ear' (1.5.22–4). More menacingly, these masquers, accompanied like those in *Much Ado* with a masculine drum,[50] are using disguise not merely as part of a social convention, but to infiltrate the house of their enemies. Furthermore, the dance is prefaced by Romeo's rather heavy-handedly proleptic fears that the night's revels will lead to death (1.4.106–11).

Romeo does not participate in the dance himself, but is entranced by Juliet, and speaks to her as she steps out of the measures. Alan Brissenden suggests that:

> she comes to him out of the dance, the symbol of harmony, which probably continues behind them; they meet, speak and kiss against a background of dance and music. This powerfully metaphysical ambience enhances the supremely important moment; it also provides a strong ironic contrast to the discord and tragedy which follow.[51]

This account perhaps rather too readily fixes the dance as a stable 'symbol of harmony'. One does not necessarily have to go so far as associating it with the Dance of Death, as some have done,[52] to recognize that the signification of dance could be much more ambiguous in general, and that this dance in particular is introduced in ways which render it much more problematic than Brissenden suggests. Romeo's mistake, one might say, is not merely to go along with the laddish bravura of entering his enemies' house under the disguise of a mask, but to stand outside the dance itself and therefore not to participate in its controlled and licensed youthful flirtatiousness.

In one other dance in the canon we see flirtation again turn to something more serious. In *Henry VIII*, 1.4, Henry enters with his companions, masked and disguised as shepherds, dances, and is attracted to Anne Bullen, with momentous consequence. The scene is generally attributed to Fletcher, but it replicates some significant features of the masked dances already discussed. First, Henry enters with a noise of drum, trumpet and ordnance[53] which is interpreted as a 'warlike voice' by Wolsey (1.4.50), continuing the sense of masculine aggression that has been implied by the drums in the earlier plays. Second, Wolsey comments that Henry 'with dancing is a little heated' (1.4.100), and evidently not only by exercise; dance has fulfilled the fears of its opponents, and provoked love's heat.

The dances so far discussed initiate or are part of continuing action. One might expect that the dances which bring action to a close and celebrate the achieved harmony of marriage would be much less compromised. But even here Shakespeare characteristically complicates a straightforward, symbolically informed response. The dance which ends *Much Ado About Nothing* undoubtedly works in the theatre to round off the play in high spirits, but one might argue that a faint shadow hangs over it. Benedick demands: 'Let's have a dance ere we are married, that we may lighten our own hearts and our wives' heels', to which Leonato crisply responds 'We'll have dancing afterward' (5.4.116–19). Dance should follow, not precede marriage, as a celebration of legitimized sexuality.[54] But this is perhaps to quibble, for it would seem that this, like the dance that rounds out the ceremonious mating at the end of *As You Like It*, and the fairy blessing in the final dance of *A Midsummer Night's Dream*, are the least ambiguous of closural gestures, uncomplicated in their suggestion of harmony.

Skiles Howard, however, has strongly objected to too ready an identification of these dances with cosmic order.[55] She argues that during the period there is an increasing separation between courtly and popular dance, and that 'courtly dancing reinscribed hierarchy through codified movement, and popular dancing celebrated affinity with traditional motions'.[56] From this perspective, the dance at the end of *As You Like It* confirms that Rosalind surrenders her autonomy as she reassumes her female garments, and Benedick's urgent pleas for a dance only demonstrate that what Harry Berger in his influentially gloomy reading of the play calls 'The Men's Club' is still in control.[57] In Howard's account the dancing in *A Midsummer Night's Dream*, far from celebrating cosmic order, manifests Oberon's triumph over Titania, as gendered hierarchy is restored in the courtly couple-dance (4.1.84–5), standing in opposition to the 'round dance' typical of Titania and the fairies, which Howard characterizes as popular and egalitarian.

In her account of this contest of dance codes the Bergomask with which the mechanicals end their play (the only dance not performed by the fairies) assumes a particular importance. It is not only a popular dance, but one often supposed to be 'a clumsy dance in ridiculous imitation of the movements of the peasants of Bergamo'.[58] Howard is surely right to suggest that in the theatre, especially if originally performed by Kempe, whose fame as a dancer equalled his popularity as an actor, this dance would have been a crowd-pleaser, rather than simply a further demonstration of the mechanicals' ineptitude. So too, she is right to insist that the interpretation of dance in the period must be more complex than simply classifying it as an image of 'harmony'. But there are a number of qualifications one might want to offer of her analysis as it applies to *A Midsummer Night's Dream*. First, although movement codes were undoubtedly becoming increasingly stratified in the period – the distinction between antimasque and masque dances at court embodied that class differentiation – yet Queen Elizabeth's courtiers danced country dances as well as galliards, and she, like Titania, was pleased to watch them do so.[59] The boundaries between different kinds of dance, as between different kinds of music, were not necessarily as rigid and impermeable as Howard suggests. Second, the binary within which Titania's fairies' round dances are classed as 'popular' does not properly allow for the evident contrast between their world and the undoubtedly working world of Bottom himself. The fairies may employ 'popular' dance forms, but they inhabit another and distinct world, and in folklore and theatre alike their difference is conventionally signalled precisely through the presence of music and dance.[60] The verse, 'You spotted snakes', that accompanies their dance for the sleeping Titania is very different from the songs that Bottom sings to himself to keep his spirits up,[61] and there is surely an instrumental differentiation between the accompaniment of their dances and the unmistakably low-life 'tongs and bones' which Bottom demands (4.1.29), and which might have featured in the Bergomask at the end.[62]

It is obviously important that we, like the Princess of France in *Love's Labour's Lost*, are aware of the politics implicit in courtly dancing; but, equally, we have to beware lest in importing contemporary anxieties about class and gender back into our readings of the dances of the plays we impose upon them an ideology as fixed and stern as Puritan disapproval itself was. Shakespeare is the master of equivocation, as the ending of *As You Like It* amply demonstrates. Hymen enters to 'still music',[63] and patterned, dance-like dialogue aligns the quartet of partners. The music

– perhaps of recorders – drawing upon the vocabulary of courtly entertainment and conventional notions of its supernatural associations, persuades us to accept the irruption of the pagan god into the pastoral world of Arden, even as the ceremoniously parallel interchanges of the speakers signal a movement into a new linguistic and theatrical register. But before the final dance, surely called for although not specifically demanded by a stage direction in the Folio text, we have Jaques's decision to absent himself from the play's conclusion. Before he departs, in language quite as patterned as the earlier exchanges, Jaques addresses himself solely to the men (where Hymen spoke to both partners) and concludes with a cynical expectation that Touchstone's marriage 'is but for two months victualled' (5.4.189). Only then does the concluding dance take place, presumably a decorous couple-dance of the kind depicted in Figure 9, p. 61. There is a precarious balance in this daring closing scene which makes us fully aware of its generically determined and theatrically embodied artificiality, and in the figure of the departing Jaques 'a tremor appears in the balance of the comedy', as Anne Barton puts it. She goes on to assert: 'Yet the balance holds. It would be wrong to over-stress the fairy-tale elements in the conclusion, even as it would be inaccurate to see its joyousness as impaired by Jaques' decision to seek a kind of experience unavailable within the comic dance.'[64] The balance is not necessarily easy to achieve on the modern stage, as the very varied Stratford representations of it since the Second World War indicate.[65] The most obvious source of difficulty for the modern audience is the appearance of the mythological figure of Hymen (often cut, especially in earlier productions); but it is at least as significant that modern attitudes to dance are less capable of summoning up notions of cosmic harmony that endorse and support this theatrical theophany, and at the same time lack the awareness of the cultural precariousness of dance that gives weight to Jaques' statement 'I am for other than dancing measures' (5.1.191).

If there are ambivalences and ambiguities surrounding many of the dances in the plays, and if one should be cautious in too readily identifying them simply as emblematic of human and cosmic harmony, one dancing scene – the vision in *Henry VIII*, 4.2.79, where, to 'sad and solemn music' six 'personages, clad in white robes' dance and hold a garland over the head of the sick and sleeping Queen Katharine – functions in a much more obvious fashion. It represents, as she herself interprets it, a vision of the heaven to which she is shortly to ascend; the dance is an angelic performance and simulation of celestial harmony. How this apotheosis of the queen might have been received is not easy to decide – its visionary vocabulary might well have been uncomfortable for many in a Protestant audience – and it has been argued that it is open to question whether the vision 'is just another anodyne or is true inspiration'.[66] But in its basic function this scene (probably written by Fletcher) seems to pick up and elaborate, even over-elaborate, the conventional function of music as sign of curative or cosmic harmony that is deployed in a number of plays to powerful effect.

Music conventionally offered comfort to the diseased mind and body.[67] That is what the dying Henry hopes for when he asks:

> Let there be no noise made, my gentle friends,
> Unless some dull and favourable hand
> Will whisper music to my weary spirit. (*2H4*, 4.5.1–3)

It is not clear for how long music sounds, but its effect is less to focus on Henry (who is beyond cure) than to intensify the contrast between his ebbing life and the noisiness of Prince Henry's entry and to prepare for the melancholy meditation of Hal over his sleeping father. It functions, in other words, as 'incidental' music characteristically does down to the present day, to intensify the emotional impact of stage action. But when in the Quarto text of *King Lear* music is called for to cure Lear's distracted wits (4.7.25) the music itself must be assumed to be an agent in his recovery. The many other theatrical examples that might be adduced attest to the belief expressed by Brabant in Marston's *Jacke Drum's Entertainment* that music 'hath such sweet agreement with our soules, / That it corrects vaine humours, and recalls / ... stragling fancies to faire union'.[68] In *Lear* gentle music is juxtaposed with Cordelia's recollection of the tempests her father has endured to intensify and underline the pathos of the moment, but its actual curative function is central. The fact that the requirement for music was cut in the Folio text suggests, however, that the musical cure was not perceived as an essential part of the scene.[69] In the plays from *Pericles* to *The Tempest* music could much less easily be excised for, as has often been remarked, it is far more than a decorative, if emotionally effective, supplement to the text.

The most straightforward of these texts (though only from a musical point of view) is *Cymbeline*. The play is actually surprisingly reticent in its music cues – there are no flourishes for royal entries, no alarums called for in the battles of 5.2, and while the text clearly requires a hunting horn to be heard at 3.3.98 and 107, it is not specified in any stage directions.[70] The two cues for instrumental music that are present, however, are striking and significant. The first is the '*solemn music*' which suddenly sounds at 4.2.186. It follows immediately upon Guiderius's report of his killing of Cloten, and perhaps we first briefly interpret it as some otherworldly comment on his deed. Belarius immediately tells us that the sound emanates from 'My ingenious instrument', and suggests that it is Arviragus who has 'given it motion'. Guiderius's subsequent comment directs our understanding of this strange sound:

> Since death of my dear'st mother
> It did not speak before. All solemn things
> Should answer solemn accidents. (4.2.189–91)

Arviragus then enters with Innogen, apparently dead, in his arms. There is something anxious and uncertain about the introduction and explanation of this musical moment. It is as if Shakespeare wanted musically to signal the solemnity of Innogen's 'death' as a portentous turning-point in the play, was checked by the realization that, realistically, there would be no instruments in the Welsh wilds, and concocted this mechanical possibility to get round the problem. Exactly what instrument or combination of instruments might have been used is impossible to guess – perhaps the most likely, for a Blackfriars performance, might have been the organ which was certainly available there, or else recorders, or even strings at high pitch. It surely is essential here that, although the sound is naturalistically explained, it should not be too ordinary in its tonal quality.

The second musical cue, accompanying the entry of the ghosts of Posthumus's parents and brothers in 5.4.29, is elaborate but straightforward in its implication. '*Solemn music*' sounds (presumably off-stage) and then the apparitions enter in two pairs, the first '*with music before them*' the second '*after other music*'. 'Music' here clearly means 'musicians' as well as the music they play, and the scene might be staged in a number of ways. The musicians might lead in each ghostly pair, or else the older and younger apparitions might enter at opposite doors and the musicians remain at the entrances, producing a ceremonious antiphonal effect.[71] Whether or not they continue to play underneath the dialogue, in which Posthumus's relations plead with Jove to save him, is not clear – and will depend partly on the nature of their musical instruments. Recorders are the instruments perhaps most often associated with 'solemn' music, but Barnabe Barnes's *The Devil's Charter* calls for a 'solemn flourish of trumpets'.[72] In the music accompanying a supernatural vision in *Macbeth*, 4.1, it is specifically the hautboys which precede the show of eight kings, striking fear into Macbeth; and it is hautboys which similarly represent a fearful otherworldliness in *Antony and Cleopatra*. But they, with sackbuts, could equally sound a note of solemnity and signal the stately arrival of the apparitions in *Cymbeline*. Perhaps quieter music is more likely, not least because of the contrast it might make with Jupiter's descent '*sitting upon an eagle*' and throwing thunderbolts (5.4.92). In the court masque such a heavenly figure would be accompanied by 'loud music', which would also cover any noise of the winch lowering him from the heavens; here, presumably, the firecracker thunderbolts perform the same office.[73] It is important, however, to register that the apparitions in this masque-like scene are visibly accompanied by their musicians. One cannot know exactly how the ghostliness of the figures was conveyed, nor whether the musicians themselves were attired or made up to identify them as visitants from the next world, but this music and its players are located firmly within the theatre. Like the 'ingenious instrument' they have a material reality which grounds their supernatural signification, emphasizing the self-conscious theatricality of the scene.

The significance of this fact is perhaps more apparent in *The Winter's Tale*, in one of the most wonderful of all musical moments in Shakespeare, as Paulina speaks to the statue of Hermione:

> Music, awake her; strike!
> 'Tis time; descend; be stone no more; approach;
> Strike all that look upon with marvel. Come!
> I'll fill your grave up: stir, nay, come away:
> Bequeath to death your numbness; for from him
> Dear life redeems you. (5.3.98–104)

This speech, built of weighty imperatives, is given its emotional syntax by the music which accompanies it, and to the theatre audience it does indeed seem that the music itself causes the transformation of the statue into the living Hermione. But Paulina has prefaced her invocation with anxious disclaimers, protesting that she is not 'assisted / By wicked powers', and ordering 'those that think it is unlawful business / I am about, let them depart' (5.3.90–1, 96–7). Paradoxically these disclaimers work to persuade us, in the theatre, that we are in fact witnessing a marvel. The musical heightening of the scene also inhibits us from asking mundane questions about why and how Paulina had kept Hermione concealed for sixteen years and pushes us towards the aching joy with which we greet the demonstration that the past may indeed be redeemed.[74] The scene, then, both invokes and disclaims the belief that music had magical properties. For a Renaissance audience, much more than a modern one, these beliefs in music's powers were possible and powerful. The music is essential to the explicitly theatrical magic that the scene enacts.[75]

Pericles offers an interesting gloss on Paulina's anxieties. This problematic play – almost certainly of mixed authorship and textually very much less than satisfactory – draws on symbolic music more than any other of the late plays except *The Tempest*, but it does so without the anxieties that we have noted in *Cymbeline* and *The Winter's Tale*. The play's opening scene emphatically recognizes that human music may be duplicitous, as Antiochus' daughter enters in a halo of musical sound (rather like Marlowe's and possibly Shakespeare's Helen of Troy), which helps to generate Pericles' 'inflamed desire' for her (1.1.21), only for her to be exposed when he works out the riddle that convicts her of incest with her father. But in the play's later scenes music is not shadowed or qualified.

When Thaisa's apparently dead body is brought to Cerimon this learned physician demands:

> The rough and woeful music that we have,
> Cause it to sound, beseech you.
> The viol once more. How thou stirr'st, thou block!
> The music there! (3.2.87–90)

As is typical of this play, a good deal of uncertainty hangs over the text here – many editors have chosen to emend 'rough' to 'still', and the 'viol' might equally well be modernized as a 'vial' containing medicines.[76] What is not at issue is that it is the music itself which works the wondrous cure and brings Thaisa back to life. Where, in *Winter's Tale*, the music provided the rhythmic syntax for Paulina's invocation of the statue, here it supports and underscores the high poetic conceitedness of Cerimon's account of Thaisa's awakening:

> Behold
> Her eyelids, cases to those heavenly jewels
> Which Pericles hath lost, begin to part
> Their fringes of bright gold ... (3.2.95–7)

There is no disavowal here; the music – which surely cannot be too 'rough' in its performance – simply works its healing function.

Music then assists at a further cure as Marina, who we are told more than once has an excellent skill in music, sings to the catatonically withdrawn Pericles at 5.1.72. Hers is a 'blank' song, for which no words are given, and she is that comparative rarity, a female singer. Her conspicuous chastity, already demonstrated in the brothel scenes, means that her music is the antithesis of the play's opening, erotically charged sounds. The music does not immediately work – Marina says that Pericles does not 'mark' her music (5.1.73) – and it is only as she begins the narrative of her life that gradual recognition steals over him. The most problematic moment comes, however, when, full recognition of his daughter established, Pericles suddenly observes 'But hark, what music?' (5.1.212). Helicanus says he hears nothing, and Pericles replies: 'None? / The music of the spheres' (5.1.216–17). Symbolically this music is, as it were, that which Marina's earthly singing reflects, but the episode presents directors with a difficult choice – either we, and Pericles, actually hear some musical sound – in which case Helicanus and the rest, like Antonio and Sebastian in *The Tempest*, are represented as in some way tainted by their inability to hear it, or else we, like them, hear nothing, which risks making Pericles appear still distracted. Its immediate effect is to put Pericles to sleep and thereby enable the vision of Diana which persuades him to go to Ephesus and rediscover his lost wife. The selective sleepiness that the music, whether heard or not, enforces is an interesting anticipation of its deployment by Ariel in *The Tempest*, 2.1, but the dramatic clumsiness in this scene in *Pericles* serves only to highlight the way in which, elsewhere, Shakespeare is very clearly in control of the difference between the image of the music of the spheres, and the reality of music performed in the theatre. In *The Tempest* he undertakes his most thorough-going exploration of the nature of music's power and its relationship to magic on the one hand, and human reality on the other – and to this we will return in Chapter 5.

For the moment it is sufficient to observe that in his deployment of instrumental music Shakespeare is ever alert to its dramatic potential, to the ways in which it can both support dramatic action and heighten an audience's response to it. Crucially, he is also always ready to explore its ambiguity and test out its disturbing and ironic possibilities. As we turn to his use of song, we will find this same mobility and elusiveness of signification and the same readiness to exploit ambiguity for dramatic and thematic effect.

Chapter Four

SONG

The songs in Shakespeare's plays are of many different kinds, and serve a variety of dramatic purposes. In order to offer some sort of productive grouping I want to deploy two related categorizations – neither of them absolute, and neither without its problems – which nonetheless provide a convenient underpinning for what follows. The first is a distinction between 'popular' song and what, for want of a better term, one might call 'formal' or 'art' song. As has repeatedly been emphasized, this was a distinction much less obvious in the sixteenth and seventeenth centuries than it is now in terms of musical style. It may well be, indeed, that many of the song lyrics which seem, on the page, to belong securely in the category of 'art' song might, in fact, have been written to fit well-known 'popular' tunes.[1] The difference, then, is one not only of musical vocabulary (as it is more clearly, for example, in the contrast between masque and antimasque song in court entertainments), but also of the way in which the citation of familiar fragments and snatches of popular song differs from a complete and formally delivered song in the relationship it sets up with an audience. The distinction that W.H. Auden offers between the 'called-for song' and the 'impromptu' is useful here. He defines the first as:

> a song which is sung by one character at the request of another who wishes to hear music, so that action and speech are halted until the song is over. ... On the stage, this means that the character called upon to sing ceases to be himself and becomes a performer; the audience is not interested in him but in the quality of his sing

In the second, however:

> The impromptu singer stops speaking and breaks into song, not
> because anyone else has asked him to sing or is listening, but to
> relieve his feelings in a way that speech cannot do or to help him
> in some action. An impromptu song is not art but a form of personal
> behavior. It reveals, as the called-for song cannot, something about
> the singer.[2]

The song performed to an audience on stage invites us to attend not only
to the music in and for itself, but to register its effect upon those to whom
it is directly addressed within the world of the play, so that:

> A song, set in a play, but set out of the play too by its music, facili-
> tates our indulgence in feelings that may be undercut before and
> after the music plays.[3]

Precisely because of their different relationship with the audience it is
important that the singer of a performed song has a good voice and performs well, whereas the involuntary singer needs no such expertise. This
distinction, like that between popular and formal song, is not absolute; and
we shall find that some of the most interesting dramatic uses of song in
the plays are the product of moments when categories overlap and
collide; but, taken together, these two categorizations provide a convenient structure for the ensuing discussion.

'POPULAR' SONG AND BALLAD

The ballad belongs, as we have seen, in popular culture, but might, in the
real world and in Shakespeare's plays alike, be either 'called-for' or
'impromptu'; on the one hand performed by professional musicians or
ballad-sellers (see Figure 11 on p. 75) or, on the other, providing the fund
of familiar tunes and words on which people, then as now, are likely to
draw when they wish to express or 'relieve' their feelings. When the
'performed' ballad is invoked by individuals in plays of the period the associations are largely negative, and their character as songs commenting
satirically on people or events is perceived as threatening. The vehement

persuasion that Matheo offers to Hippolito to moderate his behaviour in the First Part of Dekker's *The Honest Whore* is typical: 'doe you long to have base roags that maintaine a saint *Anthonies* fire in their noses (by nothing but two peny Ale) make ballads of you?'[4] These sentiments are echoed in various places in Shakespeare. Helena, in *All's Well*, tells the King of France that if her cure does not work she is prepared to undergo:

> Tax of impudence,
> A strumpet's boldness, a divulged shame,
> Traduc'd by odious ballads; my maiden's name
> Sear'd otherwise ... (2.1.169–72)

Cleopatra imagines as one of the horrors of being led captive through Rome that 'scald rhymers' will 'ballad us out o'tune' (*AC*, 5.2.214–15); Benedick visits on himself the curse:

> prove that ever I lose more blood with love than I will get again with drinking, pick out mine eyes with a ballad-maker's pen, and hang me up at the door of a brothel-house for the sign of blind Cupid. (*MA*, 1.1.237–9)

Falstaff rages at Hal and his companions when they refuse to provide him a horse: 'An I have not ballads made on you and sung to filthy tunes, let a cup of sack be my poison' (*1H4*, 2.2.44–5), his adjective firmly characterizing ballad tunes as both morally and socially disreputable. Falstaff also threatens, if he is not given his proper due for the capture of John Colevile, that:

> I will have it in a particular ballad else, with mine own picture on the top on't, Colevile kissing my foot: to the which course if I be enforced, if you do not all show like gilt tuppences to me ... believe not the word of the noble. (*2H4*, 4.3.47–54)

One might take this speech in a number of ways. At one level, perhaps, it can be construed as a threat whose vulgarity would upset Prince John; at another, however, it represents a self-aggrandizement which echoes that of Bottom the weaver, who actively seeks memorialization in a ballad. When he wakes from his vision of Titania he proudly says:

I will get Peter Quince to write a ballad of this dream: it shall be called 'Bottom's Dream', because it hath no bottom; and I will sing it in the latter end of a play, before the Duke. Peradventure, to make it the more gracious, I shall sing it at her death. (*MND*, 4.1.212–17)

At one level Bottom's comfortableness with this notion is simply a mark of his social status – as, in *The Winter's Tale*, the eagerness of the rural population to inspect the ballads of Autolycus defines their class. But in offering to perform his ballad at the end of a play he identifies himself with the normal expectations of the theatre audience that the actor, Kempe, who probably played the part, would indeed end the entertainment with a ballad or jig.

It is this ambivalence which characterizes the various uses to which actual sung ballads are put throughout the Shakespeare canon. They are lower class, but employ a language and a music shared between characters of different social status, and with the audience. They are capable therefore of standing in various relationships with stage action. So, for example, the witty exchange between Lucetta and Julia over a lover's rhyme demonstrates their sophisticated familiarity with musical terminology; but when Julia suggests 'best sing it to the tune of "Light o' Love"' (*TGV*, 1.2.83) she nominates a tune that would probably have been familiar to all, and, perhaps, a ballad familiar enough for an audience to recognize that the original words are actually about female fickleness – even though here they poignantly foreshadow the faithlessness of Proteus who has sent the letter.[5]

References to ballads imply a knowledge shared between audience and stage characters – as, for example, in the two casual mentions of perhaps the best-known of all ballad tunes, *Greensleeves*, in *Merry Wives of Windsor*. In the first, Mistress Ford comments ironically on the disparity between Falstaff's behaviour and his words: 'they do no more adhere and keep place together than the hundred psalms to the tune of "Greensleeves"' (2.1.54–6). In the second, Falstaff greets the approach of Mistress Ford with a call for aphrodisiacs: 'Let the sky rain potatoes, let it thunder to the tune of "Greensleeves", hail kissing-comfits and eringoes.

Let there come a tempest of provocation' (5.5.18–21). There are, however, some basic problems in detecting and interpreting such references.
In the first place, the fact that many ballads have been lost means that we
cannot always be sure whether what appears to be a citation or quotation of a popular song is not in fact an impromptu invention (or, conversely,
be confident that we have not missed an allusion altogether). More
important, the textual and musical malleability of ballads means that it
is important not to treat recollections or citations of them in the same way
as one might discuss the uses Shakespeare makes, for example, of references to stable classical texts. The intertextual dialogue is altogether less
precise in the citation of a ballad text. Second, it is not always explicit
whether ballad-fragments are intended to be sung or spoken.

   Both of these problems are illustrated in *Love's Labour's Lost*. At 4.1 the
witty banter between Boyet and Rosaline concludes with the lines:

> ROSALINE
>   Thou canst not hit it, hit it, hit it,
>   Thou canst not hit it, my good man.
> BOYET
>   An I cannot, cannot, cannot,
>   An I cannot, another can. (4.1.126–9)

The Arden2 edition suggested that this was a dance tune and cited a
number of parallel phrases; Arden 3 simply notes that it is 'a popular song
and dance, with the innuendo of "hitting" as having sex'. Ross Duffin,
however, observing that 'no text survives for this song, aside from the lines
in Shakespeare', suggests that 'this may have been a rhyme to accompany a game'.[6] Without a clear sense of exactly what original the two
characters might refer to, the full implication of the exchange is lost. The
difference between the adoption of a song which already has an amatory
or sexual content, and the conversion of an innocent game into bawdy
implication is perhaps slight, but not insignificant. More interesting is the
question whether or not the characters here actually burst into song.
Seng[7] does not list this as a song, though the editors of *A Shakespeare Music
Catalogue* do. If the characters do sing, it makes a difference to the dramatic
effect. In particular, the impropriety of admitting low-life song into courtly

word-play becomes more marked. Berowne's later ridicule of Boyet includes the assertion 'he can sing / A mean most meanly' (5.2.327–8) – and he clearly does not intend this as a compliment, but rather to intensify the suggestion of Boyet's effeminacy which runs through his speech. Rosaline's transgressive indecorum would be increased by her singing in public. It is perhaps significant that it is the lowly Costard who applauds their exchange with the words 'By my troth, most pleasant', for much earlier in the play when Armado asks 'Is there not a ballad, boy, of the King and the Beggar' which will serve as a model for his falling in love with Jacquenetta the dairymaid, his page, Moth, is haughtily contemptuous of such lower-class and outdated material: 'The world was very guilty of such a ballad some three ages since, but I think now 'tis not to be found, or, if it were, it would neither serve for the writing nor the tune' (1.2.104–9).[8] The brief moment of Boyet and Rosaline's exchange, then, illustrates some of the very real practical problems in pinning down ballad references and the nature of their performance. It also raises significant questions as to how a contemporary audience might have received and responded to such a citation – would they have identified with Costard's pleasure, or would they have perceived it primarily as overstepping the boundaries of decorum?

Questions such as these attend many of the citations of popular song throughout the canon. Rather than track all the references to and uses of ballads, however, it seems most profitable to focus on five plays where their function is particularly significant. In *2 Henry IV*, *Othello*, *Hamlet*, *King Lear*, and *The Winter's Tale*, popular song figures prominently, making important yet very distinct contributions to each of them.

While in both parts of *Henry IV* the tavern stands in opposition to the world of the court, and while the tavern was above all the place of convivial music and balladry, it is notable that there is virtually no music in Eastcheap in *Part One*. In *Part Two*, however, music has a vital role, not, as one might perhaps expect, simply as sign of riot and drunkenness, but as a melancholy reinforcement of the darkening world of this play. In 2.4 an anonymous tavern servant is sent to find the memorably named 'Sneak's Noise'[9] because 'Mistress Tearsheet would fain hear some music' (2.4.10–12). Before they arrive, Falstaff enters singing the first lines of the ballad 'When Arthur first in court began, and was a worthy king', which, in the version Duffin quotes, continues 'By force of arms great victories won and conquest home did bring'.[10] If sung with a certain bravura, as one might expect of an entrance song, this would suggest that Falstaff, whom we have earlier seen sick and conscious of his age, has recovered his spirits and sense of his own importance; but the entry and furious language of the braggart Pistol soon overfaces him, and he wearily says 'Pistol, I would be quiet' (2.4.183), before thrusting him out of doors with his rapier. Shortly afterwards the musicians enter and begin to play (2.4.224). A band of this sort would, presumably, play music from a popular repertoire, and if their performance continues throughout the scene then the effect is potentially a powerful and mixed one. At one level, requested as they are by the prostitute Doll Tearsheet, they represent the familiar association of brothel and music, dramatically represented in Middleton's *Your Five Gallants*, where, under pretence of providing a music school for young ladies, Primero runs a bawdy-house. His courtesans are indeed musical, but, as the bawd observes, 'They're natural at pricksong'.[11] Yet since Prince Hal, overlooking Falstaff and his whore, later observes: 'Is it not strange that desire should so many years outlive performance?' (2.4.260–1), the effect, particularly if the music is of a gently melancholic character, is rather to underline Falstaff's wistful observation 'I am old, I am old' (271) than to suggest the incitement of lust. Exactly when the musicians stop is not indicated, but most obviously they might end when Hal reveals himself at line 290. Falstaff's command to pay the musicians at line 373 then comes as an afterthought (typically avoiding his own expenditure). But whenever it stops, the music is here associated with old age and declining performance in a fashion that is picked up again in the final Gloucestershire scene.

The first two Gloucestershire scenes emphasize the senescence of Shallow and Silence – and of Sir John himself, vainly though he resists it. They contain no music – unless Shallow's reminiscence 'Our watchword was "Hem, boys"' following Falstaff's 'We have heard the chimes at midnight' (3.2.214–18) is an allusion to the refrain of the ballad 'There was an old fellow at Waltham Cross' which concludes 'with a Hem, boys, hem, and a cup of old sack'.[12] But in the final Gloucestershire scene, ballads become crucial to the dramatic effect, as Silence incessantly picks up words from the dialogue and responds with snatches of song. Only two of his five songs have been identified, but there is no reason to doubt that the others were either citations or variations of known ballads. The effect here is poignantly comic. That Silence sings is a symptom of his drunkenness – and his increasing inebriation is charted by the fact that he sings less and less of each ballad, finally uttering the single line 'And Robin Hood, Scarlet and John' (5.3.103) after which he says nothing further. But more than that, these are songs of recollection; the characters call to mind ballads with which we might assume the audience are familiar, and at the same time function, like the earlier reminiscences by Falstaff and Shallow of their youthful escapades, as painful reminders of a time that is irrevocably gone. The identification between audience and singing character which the songs necessarily generate – however comic they may be in their drunken performance – both prepares for, and contributes to, the shock of Hal's rejection of Falstaff: 'I know thee not, old man' (5.5.47).

The association of music and the past may be given weightier significance. Robin Headlam Wells has suggested that there is a religious iconology underlying the tavern music surrounding Falstaff, which 'underscores the link that Hal makes between him and the devil'.[13] In this account, Falstaff stands for the 'old music' of the unregenerate soul, 'the music of the unenlightened, the melody of the flesh rather than of the spirit'.[14] Hal in his reformation casts off the 'Old Man', has 'turn'd away from my former self' (2H4, 5.5.58), and associates himself with the New Man of St Paul. Headlam Wells is fully aware that this is an identification which Hal manufactures and exploits for political purposes, and he does not see it as rendering the rejection of Falstaff less problematic an experience for the theatrical audience. Indeed, I would argue that even if the music which surrounds Falstaff in the tavern and the songs which Silence sings are 'the music of the unregenerate', the fact remains that in the theatrical experience of the play they elicit from us a response that ensures our emotional complicity with its senescent characters. The music and fragments of song thus offer a counterpoise to the exposure of corruption in Falstaff's impressing of his soldiers, and ameliorate our increasingly judgemental sense of his abandonment of knightly responsibility as the play heads towards its close. In the complex interplay of alienation and empathy which leads up to Falstaff's rejection, music has a significant function.

Recollection and melancholy also characterize Desdemona's 'willow song' in *Othello*. She introduces it with the words:

> My mother had a maid called Barbary,
> She was in love, and he she loved proved mad
> And did forsake her. She had a song of 'willow'.
> An old thing 'twas, but it expressed her fortune
> And she died singing it. That song tonight
> Will not go from my mind. (4.3.24–9)

The association of music and love-melancholy is a standard one; more interesting here is the way the ballad is placed in terms of social class – it is the maid, not the mother, who sang it. It is important, too, that it is offered as an old song, a song heard in childhood, which forces its way into Desdemona's memory, and then into her voice as she sings it to accompany her preparations for bed.[15] Or, at least, it does so in the Folio text of the play, for in the Quarto the song itself is cut, as is the later recollection of it by Emilia at her death (5.2.247–8).

It has been suggested that these cuts should be linked to the apparent change of mind which sees 'Come away death' in *Twelfth Night* reallocated from Viola to Feste,[16] and that the reason for both was that 'the original boy actor's voice broke earlier than expected, and that adjustments were hurriedly made in both plays at the same time'.[17] Attractive as the hypothesis might be, it is by no means uncontroversial, requiring a modification of the usually accepted date of the composition of *Othello* and resting on an unproveable hypothesis about acting personnel. Few critics, however, would want to deny that the scene reads awkwardly and loses immeasurably in its pathos without the song.

This ballad illustrates nicely the variety of problems which attend such musical moments in the plays. Although Desdemona invokes it as an old song, and although 'willow' refrains have been found in lyrics which pre-date the play, the only surviving versions close to her text come from unregistered broadsides of the early seventeenth century. There are at least two candidates for the melody to which it might be sung, the more famous of which is preserved in a manuscript which post-dates the play.[18] It therefore becomes difficult to assess precisely what kind of intertextual dialogue, if any, a member of the original audience might have perceived in Desdemona's version. How far does it matter that the surviving texts are in a male, not female persona? How many of the audience would have registered Desdemona's revision of 'Let nobody blame me, her scorns do I prove' to 'Let nobody blame him, his scorn I approve', a modification which Honigman annotates as: 'A Freudian slip (unconsciously she wants to shield Othello from blame)?' So too, one might wonder whether the fact that 'she first muddles the order of the stanzas before finally stopping altogether, unable to go on'[19] would have been perceptible in the theatre.

There are questions, too, about the manner of the song's performance. Othello has earlier remarked that his wife 'sings, plays and dances well' (3.3.188) and it is just possible that she might sing to a lute. The version of the song in British Library Additional MS 15117 has a lute accompaniment, and King suggests that 'some striking harmonic modulations in the lute accompaniment ... greatly increase the impact of the tune, while cadences in the lute part sound through rests in the vocal line to give the effect of sighs'.[20] But Sternfeld objects that 'it would not be feasible, either for Desdemona or for Emilia, to manage a lute while Emilia undresses her mistress. The entire character of her recitation, the spontaneous way in which she breaks into her swansong, modifies and breaks it off, precludes forethought or an elaborate instrumental accompaniment.'[21] My own view coincides with Sternfeld's, but for rather different reasons: to introduce accompaniment would tend to turn this from involuntary song into performance, and any sense of self-consciousness would convert its pathos into a stagy sentimentality – a danger which, even if Desdemona sings unaccompanied, is only narrowly averted.

Nonetheless, the song, as a brief hiatus in the terrible inevitability of the prosecution of Othello's jealous rage, has enormous dramatic power and a great capacity to move an audience both for what it shows of Desdemona's emotional state and because its very vulnerability of expression heightens our sense of her self-sacrificial state of mind. The liveliness and independence which characterize Desdemona in the earlier part of the play are lost as, the swan singing before her death, she seems to assent to her inevitable fate. The force of the scene is more fully to be comprehended if it is set within the other musical references and events in the play. At Othello's arrival in Cyprus he is greeted by the sound of the trumpet, as befits his dignity; he then turns to Desdemona, greets her, and sums up his state of mind:

> I cannot speak enough of this content,
> It stops me here, it is too much of joy.
> And this, and this the greatest discords be   *They kiss*
> That e'er our hearts shall make.

On which Iago comments, aside:

> O, you are well tuned now: but I'll set down
> The pegs that make this music, as honest
> As I am. (2.1.194–9)[22]

It is the measure of his success that the mutual music of love turns into the solo lament of Desdemona singing a lyric of desertion.

A crucial stage in Iago's persuasion is reached at the moment when Othello characterizes the consequence of Desdemona's imagined unfaithfulness on his own sense of self explicitly in musical terms:

> Farewell the tranquil mind, farewell content!
> Farewell the plumed troops and the big wars
> That makes ambition virtue! O farewell,
> Farewell the neighing steed and the shrill trump,
> The spirit-stirring drum, th'ear-piercing fife,
> The royal banner, and all quality,
> Pride, pomp and circumstance of glorious war!
> And, O you mortal engines whose rude throats
> Th'immortal Jove's dread clamours conterfeit,
> Farewell: Othello's occupation's gone. (3.3.351–60)

The familiar opposition between the music of war and of love is reflected here in Othello's definition of himself by the martial instruments of battle; the music of love is forgotten as the threat of Desdemona's infidelity figures a loss of masculine identity.

Iago's manipulation is not only practised on the Moor; the entrapment of his other victim, Cassio, is also characterized in part in musical terms. Iago first plots his downfall as they set out on the watch – incidentally and salaciously characterizing Desdemona's speech as 'an alarum to love' (2.3.24) – by enticing the weak-headed Cassio to drink, which he does by singing the song 'And let me the cannikin clink' (2.3.64–8). No tune survives, but this is clearly a song the tavern, which Iago claims to have learned in England, where they are 'most potent in potting' (2.3.72). Its swaggering lyric identifies manliness with the life of the soldier and with drinking, and it is, no doubt, precisely that identification which persuades the nervous Cassio that it is ''Fore God, an excellent song!' (2.3.70). Iago then incites him further with a stanza taken from a longer Scottish ballad, varying the original 'King Harry was a very good king' to 'King Stephen was and-a worthy peer' (2.3.83–90).[23] While the lyrics seem to speak of impatience with class privilege, which is appropriate enough to Iago, they have no particular relevance to the moment – unless, as Honigman suggests, Iago aims the lines 'He was a wight of high renown / And thou art but of low degree' as a direct insult to Cassio. The significance is rather that Cassio indicates his inebriation by admiring it as 'a more exquisite song than the other' (2.3.92–3). If Iago's success with Othello comes through exploitation of a soldier's sense of vulnerability in love, his success with Cassio comes by preying upon his anxiety over his own soldierly masculinity expressed in his confessed inability to take his drink. Popular music is Iago's persuasive means to entice Cassio with the illusion of conviviality and belonging to the crowd. What might appear to be impromptu song is in fact carefully staged and performed with duplicitous intent. In the theatre, however, the audience's response is complicated because, although they are aware of Iago's purposes, they are at the same time likely themselves to identify with a familiar drinking song, and therefore with the conventional masculine attitudes it embodies. This then renders Cassio's inability to take his drink comic, or even contemptible in our minds. Iago seduces us, briefly at least, to complicity with his scheming through the agency of song.

And there is comedy, too, in Cassio's next musical humiliation, as he tries to recover his position by providing an aubade at Othello's door (3.1). The musicians play, but the Clown enters and ridicules the noise of their reed instruments (perhaps including bagpipes), telling them that the general doesn't want them, and the musicians quickly pack up and leave. 'Cassio behaves correctly in considering that music is necessary for the occasion, but he displays an inordinate lack of taste in his choice of musicians.'[24] This might seem a rather clumsy and unnecessary scene, and it is often cut, but Lawrence J. Ross has argued at length that it is a hinge in the play, functioning as a prelude to Iago's efforts to untune the music of Othello and Desdemona's love.[25] Crucial to his argument is what he perceives as the opposition between the music that Cassio provides, and the Clown's statement: 'If you have any music that may not be heard, to't again' (3.1.15–16). Cassio's bagpipes (or other reed instruments) are associated with lechery and the grossly human, whereas the 'music that may not be heard' is read as a reference to the heavenly music of the spheres, so that the scene functions symbolically and emblematically to set these two musics one against the other. One might wonder whether the Clown's jocular comment will really sustain the enormous learning expended in substantiating this argument, yet Ross makes an important and simple point when he observes that the comment 'to hear music the general does not greatly care' (3.1.16–17) is a sign of the way that 'under Iago's "rule" Othello lacks "true musick" more and more, and an ironic measure of his tragic degeneration is provided by his growing incapacity to "hear" it as the action progresses'.[26]

It is the surrounding variety of these musics, literal and figurative, in the drunken songs of Iago, the earthy sounds of Cassio's failed aubade, the recollection of the masculine music of war and the loss of love's music, that reinforces the fragility of Desdemona's private and melancholy song. It is significant also that her music-making stands as a mark of female disempowerment in the play, as is emphasized painfully when Emilia, after her outburst 'No I will speak as liberal as the north, / Let heaven and men and devils, let them all, / All cry shame against me' (5.2.218–20) is stabbed by her husband and dies singing 'willow, willow', and calling out 'Canst thou hear me' to Desdemona.

In *Hamlet* another marginalized woman abused in love dies chanting 'snatches of old tunes'. Ophelia's singing in her mad scene is more troubling than Desdemona's, and richer in its theatrical effect. In order fully to understand its effect it is important to juxtapose it with the earlier scenes of Hamlet's distraction. After being subjected to Hamlet's rejection, Ophelia comments on the spectacle of his madness:

> And I, of ladies most deject and wretched,
> That suck'd the honey of his music vows,
> Now see that noble and most sovereign reason
> Like sweet bells jangled out of tune and harsh,
> That unmatch'd form and feature of blown youth
> Blasted with ecstasy. (3.1.156–61)[27]

Ophelia characterizes Hamlet's 'ecstasy' in musical terms, but she essays no explanation of his madness, which she clearly believes is genuine. The reactions of the listening Claudius and Polonius, however, are very different. While Polonius interprets Hamlet's conduct as a consequence of love-melancholy, Claudius suggests that 'what he spake, though it lack'd form a little, / Was not like madness', and fears that 'the hatch and disclose / Will be some danger' (3.1.164–5, 167–8). Each of the beholders reads the spectacle of insanity differently, and when Ophelia herself later appears in a state of distraction we, and the audience on stage, are faced with very similar problems of interpretation.

Ophelia enters, according to the stage direction of the first Quarto, '*playing on a Lute, and her haire downe singing*'.[28] In some respects this entrance works within familiar theatrical conventions. Hair let down was a conventional sign of a woman in a high emotional state, if not necessarily one of madness,[29] her broken and fragmentary speech is of the same kind that characterizes the madness of Edgar as Poor Tom in *King Lear*.[30] These, and her inability to recognize people, are symptoms that were widely recognized as signifying madness in the medical discourse of the period.[31] Singing, however, seems to have been the theatre's, or perhaps Shakespeare's, addition to the iconography of the mad woman. The representation of Ophelia's distraction by her singing established it as a theatrical norm, imitated in the later Fletcher-Shakespeare collaboration,

Two Noble Kinsmen, and thereafter to become not only a theatrical convention, but the foundation of a sub-genre of later seventeenth-century song.[32] Ophelia's songs, although exact sources have not been found for them, clearly belong to the popular ballad tradition.[33]

In approaching this powerful dramatic episode, there is a whole series of questions that need to be raised. First, the question of the manner of Ophelia's performance. Auden observes:

> no producer ... would seek to engage Madame Callas for the part of Ophelia, because the beauty of her voice would distract the audience's attention from the real dramatic point which is that Ophelia's songs are to the highest degree *not* called for.[34]

It is presumably because Harold Jenkins also sees this as impromptu song that he objects to the lute specified in the First Quarto stage direction as 'uncalled for in the text and incongruous with the ballad snatches Ophelia spontaneously breaks into'.[35] Yet, unlike the situation of Desdemona's song, there is no practical reason here why Ophelia should not carry a lute – and the lute can be played, as the songs can be sung, in very many different ways. The majority of actresses have chosen to generate through their singing a withdrawn, introspective pathos in a contained and musical rendition of the songs, and at least one early twentieth-century performer did accompany herself on the lute.[36] Glenda Jackson in the RSC performance in 1965 deliberately did not – the songs were barely sung, and the words harshly thrown at the characters on stage. This performance eschewed the poignant effect that the music can certainly have; but in doing so it drew attention to the way these songs, unlike Desdemona's, carry the potential to suggest something more than the impromptu expression of unspeakable feeling.[37] For just as in her speech Ophelia addresses people directly, although not apparently knowing who they are, so there is the possibility that her songs are sung to, or appear to be aimed at, an audience that exists at least in her mind. When represented on stage, madness, like death, must always be a 'performance' and therefore to some extent focus our attention on the performer-as-actor.[38] It is this, I would argue, that gives this scene its theatrical edge. Neither the characters on stage nor the audience in the theatre are sure how to interpret Ophelia's songs and speeches.

The anonymous Gentleman who prepares us for her entrance remarks:

> Her speech is nothing,
> Yet the unshaped use of it doth move
> The hearers to collection. They aim at it,
> And botch the words up to fit to their own thoughts. (4.5.7–10)

Just as Polonius had earlier interpreted Hamlet's madness as a consequence of love melancholy, so Claudius suggests 'it springs / All from her father's death' (4.5.75–6). A good deal of literary criticism has been preoccupied with identifying the 'source' of Ophelia's madness by means of the subjects of the songs she sings, debating whether they speak of her father, or of Hamlet. They surely refer in some way to both, and articulate Ophelia's desperation at the death of one and desertion of the other. But interpreting the songs solely as the impromptu expression of her feelings, and seeing them only as significant insofar as they embody her psychological state, obscures the different ways in which her songs might be read by the on-stage audience. For just as Claudius is fearful of what Hamlet's madness might portend, so Horatio fears that Ophelia 'may strew / Dangerous conjectures in ill-breeding minds'[39] (5.4.14–15), and Gertrude confesses that 'each toy seems prologue to some great amiss' (5.4.18).

Ophelia's first line, 'Where is the beauteous Majesty of Denmark?' (4.5.21), is resonantly ambiguous – it might refer, with conscious or unconscious irony, to the queen or to the king, or might be taken to recollect her earlier description of Hamlet. Gertrude certainly seems to think it is addressed to herself, and responds with the uneasy question 'How now Ophelia?' We might then readily imagine that the opening of Ophelia's first song, 'How should I my true love know / From another one' could be taken by a nervous Gertrude to refer to her own dead first husband – an impression which might be fortified by an anxious delivery of her question: 'Alas, sweet lady, what imports this song?' (4.5.27). To others on-stage, however, the partial referents might be more obviously Hamlet (true love, but not dead) or Polonius (dead, but not a true love).

As the song continues with the narrative of a burial Claudius enters, and
Ophelia makes a pointed modification of expectation as she sings:

> White his shroud as the mountain snow
>> Larded with sweet flowers
> Which bewept to the grave did not go
>> With true-love showers. (4.5.36, 38–40).

The 'not' in the third line 'violates both the metre and the expected sense',
and Jenkins conjectures that 'the song thus reflects the actual short-
comings of her father's burial ... but still more, since it concerns a "true
love", her fantasies of Hamlet's death'.[40] It is equally possible that to
Gertrude, and to Claudius who has just entered, these 'maimed rites' might
speak of the death of Hamlet's father, unmourned by his unloving queen,
rather than of Polonius. This is not to suggest that Ophelia knows the truth
of the murder (though in theory she might have divined it herself from
Claudius's reaction to the 'Mousetrap'), any more than her subsequent
song of seduction, 'Tomorrow is Saint Valentine's day' (4.5.48–55), should
be taken to indicate that she and Hamlet had consummated their love-
relationship. It is, however, to recognize, with the Gentleman, that the
spectacle of madness inevitably invites interpretation, by the audience on
stage as well as in the theatre, and that we, like them, hear the words
Ophelia utters and sings as referring, however unconsciously, to more than
her psychological state.

> When Ophelia sings, she takes on a mask of performance: her per-
> sonal voice is estranged, filtered through the anonymous voices of
> the ballads, multiplying, and thereby rendering indeterminate the
> relationships between singer, personae, and audience.[41]

It is this fundamentally theatrical indeterminacy which generates a significant part of the disturbing effect of the scene.

Its power also derives from the ways in which Ophelia breaks all the
bounds of social convention by which and to which she has hitherto been
bound. The dishevelled hair is symptomatic of her indifferent confusion
of public and private worlds; the fact that she sings in public at all is an
impropriety;[42] that she performs popular songs is indecorous, and, of

course, 'Tomorrow is St. Valentine's day' in particular speaks of desire with an immodest directness.[43] She presents a mixed emblematic picture. Her disordered hair might link her to the prophetess Cassandra, who appears in *Troilus and Cressida 'with her hair about her ears'* (2.2.97), and thereby underscore the anxiety with which Gertrude and Claudius greet her; but her entry in a state of undress, and her singing, especially if she does carry a lute, associates her both with music's irrational force, and perilously with the prostitute.[44] The conventional association of music with madness and melancholy – which it might express, incite or cure – underlies Shakespeare's adoption of song as the medium of expression of Ophelia's distraction, and it has often been suggested that it signals that she suffers from love-sickness, or 'erotomania', to which women were adjudged particularly prone.[45]

A number of recent critics have focused particularly on the way in which the mapping of music, madness, and gender one onto the other is important for this scene. Dunn suggests: 'if music arouses excessive "feminine" passions, then it is also an ideal vehicle for representing feminine excess', and is therefore 'an apt marker of the mad Ophelia: a frightening figure of female openness, of uncontrolled generativity'.[46] Fox-Good arrives at a similar verdict, suggesting that 'through music – which means so much partly because it appears to mean either nothing or an inexpressible everything – Ophelia builds a secret, subversive power beneath a public, conventional appearance of passivity and vulnerability'.[47] Readings such as these suggest strongly the way in which Shakespeare's use of song to characterize Ophelia's madness taps into Renaissance cultural anxieties about the relationship of music and the feminine that we have noted repeatedly in the course of this study.

In this context it is of more than passing interest that in at least two of the songs, 'How should I your true love know', and 'Tomorrow is Saint Valentine's day', Ophelia, like Desdemona, seems to adopt what, in analogous lyrics, is a male position – the first of a man deserted by his lover, the second the song sung at a beloved's window. Given the uncertainty about what versions of the songs Shakespeare and the original audience might have known it would be wrong to read too much in to this variation, but that Ophelia in her distraction can only find expression for her grief by usurping a traditionally male lyric position intensifies the sense of her alienation.

There is, however, one potential complication which the play offers to an exclusively gendered reading of Ophelia's songs. Hamlet in his assumed madness taunts Polonius with quotations from a popular ballad of King Jeptha in 2.2.403–4, 412, 414. No editor seems ever to have suggested that he sing them, although there is no obvious reason why he should not chant this 'pious chanson'. Were he to do so it would both accentuate his 'madness' through its indecorum, and enforce a connection between the two representations of distraction. At the very least, it suggests that both Hamlet and Ophelia draw upon the way in which the citation of popular song might offer an indirect and often critical perspective on action or character. It is, however, equally possible to read the fact that Hamlet is assumed by editors to speak, not sing, as further supporting the way in which singing itself is a gendered activity, and has not lost that quality even in recent years.

At the simplest level the scene emphasizes the contradiction between Ophelia's distracted mind and the melody she sings. As with other popular songs, the familiarity of the tunes to an audience stirs identification and compassion.[48] It is part of her tragedy that she can elude the social controls that inhibit her speech, and can speak of her father and of her lover only in the indirection of madness and song. Gertrude's narrative of Ophelia's death recuperates her singing as simply the sad sign of mental disorder:

> Her clothes spread wide,
> And mermaid-like awhile they bore her up,
> Which time she chanted snatches of old lauds,
> As one incapable of her own distress,
> Or like a creature native and indued
> Unto that element. (4.7.175–80)

In this account all the dangerous implications of her songs are leached away; but it would be wrong to let this retrospectively diminish the problematic and challenging nature of the earlier scene. Ophelia subsides here into the absent occasion of male revenge, but in her mad singing she critiques and exposes, however allusively and enigmatically, the penalty of her subservience to father and lover alike. In this play, so preoccupied with the reading of ambiguous signs, the scene of Ophelia's singing involves us actively, and painfully, in the dilemmas of interpretation.

By contrast, the other song in the play, the Gravedigger's in 5.1, is much more readily placed. He sings when, as far as he knows, he is alone on-stage, and the song functions as a rhythmical counterpart to his digging, lightening the burden of his toil exactly in the way that countless defenders of the utility of music said it should. Whereas no clear originals for Ophelia's songs have been located, this 'ballad' is an extract from a published poem, Lord Vaux's 'The aged lover renounceth love', published in *Tottel's Miscellany* (1557). Some thirty years later *A Gorgeous Gallery of Gallant Inventions* (1578) contains another ballad that calls for the tune 'I loathe that I did love'.[49] Apart from the example this gives of the way 'courtly' and 'popular' could slide one into the other, the Gravedigger's much-discussed freedom with the 'original' text (he selects only three stanzas, and scrambles lines from others in his version) is also a mark of the ease with which such texts were always appropriable. The detail of his variation is not significant, though presumably those in the audience aware of the context of the original words would have seen an appropriateness in his choice of a poem of old age for singing in a graveyard. They might, too, have recognized a connection between the words of this song of death and the subject of some of Ophelia's earlier ballads. The gravedigger's singing, like Ophelia's, is perceived as indecorous – Hamlet objects: 'Has this fellow no feeling of his business a sings in grave-making' (5.1.65–6) – but it is precisely the indifference of the workman which prepares for the lack of differentiation in death that is the dominant topic of the first part of this scene. The mixed reaction of an audience who might recognize and mentally sing along with the tune even as they were disturbed by the context of the singing prefigures the tonal uncertainty of Hamlet's meditation on the skull of the dead jester, Yorick. The disjunction of song and situation prepares for the grotesque comedy of Hamlet's exclamation 'Why may not the imagination trace the noble dust of Alexander till a find it stopping a bung-hole' (5.1.201–2). Where Ophelia's songs are laden with the burden of a desperate attempt to communicate that which she cannot speak, the point of the gravedigger's song is its insouciance, 'allowed' by his occupation. Yet, in very different ways, both exploit the involvement between singer and audience that the use of popular melody inevitably generates, to intensify our implication in the indecorum which characterizes both scenes.

Hamlet is, of all the tragedies, that which uses popular song to the greatest effect. In *King Lear*, by comparison, song is much less prominent; but the Fool's few ballads usefully raise one or two further questions. Unlike all the characters so far considered, the Fool is one from whom singing might be expected. In neither of the texts of *King Lear*, however, does any stage-direction explicitly demand that the Fool's rhymes be sung. The only indication that they might be is given by Lear's comment 'When were you wont to be so full of songs, sirrah?' (1.4.162), which follows the stanza 'Fools had ne'er less grace in a year'. This has been taken by editors to indicate that this, and the following rhyme 'Then they for sudden joy did weep' should both be sung. The latter adapts lines from a printed 'godly ballad' by John Careless, a Protestant martyr, and Seng discovered a tune added in the margin of Ravenscroft's *Pammelia* (1609) to words which are close to those of the original.[50] It would seem probable that the stanza in 3.2.73–6, which offers a variant on the epilogue song of *Twelfth Night*, should be sung, especially if, as is often suggested, the actor Robert Armin played both parts. Some editors have thought that other of the Fool's stanzaic lyrics might be sung, and Duffin shows that they can readily be accommodated to ballad tunes. It is also possible that the stanza beginning 'Come o'er the burn Bessy to me', shared between Poor Tom and the Fool in 3.6.25–8 – which alludes to a well-known ballad – and Poor Tom's subsequent lyric 'Sleep'st or wak'st thou, jolly shepherd' (3.6.41–4) could also be sung.[51]

There is no way of resolving the issue; it is certainly possible that these lyrics could be spoken, as other rhyming proverbial lyrics such as 'Have more than thou knowest' (1.4.116ff) almost certainly are. It might seem that frequently to launch into song would unacceptably slow down the interchanges between Lear and his 'all-licensed fool' (1.4.191). Nonetheless, even if they do not actually sing, 'actors often speak the lines, though in a sing-song fashion'.[52] These stanzas seem to demand, if not the absolute differentiation of song, some kind of delivery that emphasizes their distinct quality. The Fool responds to Lear's question about why he suddenly sings with the words:

> I have used it, nuncle, e'er since thou mad'st thy daughters thy mothers; for when thou gav'st them the rod and putt'st down thine own breeches,
>
>> Then they for sudden joy did weep
>>> And I for sorrow sung
>> That such a king should play bo-peep
>>> And go the fools among. (1.4.163–9)

He here suggests that his singing is directly a consequence of Lear's folly and inversion of normal familial hierarchy. This invests his critique of Lear with the emotional force that bursting into impromptu song implies. At the same time, characterizing him through the language of popular song implies, as does his frequent use of quasi-proverbial language, that there is a wisdom to which Lear is deaf – the wisdom that finally he is to acquire as the storm prompts him to recognize that he has 'ta'en too little care' (3.4.32–3) of the world outside the ceremonies of court. Singing, then, suggests simultaneously the urgency of the Fool's feelings and a subversive critique which is both expressed and mitigated by being cast in such a form.

In some ways the Fool's songs function as do Ophelia's mad songs to express that which cannot otherwise be said, although, unlike her, he is in control of their meaning and focused in aiming them at his audience. The Fool's alienation, as well as his desperate need to penetrate the mind of his master, might be even more strongly suggested if the lyrics be fully 'framed' in sung performance. The Fool's audience is not only Lear, however, for he also implicates Goneril's undaughterly behaviour in two snatches which might be sung: 'He that keeps nor crust nor crumb', and 'The hedge-sparrow fed the cuckoo so long' (1.4.188–9, 206–7). Clearly she finds him an irritant, lumping him together with 'other of your insolent retinue' who 'Do hourly carp and quarrel' (1.4.192–3), and in her criticism of her father's retainers she suggests that they have made the court 'like a riotous inn' and 'more like a tavern or a brothel / Than a graced palace' (1.4.235–7). If the Fool were actually to sing at her, then something of the antipathy between popular ballad and the upstairs world that is so crucial in *Twelfth Night* would also come into play here.

A 'natural' fool hovers always at the edge of the rational, but there is no sense that the Fool's songs are to be interpreted as signs of madness rather than of marginality. Indeed, with the entrance of Edgar playing the part of Poor Tom, and as Lear's own madness grows, the Fool disappears from the play. Edgar takes over the communication in rhyming jingles that the Fool had earlier used (and might, possibly, adopt a sung or chanted delivery). His commentary on events, however, is much more obviously on the edge of sanity, and at this stage of the play, dominated by the 'music' of the storm, the effect of song would perhaps seem less appropriate.

In both *Hamlet* and *Lear*, then, popular song acts as a critique of the court-world, and is delivered as impromptu song which thereby suggests the power of feeling in its singer. In the last of the plays to be considered in this section, *The Winter's Tale*, popular song still functions as contrast to, and potentially as critique of the court, but it reaches us through the mouth of Autolycus, a character much more problematically located in the play's world, and one to whom, therefore, we respond much more equivocally than to the mad Ophelia or desperate Fool.

Autolycus tells us that he once served Prince Florizel but is now 'out of service' (4.3.14); he confesses that he is a 'snapper-up of unconsidered trifles' (4.3.26), and his language is coloured with the 'cant' or thieves' slang that numerous treatises on rogues had made current in the period. We see him picking the purse of the Clown, and after the festivities he claims that he 'picked and cut most of their festival purses' (4.4.616). In his conduct he amply bears out the stereotypical assumption that the ostensible trade of chapmen and ballad-sellers was a cover for petty crime. One can easily imagine many contexts in which such a figure would carry a threat to social order, yet in this play Autolycus's roguery seems to be offered primarily for our amusement. Its challenge is defused in part by the way he speaks directly to us, inviting our complicity (the standard theatrical technique for rendering vice at least temporarily palatable), in part by his eventual discomfiture by his erstwhile victims, the Shepherd and Clown, and, crucially, by his singing.

He enters with the song 'When daffodils begin to peer' (4.3.1–12), a mixture of pastoral images and thieves' slang, which sets the song of sweet birds alongside his desire for ale and for the comforts of his 'aunts' tumbling in the hay. No other version of this song survives, nor is any tune associated with it, and it would seem most likely that it is an example of a new-written ballad sung to a well-known tune. Auden firmly characterizes this as an impromptu song:

> He sings as he walks because it makes walking more rhythmical and less tiring, and he sings to keep up his spirits. His is a tough life, with hunger and the gallows never very far away, and he needs all the courage he can muster.[53]

While the song could, no doubt, be performed this way, I think that, for once, Auden has got it slightly, but significantly, wrong. Autolycus, entering onto an empty stage, is singing not just to himself, but explicitly to the audience. If they know the tune but are unfamiliar with the words, this might predispose them to careful attention to what he sings, and on the bare Elizabethan stage he must surely sing the song directly to them, so that it becomes a kind of musical soliloquy. This is even clearer in his second song, 'But shall I go mourn for that, my dear?' (4.3.15–22), where he is offering us a ballad which speaks exactly to his present situation, consoling himself for his loss of position as Florizel's servant, and justifying his own itinerant and shady life. The first person pronouns in both songs invite us to identify with the singer, while his self-presentation to us asserts Autolycus's own identity with the persona of his song. This is clarified by the difference of the final song Autolycus sings as he exits after picking the Clown's pocket. 'Jog on, jog on' (4.3.121–4) seems much more likely to have been one whose words and tune would have been familiar to an audience (although surviving versions are later than the play), and the absence of a first-person pronoun generalizes its sentiments, so that it seems much more a case of Autolycus appropriating a lyric of good cheer as a song of triumph for the success of his thievery. We identify with his feelings, but this is much more of an 'impromptu' song than the first two, which are offered as self-conscious performances and therefore as part of Autolycus's self-presentation.

It is often – and rightly – said that the introduction of song in this scene is a vital ingredient in transforming the tone of the play after the claustrophobic atmosphere of Leontes' court. But in the scene which precedes it Polixenes and Camillo discussed Florizel's absence from court, and the shepherd's daughter who is the 'angle that plucks our son thither' (4.2.46). Polixenes' sense of Perdita as bait which has lured his son from his proper exercises, and his contempt for the 'simplicity' of the shepherd which will make it easy for him to extract a confession, hang threateningly over the later celebrations. Autolycus's thieving, and his contempt for the 'cheats' he so easily defrauds, even as he presents himself to us agreeably as the singer of songs, similarly complicates any too simple and idealized a reading of the pastoral scenes as a contrast to and retreat from the Sicilian world of the play's first half.

Autolycus enters the sheep-shearing feast preceded by the praise of the servant:

> O master! if you did but hear the pedlar at the door, you would never dance again after a tabor and pipe; no the bagpipe could not move you: he sings several tunes, faster than you'll tell money; he utters them as he had eaten ballads, and all men's ears grew to his tunes.
> (4.4.183–8)

and he then describes his wares:

> he has the prettiest love-songs for maids, so without bawdry (which is strange); with such delicate burdens of dildoes and fadings, jump her and thump her; and where some stretch-mouthed rascal would, as it were, mean mischief and break a foul gap into the matter, he makes the maid to answer 'Whoop, do me no harm good man'.
> (4.4.195–201)

These comments are revealing in a number of ways. First, they suggest that Autolycus appears to the shepherds a man of urban sophistication, one who surpasses the rural music to which we have already seen the rural inhabitants dance. The servant's innocence in describing as 'without bawdry' lyrics which are clearly highly sexualized in their implication

positions the audience themselves as knowingly superior to his rustic ignorance (although Perdita herself demands that Autolycus be forewarned
'that he use no scurrilous words in's tunes' (4.4.214–15)). We are being
encouraged towards a double vision of the rural scene, in which we
respond positively to its innocence as a contrast to the sexual suspicion
which has dominated the first part of the play, and yet at the same time
gently mock its credulity. Shakespeare seems determined to rescue the
Clown's sheep-shearing celebrations from the condemnation meted out
to rural festivities by many of the religiously minded, suggesting that
any moral contamination issues from the ersatz sophistication of which
Autolycus is the representative, while at the same time preserving an
ironic distance from any tendency to idealization.

Autolycus, of course, is not merely a ballad-singer but a chapman with
a variety of things to sell. He enters the feast again singing, but here, in
'Lawn as white as driven snow' (4.4.220), as later in his exit song 'Will
you buy any tape' (4.4.317), he imitates the standard musical cries of
vendors of all kinds of goods which resounded through London's streets.
These cries were absorbed into compositions by musicians as distinguished
as Orlando Gibbons and Thomas Weelkes, and were imitated in 'art' songs
such as Thomas Campion's 'Cherry ripe' and Dowland's 'Fine knacks for
ladies'.[54] Autolycus's songs are specifically calculated to drum up business.
The ballads he offers for sale are those containing improbable 'news' – of
'a usurer's wife was brought to bed of twenty money-bags at a burden'
(4.4.263–5) and of 'a fish that appeared upon the coast ... and sung this
ballad against the hard hearts of maids' (4.5.276–9). Like Nightingale's
list of his wares in Jonson's *Bartholomew Fair*, which includes '*A delicate
ballad o' the* Ferret *and the* Coney' and '*The Wind-mill blowne downe by the
witches fart*' (2.4.12, 18), these exaggerate – but only just – the titles of
surviving ballads. The credulity of Mopsa and Dorcas is mocked as they
ask 'Is it true?' (4.4.267, 283), but this invocation of tall tales takes an
ambiguous place in a play which turns on the nature of stories and belief
in them, from Mamillius's 'sad tale ... of sprites and goblins' (2.1.25–6),
through the twisted fantasies of Hermione's infidelity that are fashioned
in Leontes' frantic brain, to the final marvel of Paulina's giving life to the
statue of the 'dead' queen.

We do not, in the event, hear any of these ballad narratives. Instead, reversing Mamillius's dictum that a 'sad tale's best for winter', the Clown and Mopsa reject the 'pitiful' tale of the fish, and request a 'merry' ballad. They are offered 'Two maids wooing a man'. Autolycus assures them that 'there's scarce a maid westward but she sings it; 'tis in request, I can tell you' (4.4.291–2). Mopsa and Dorcas offer to perform it with Autolycus, since they 'had the tune on't a month ago' (4.4.296). This reflects the way ballads were circulated with new words to known tunes, as does Autolycus's later report that the Clown 'grew so in love with the wenches' song, that he would not stir his pettitoes till he had both tune and words' (4.4.607–9). But the realistic image this presents is complicated by a contemporary setting of the words which may be by Robert Johnson. The song survives in two manuscripts, and contains ornamentation of the vocal line which, one might think, would make it more appropriate to courtly professional singers than to Autolycus and two shepherdesses. Even in the version Duffin advances,[55] stripped of this elaboration, the song seems to me not to have the character of a popular song that might readily have been got by heart and sung to other lyrics, as the text implies this is. The rhythmic contours of the song are by no means straightforward, and it demands a lute or other accompaniment to establish the rhythmic foundation for the 'whither? O whither?' exchanges of the three voices. Such an accompaniment might have been supplied by Autolycus himself (though there is no mention of his carrying an instrument) or by the on-stage musicians who had already played for the rural dancing (so they, like Mopsa and Dorcas, must be imagined as already having learnt the tune). It is, of course, possible that this setting was not intended for theatrical use, or that it was composed for a later production of the play, but if it is indeed the song heard by the original audience, then its character is somewhat surprising. Seng suggests that 'to modern ears the tune sounds more like a funeral march than a merry tune' (245). The performance on the CD that accompanies Duffin's book is not as dirge-like as this implies, although the song still seems rather more melancholy in its figuring of the disappointment of the two women at their lover's indifference than might be expected. More important, its relative musical sophistication requires that we suspend for the duration of the song the impression we have already formed of the naive characters of the two shepherdesses. Instead the song becomes a self-contained set-piece, to be indulged in for its own sake, rather than being a direct expression of the dramatic situation or of the character of its singers. For these reasons I am inclined to believe that this is unlikely to have been the setting rendered at the original performances – but it must remain a possibility that Shakespeare was happy to insert what, in modern terms, one might call a 'production number', and that it offers a further ingredient in this scene's exploration of the relationships between courtly sophistication and rural simplicity.

All this may be to make a mountain out of a molehill, but, if nothing else, it is a useful reminder of how much conjecture there must inevitably be about the precise effect of songs when for so few of them, even those which seem to belong to the popular repertory of lyrics and tunes that we assume a contemporary audience would have known, does the music survive. Nonetheless, the participation of the music in this tonally complex scene is significant. At a sheep-shearing feast where the radiance and innocence of its queen, Perdita, both is and is not a product of her rural situation, where the courtly audience of Polixenes and Camillo are simultaneously enchanted by the 'queen of curds and cream' (4.4.161) and appalled at the idea of her as a mate for the princely Florizel, where the chief singer is a trickster, and the Clown a gullible, if lovable, fool, the music, at one and the same time appealing to yet satirizing popular taste, forms an important constituent in the scene's ambiguity of effect.

FORMAL SONG

Autolycus's songs – and the possibility that 'Get thee hence' was performed to a specially composed tune – move us from the territory of impromptu song to the more formal songs in the plays. These are explicitly called for and performed as complete wholes to an audience on-stage and off. While contributing to the mood and character of a particular scene; they condition our understanding, not primarily of their singer, but of the persons to and for whom they are performed; and they work to define the society within which they function. They are 'framed' events, and often the way they are situated and commented upon may be as important as the direct effect they have as musical performance.

So, for example, Act 4 of *Measure for Measure* opens with the first appearance of Mariana, Angelo's rejected betrothed. She is accompanied by a boy who sings, presumably to the lute,[56] the song 'Take, O take those lips away'. Upon the entrance of the Duke, however, Mariana embarrassedly despatches the singer and excuses herself:

> I cry you mercy, sir, and well could wish
> You had not found me here so musical.
> Let me excuse me, and believe me so,
> My mirth it much displeas'd but pleas'd my woe.

To which the Duke replies:

> 'Tis good: though music oft hath such a charm
> To make bad good and good provoke to harm. (4.1.10–16)[57]

The authorship of this scene has been questioned, with suggestions that it is a later interpolation importing a song from *Rollo, King of Normandy* (where it appears with a second stanza), probably by John Fletcher.[58] But even if it is – and its detachability from the action of the play lends some support to the hypothesis – it is a useful starting point for this discussion.

As a song of disappointment in love it is entirely characteristic of the association of music with love-melancholy, as Mariana herself implies. At the simplest dramatic level it creates a wistful mood which marks out the difference of the isolated world of the moated grange from the urban world of Vienna.[59] It comes as a relief from that foetid atmosphere, something to be savoured by Mariana and the audience alike with uncomplicated pleasure. But the comments that follow its performance undercut any simple delight. Mariana is embarrassed at being caught in musical indulgence, fearful that it would be interpreted by the Duke as a sign of frivolity. She has fully internalized some of the negative attitudes to music and its association with enfeebling love and femininity that we have already seen were characteristic of the period, attitudes embodied in the Duke's sententious commonplace. Sternfeld justifies the Duke's comments by suggesting that:

> Mariana's purpose is 'to make bad good' as the boy's song of
> deserted love consoles her ... But to give oneself up to this melan-
> choly stanza ... is also an act of self-indulgence and therefore
> likely to provoke good to harm.[60]

But the detail matters less here than the general situation in which music's
consolation – for character and for audience – is hedged with qualifications. This is a common, almost a constant feature of the songs of love
that are scattered through the plays.

Most obviously is it the case with Pandarus's 'Love, love, nothing but
love' in *Troilus and Cressida*. The instrumental music in the scene has
already been discussed, but the song itself deserves attention. In the first
place, Pandarus's modesty about his musical abilities, which he calls 'rude
in sooth; in good sooth, very rude' (3.1.55) must not be taken to indicate
that his singing is anything but polished – he simply voices the conventional hesitation of the courtly male about performing in public. He calls
for an instrument (3.1.91–2), presumably either a lute or a bass viol, and
must accompany himself in the song. No setting survives, and the complex versification makes it difficult to accommodate to any existing tune.[61]
This might imply that a setting was specially composed – and given the
enigmas that surround the circumstances of its original performance, it
is possible that this might have been a play which broke what seems to
have been the more usual custom of writing lyrics to fit existing
melodies. Certainly, for all the vulgarity of the words, a setting that derived
from a relatively courtly style would be particularly appropriate. The published song collections of Robert Jones, for example, contain a number
where double entendre speaks euphemistically of sexual encounter.[62] An
instance is 'Sweet Philomell' from the *First Booke of Songs or Ayres*, which
says of the 'nightingale':

> but then her tunes delight me best,
>   when pearcht with prick against her breast
> shee sings 'fie, fie' as if shee suffred wrong
> till seeming pleas'd, 'sweete sweete' concludes her song.[63]

Something of the archness of a song like this, which is in part at least
derived from the tension of bawdy expression contained in elegant musical

form, would seem apposite for Pandarus's lyric, in which the first stanza speaks decorously enough of the 'buck and doe' wounded by love's arrow, but the second turns to the cries of human lovers engaged in sexual activity:

> These lovers cry, 'O! O!', they die!
>   Yet that which seems the wound to kill
> Doth turn 'O! O!' to 'Ha, ha, he!' (3.1.117–20)

It is important to the effect of the scene that just as the music of its opening puts a false gloss on the entry of Paris and Helen, this song should at least temporarily involve the audience in the overripe sexuality of the scene. If we do not smile at its double entendres, and are not led to surrender some of our moral disapproval by Pandarus's singing, then the song seems too immediately and obviously that of 'a depraved Elizabethan gentry'.[64] The words of the song are consistent with, and contaminated by, Pandarus's oppressive voyeurism throughout the play; but to some extent at least, the fact that he sings lightens, however briefly, the cloying sense of decadence that envelops him, and this scene in general.

A similar ambivalence of theatrical effect surrounds the serenades in *Two Gentlemen of Verona* and in *Cymbeline*. The device of wooing by singing beneath a beloved's balcony is one that occurs in many plays, though 'the serenading amorists of the children's stage cause few moral dangers for the women they love. Almost invariably, they are doltish lovers for whom the ladies have at best pity and at worst contempt.'[65] (The frontispiece by Jost Amman, itself within a tradition going back at least to Dürer's illustration of the *Ship of Fools*, indicates that this was not merely a literary convention.) Both Shakespearean examples play variations on this common theme. In the first, the song 'Who is Sylvia' (4.2.38–53) is sung under Silvia's window ostensibly to further the ambitions of her suitor, Thurio, but in fact to promote the cause of the faithless Proteus whose abandoned love, Julia, watches in dismay. She had been brought to the place by the Host, who promised she would see Proteus – to which her initial reaction is: 'That will be music' (4.2.34), but after observing the performance she is discomfited, and to the Host's statement 'The music likes you not' responds 'You mistake: the musician likes me not', because 'he plays false' (4.2.54–7). The dialogue between the Host and Julia continues, emphasizing the contrast between his delight in the performance, and her discomfiture and grief – divided perceptions that the audience is invited to share. (This exchange also makes it clear that Proteus himself sings the song.) Apart from Julia, the other listeners to the song, including Silvia, who appears above on the balcony to thank the gentlemen for the music (4.2.83), express pleasure in it. That Julia uses musical conceits to hide her pain from the well-intentioned Host poignantly contrasts with the confidence she had earlier shown in rejecting Proteus's letter to her in musical images exchanged with Lucetta in 1.2.90–98. Silvia's immediately following dialogue with Proteus, once she recognizes that he was singing for himself, underlines the treachery of his actions.

There is very little complication in this scene. The song itself is un-exceptionable as a serenade, and was presumably sung to a graceful tune with instrumental accompaniment, though no contemporary setting survives. Its five-line stanzas are not easily accommodated to surviving tunes in the ballad repertoire,[66] raising the possibility that it might have been specially composed. But whatever the setting, the point of the scene is to expose Proteus's treachery to his faithful love, and the function of the music is to amplify the poignancy of our participation in her suffering. When Shakespeare uses the device of a serenade again in *Cymbeline* the effects he generates are far more complex. The aubade which Cloten commands, 'Hark, hark, the lark' (2.3.20), exists in a setting attributed to Robert Johnson, perhaps the first of his surviving songs for the King's Men, and possibly a mark of the new musical arrangements made possible by the acquisition of Blackfriars and its musicians. It is an elegant rendition of the words, with an introductory flourish on the repeated word 'hark', whose octave leap is echoed and extended in the steady rise up the octave on the words 'arise, my lady sweet, arise' at the end. Two lines are, however, omitted in Johnson's setting. In Duffin's transcription the words 'His steeds to water at those springs / on chalic'd flowers that lies' are plausibly set to a repeat of the first two lines of music, whereas James Walker in his version composes a new musical insertion, assuming that the lines have simply been lost at some stage in the song's transmission.[67] In the sole surviving manuscript there is some simple ornamentation of the vocal line[68] – but unlike the ornamented version of 'Get you hence' in *The Winter's Tale*, this seems entirely appropriate to the song, the occasion and the singer. Or at least this would be straightforwardly the case if it were performed by one of the musicians who enter at 2.3.13. There is no speech-heading for the song in the Folio text, and some modern productions have given the song to Cloten himself. While it is not impossible that we might think that Cloten had 'acquired the accomplishments of a prince and so be able to perform the song',[69] for reasons that will become clear, I think it both unlikely in itself, and a potentially disastrous weakening of the effect of the scene.

Cloten enters at the beginning of 2.3 from a long night at the gambling table, and attendant lords congratulate him on his patience when he loses, since he is 'most hot and furious' when he wins. He takes it as a compliment, observing: 'Winning will put any man into courage. If I could get this foolish Innogen, I should have gold enough' (2.3.7–9). The contemptuous way he speaks of the woman he is attempting to woo prepares us for the instructions he gives to the musicians he has only commissioned because 'I am advised to give her music a mornings, they say it will penetrate' (2.3.11–13). He impatiently orders them:

> Come on, tune: if you can penetrate her with your fingering, so: we'll try with tongue too: if none will do, let her remain: but I'll never give o'er. First, a very excellent good-conceited thing; after, a wonderful sweet air, with admirable rich words to it, and then let her consider. (2.3.14–19)

In believing that music achieves its effects by its penetration of the ear, and in accepting the advice that women are particularly susceptible to music, Cloten is, of course, echoing commonplace beliefs. His expression of them, however, reveals him as a boor. Whether his double entendres here are construed as deliberate, or are simply the product of his asinine mind, their unpleasantness is made manifest by comparison with the instructions given by a character in Cooke's *Greenes Tu Quoque* (1614), for a similar aubade:

> Musitions, give to each Instrument a tongue,
> To breathe sweete musicke in the eares of her
> To whom I send it as a messenger. (sig. F1r)

Cloten asks for 'a very excellent good conceited thing', which might imply that the musicians played an instrumental prelude before launching into the song. After it, Cloten continues in his boorish fashion:

> So get you gone: if this penetrate, I will consider your music the better: if it do not, it is a vice in her ears, which horse-hairs, and calve's-guts, nor the voice of unpaved eunuch to boot, can never amend. (2.3.27–31)

This is, no doubt, his idea of a compliment to the musicians, asserting that the song ought to have had its effect, and if it did not, then it is Innogen's incapacity which is to blame. But delivered in this way – with the third use of the word 'penetrate', insulting characterization of voice and instruments, and peremptory 'get you gone' – it scarcely suggests that Cloten himself has responded in any way to the music. It is also a speech that would seem unlikely if Cloten himself had sung, since the comment on the 'unpaved eunuch' is surely intended to characterize the (boy) singer.

As an audience we find Cloten at best ridiculous, at worst positively distasteful; but the effect of the scene depends upon the fact that in the framed interlude that the music offers us we are drawn into it and respond positively. We measure our response against Cloten's, and at some level congratulate ourselves on our greater musical sensitivity; but the other audience of the song – the off-stage Innogen – gives no sign of having heard it at all. She does not appear immediately. After a twenty-line interlude Cloten knocks on the door, and then further evidences his loutishness in conversation with Innogen's Lady before Innogen herself enters. Unlike Silvia, she makes no comment directly on the music, though she similarly rejects the suitor. If Cloten intended his aubade as 'provoking music' it singularly fails to 'penetrate', and Innogen demonstrates her faithfulness and purity of mind precisely in her lack of response.

This scene follows immediately upon that in which we have watched Iachimo[70] emerge from the trunk into Innogen's bedchamber, note in detail the adornments of the room, and examine with erotically charged intentness her sleeping body. In crucial respects the scene of the serenade restages the ambition to possess and 'penetrate' Innogen that Iachimo narrowly backed away from. And just as we are complicit with the voyeuristic intensity of Iachimo's gaze, so the music here implicates us in its desires. As Martin Butler observes: 'in context, the song is problematized by the fact that Cloten presents it. His commentary sexualizes its compliments, activating their erotic undertow, and complicating the song's generic signals: is it an innocent aubade, or a sensual appreciation of Innogen's seductiveness?'[71] However subliminally, as we enter into the song's spell we too are in danger of being found guilty of the charge that music provokes to harm.

In both of these scenes the different levels of awareness of the characters on-stage complicate the workings of the songs, while our own temporary immersion in the musical event adds a further layer to its effect. The music itself, well-performed as it must be, stands as a kind of morally neutral centre, while the text and action which surround it invite us to self-consciousness about the nature and consequence of our involvement with it. This discrepant awareness is exploited to comic effect in *Much Ado About Nothing*. In 2.3 Don Pedro and his companions carry out their plot to induce Benedick to fall in love with Beatrice, announced at the end of 2.1, and they choose as part of their strategy to engage a singer to perform. Balthasar apologizes lengthily for his lack of ability, and some have taken him to speak true, so that the comedy of the scene lies in part in his massacre of the song. But so conventional is the apologia that it seems best to read Benedick's comment 'an he had been a dog that had howled thus, and I pray God his bad voice bode no mischief' (2.3.78–80) as a sign of his resistance to music in general and to this song in particular. He exploits for the audience's benefit the opportunity offered him for witty display by Balthasar's second apology for his poor voice, rather than describing the performance we have just heard.

But at least in one respect Benedick speaks truer than he knows in fearing that the song 'bodes mischief', for the lyric of 'Sigh no more ladies' speaks of men's falsehood, and advises women to be cheerful by dismissing them and 'Converting all your sounds of woe / Into Hey nonny nonny'

(2.3.67–8). On the face of it, it seems a strange lyric to choose to persuade Benedick to fall in love, but Auden persuasively argues: 'If one imagines these sentiments being the expression of a character, the only character they suit is Beatrice ... I do not think it too far-fetched to imagine that the song arouses in Benedick's mind an image of Beatrice, the tenderness of which alarms him.'[72] Don Pedro has chosen his song carefully, paradoxically to ensnare Benedick by offering him a lyric which suggests that the fickleness he himself outwardly manifests, far from triumphing over the weakness of women as he supposes, provokes them only to a cheerful indifference. The song is not the persuasion to love we might perhaps have expected – a dreamy and romantic song to work upon Benedick's hardened heart – but one which, as his overreaction to it suggests, works to critique his own posturing.

The response of the other characters on stage is not made explicit. Claudio opens the teasing of Benedick with the comment: 'How still the evening is, / As hush'd on purpose to grace harmony' (2.3.37–8), but neither he nor anyone else comments on the song itself once Balthasar is dismissed. If Claudio responds at all, it cannot be to the threatening hint of his own future unfaithfulness to Hero – and nor can the audience, since, although they have seen Don John begin his plotting, they can at this stage have no sense of the course it will take. How an audience might react will depend, inevitably, on the character of the music. The lyric might seem to demand a contrast between a melancholy setting of the first part of the stanza, picking up the cue of the word 'sigh', which many compositions of the period delighted in illustrating by a rest before the word is uttered, and then a second section of a livelier cast, heading towards the careless, conventional 'hey nonny' refrain.[73] Unfortunately no music survives, except for a later version by Thomas Ford, which modifies the lyric. But whatever the setting, and, indeed, however well Balthasar sings it, the simple dramatic point is precisely that it is being deployed as part of a trap, intended to contribute to the ensnaring of Benedick. We are as interested in observing his response to it as we are in being ourselves involved in the music. It functions, therefore, as part of an intricate stage picture.

The same is true of a very different song, 'Tell me where is fancy bred', in *The Merchant of Venice*. As Bassanio prepares to make his choice of casket, Portia commands music – which she pointedly had not for the previous suitors. She offers two reasons: first that if Bassanio loses 'he makes a swan-like end, / Fading in music'; but, second, that if he succeeds it will be:

> Even as the flourish, when true subjects bow
> To a new-crowned monarch: such it is,
> As are those dulcet sounds in break of day,
> That creep into the dreaming bridegroom's ear,
> And summon him to marriage. (3.2.49–53)

She here anticipates her later comments on the way the character of a piece of music depends as much upon the circumstances of its hearing as its intrinsic merit. The question, however, is whether she is attempting to ensure that the song will in fact 'summon' her wished-for mate to make the right decision. The lyric runs:

> Tell me where is Fancy bred,
> Or in the heart, or in the head?
> How begot, how nourished?   Reply, reply.
> It is engend'red in the eyes,
> With gazing fed, and Fancy dies
> In the cradle where it lies;
> Let us all ring Fancy's knell,
> I'll begin it. Ding, dong, bell.
>   ALL Ding, dong, bell.[74]

In general the sentiments of the song encourage Bassanio not to be misled by Fancy and the judgement of the eye. At least since Fox-Strangways in 1923 it has also often been suggested that the 'ed' rhymes of the first three lines, the 'l' sound at the end of the lines in the second part, and the suggestion of coffins in the death-knell are clues that are intended to direct Bassanio to the lead casket. The suggestion has, however, been dismissed by, amongst others, Granville-Barker, who could not believe Shakespeare would indulge in such a 'slim trick', and John Russell Brown, who does not accept that Portia would attempt to subvert her father's proscription of any assistance for her suitors, and that Shakespeare would so 'cheapen the themes of the play'.[75] It is undoubtedly the case that if we had a surviving setting for the song 'it would demonstrate whether or not the song revealed the secret of the caskets'.[76] No music survives, however, and so we must be guided by the dramatic situation as it is presented to us. Crucial is the stage direction: '*A song to music the whilst Bassanio comments on the caskets to himself*' (3.2.62). This implies that the music continues under Bassanio's thirty-two line speech, and that, therefore, he himself is not attending to the song, so that any hint it offers can be at best subliminal. As with the other songs we have so far considered, the awareness of the audience and that of the characters on stage are at variance. Empson suggests that:

> the audience is not really meant to think that [Portia] is telling [Bassanio] the answer, but it is not posed as a moral problem, and seems a natural enough thing to do; she might quite well do it in the belief that he would not hear; the song is explaining to *them* the point about the lead casket, may be taken to represent the fact that Bassanio understands it, heightens the tension by repeating the problem in another form, and adds to their sense of fitness in the third man being the lucky one.[77]

If the song accompanies Bassanio's speech, however, then the possibility of the audience attending simultaneously both to what he says and to the hints the song offers is considerably reduced. For them, as for him, the argument of the lyric will almost certainly be less than obvious, for argument is precisely what musical setting absorbs and masks. The chime of the rhyme-words might be rather more apparent, but to suggest that 'the audience ... will be on tenterhooks: will Bassanio catch the clues?'[78] overstates at least the original audience's capacity to attend to two things at once. (The modern audience, many of whom are fully familiar with the play, and with the debate about the song, is, of course, in a very different position.) Nonetheless, however buried the hints of the song may be in actual performance, we still see Shakespeare not simply using song to contrast the harmony of Portia's household with the world of Venice, nor merely to provide some much-needed romantic gloss to help us forget for a moment Bassanio's mercenary motivation in undertaking the task at all – although he is doing both of these things – but wittily playing with the same kind of discrepant awareness that so often characterizes his theatrical use of song.

At the simplest level, however, this song invests Bassanio's choice of caskets with an appropriate ceremoniousness. And it is to ritual or ceremonial songs that we now turn. At the end of *As You Like It* Hymen introduces 'Wedding is great Juno's crown' (5.4.139–44) with the words:

> Whiles a wedlock hymn we sing,
> Feed yourselves with questioning,
> That reason wonder may diminish
> How thus we met, and these things finish. (5.4.135–8)

This, rather oddly, seems to suggest that the music functions not to reinforce the sense of wonder and amazement that the appearance of Hymen and Rosalind in her women's clothes have generated, but rather as a kind of winding down from it. The lyric of the song itself also naturalizes the high strangeness of Hymen's appearance, domesticating the classical god as he that 'peoples every town' (5.4.141). That it is called an 'hymn' suggests a melody of some solemnity; the question who the 'we' are who sing is open to a number of possible resolutions – Amiens, perhaps, together with the other lords who had sung earlier in the play, or the pages who have earlier appeared only to sing 'It was a lover and his lass' performing in a trio with Hymen himself. It probably should be sung in harmony, rather than as a solo, to give it an appropriate impersonality, and while it is unlikely that a contemporary psalm tune might be employed (apart from any offence it would cause, they almost all fit four-line or eight-line stanzas whereas this is of six lines), ballad tunes can have a perfectly sufficient stateliness, as is demonstrated by Duffin's setting of it to the tune 'Troy Town' (which sounds to modern ears very like an ecclesiastical melody if sung with solemnity). At the very least, however, this song, drawing simultaneously on the conventional association of music with celestial harmony and with the earthly celebration of matrimony, anchors the irruption of Hymen's heavenly visitation in recognizably human ritual.

If this is a straightforward song, the 'solemn hymn' which Claudio asks for in *Much Ado About Nothing* (5.3.11) is rather less so. After the deception practised by Don John on Claudio is revealed, Leonato, father of the slandered Hero who has been given out as dead, demands that Claudio and Don Pedro demonstrate their penitence by hanging an epitaph on her tomb and singing it 'to her bones' (5.1.277–8). In 5.3 Claudio, Don Pedro, the Prince and 'three or four with tapers' enter to the 'monument of Leonato'; the epitaph is read, and the song 'Pardon, goddess of the night' is sung. The lyric suggests that as the song is performed (presumably by the 'three or four' extras, no doubt including Balthasar) the others walk in solemn procession 'round about' the tomb. No tune survives for the song, but one might surmise that it, like the hymn in *As You Like It*, was partly or wholly sung in harmony, to give it the necessary impersonal solemnity.

It is a scene, and a song, that has come in for much criticism. J.S. Manifold thought it 'among Shakespeare's worst' and advised 'cut it out altogether',[79] an instruction anticipated by almost all productions during the nineteenth century, and by many in the twentieth.[80] Earlier commentators were worried by the fact that the hymn is addressed to a pagan deity, and felt the lyric was hyperbolic and therefore in some way 'insincere'.[81] Yet this song and the ritual it accompanies are designed, by introducing a very different dramatic mode into the play, to aid in the transition to the reappearance of Hero – itself a kind of first attempt on Shakespeare's part for the device he later employs in *The Winter's Tale*. Given the way Claudio has so easily credited Hero's faithlessness, and, especially, given the loucheness of his treatment of Leonato in 5.1, and the inappropriateness of his banter with Benedick which follows, the play urgently needs some device that will enable us to credit the transition of feeling that follows the revelation to him of Hero's innocence.

This is precisely the function of the funeral procession and song. Shakespeare deploys the melancholy that music can engender to persuade the audience that the feeling it provokes in them must also express the repentance that Claudio claims to enact. In most of Shakespeare's comedies it is the moment of recognition and resolution itself which is dressed in language of heightened formality, sometimes, as in *As You Like It* or *The Winter's Tale*, aided by music. In this play, shifting the centre of gravity back to Claudio's repentance through the use of ceremony and music is an interesting formal experiment. It is difficult for a modern audience to give full weight to the fact that Claudio remains true to the demand that he will marry, unseen, Leonato's 'brother's daughter', and easy to undervalue the submission he offers when saying 'I am your husband, if *you* like of *me*' (5.4.59, my italics). We are only too likely to feel that Hero should certainly not 'like' Claudio after what he has done, and Shakespeare makes it no easier for us by the fact that immediately before the marriage Claudio reverts to his old manner in taunting Benedick with the possibility of his cuckolding (5.4.43–7). Without the scene at the monument there would be no hope at all of reacting with pleasure to the reuniting of Claudio and Hero.

One of the factors that complicates an audience's response to this scene is that they know Hero is not actually dead. Noble somewhat improbably thought that this gives 'something of comedy in the scene';[82] yet participation in the emotion and ritual of the music surely makes us the more ready to suspend our knowledge, and diminishes the sense that the Friar's plan to stage Hero's death is merely a convenient theatrical trick. There is a parallel effect in the dirge in *Cymbeline*. When Arviragus enters with the dead body of Innogen, whom he knows as Fidele, in his arms, an audience is aware that she has taken a drug given to her by Pisanio, and may remember that this is the same potion which Cornelius had given to the Queen, informing the audience in an aside that it would not bring about lingering death as the Queen desired, but simply 'stupefy and dull the sense awhile' (1.6.37). Yet, as Roger Warren observes, 'the reaction of an audience, in all the productions I have seen or been involved in, has been the same: a hushed, tense stillness in which, so to speak, they seem to suppress that factual knowledge and respond instead to the theatrical experience: to all intents and purposes, as the Folio says, Innogen is dead'.[83] The situation then, is like, but unlike that of *Much Ado*, where our knowledge is more certain, and what we see is a tomb rather than the apparently 'real' dead body. Generically, too, *Cymbeline* is highly ambivalent, and at this stage an audience cannot be entirely certain that the situation will not turn out to be more like that of *Romeo and Juliet* than *Much Ado*.

Guiderius and Arviragus prepare to lay Innogen in her grave, and this dialogue ensues:

ARVIRAGUS And let us, Polydore,[84] though now our voices
    Have got the mannish crack, sing him to th'ground,
    As once to our mother: use like note and words,
    Save that Euriphile must be Fidele.
GUIDERIUS Cadwal,
    I cannot sing: I'll weep, and word it with thee;
    For notes of sorrow out of tune are worse
    Than priests and fanes that lie.
ARVIRAGUS   We'll speak it then. (4.2.235–42)

After a short while they speak the words of 'Fear no more the heat o' th' sun' (4.2.258–81), taking a stanza each, and dividing the third and fourth between them. The Folio text heads the lyric firmly as 'Song'.

Leaving on one side the critics who, from the eighteenth to the twentieth centuries, found the lyric itself clumsy and unappealing, a verdict few would now share, editors and others have divided over the implication of this prefatory dialogue. Gary Taylor is but the most recent to argue that: 'If anything in the canon is a theatrical interpolation due to exigencies of casting, these lines are a chief candidate. Quite apart from their evident excusing of a bad voice, they are contradicted by the direction "SONG".'[85] The play's most recent editors, however, both reject this hypothesis. Warren suggests that the reason for the lines is 'to draw attention to the words of this celebration of Innogen: they are to be spoken, not sung, so that there may be no risk of anything detracting from their hypnotic impact'.[86] This is not entirely convincing, for whatever importance the words have, they are anything but a 'celebration' of Innogen. Martin Butler persuasively points out that these lines are consonant with the play's emphasis on the adolescent state of the two princes, who are on the verge of manhood and ready to blossom into heroic warriors in the contest with the Romans. Further support for this view is to be found a few lines earlier, where, after Arviragus has descanted on the flowers he will lay in Fidele's grave his elder brother tartly observes: 'Prithee, have done, / And do not play in wench-like words with that / Which is so serious' (4.2.229–31). Arviragus in the exchange quoted above is prepared to sing although his voice has broken, and is persuaded not to by his brother. There is some suggestion, then, that Guiderius, with his sensitivity to 'wench-like words', and the self-consciousness of the adolescent elder brother, fears that he would render himself effeminate or childish by singing, and needs to mark a decisive transition from their boyish past by refusing now to sing as they once did over their dead mother.

Like the dirge for Hero, the words of the song are couched entirely within a secular and pagan world-view. Here there is more obvious justification, in that the play is set at or near the time of Christ's birth. Arviragus and Guiderius themselves are at the margins of Britain in the harsh pastoral environment of Wales, and the only consolation the lyric offers is the stoic recognition that death has removed Fidele from the trials of the world, and, in terms not so far from the gravedigger scene in *Hamlet*, that death destroys all equally. To sing the words might actually to be to ameliorate their bleakness. Whether spoken or sung, however, the ritual quality of the verse, generated by its sombre repetitions, is central to the effect of the moment. We might briefly register that the lines 'Fear no more the frown o' th' great / Thou art past the tyrant's stroke' (4.2.264–5) could, although they do not know it, refer to their own, or at least Belarius's situation, and more poignantly notice, as they cannot, the applicability of the line 'Fear not slander, censure rash' (4.2.272) to Innogen's defamation by Iachimo and Posthumus. But any such resonances are fleeting; the effect is one of generalized, almost impersonal statement. It is song-like, in that the speakers lose their individuality as they immerse themselves in their ritual observance, just as the singers of Hero's dirge submerge any personality in the act of singing.

In its final stanza the dirge turns into a kind of charm as it bans exorciser, witch, and ghost, concluding 'Nothing ill come near thee!' (4.2.279). In this respect it has something in common with a song performed in a very different situation in *A Midsummer Night's Dream*: the fairies' 'You spotted snakes' (2.2.9–23), sung to ward off harm from the sleeping Titania. Adventitious though the collocation might be, it usefully reminds us of the etymological derivation of the word 'charm' from the Latin *carmen* meaning 'song', and of the connection between music and magic touched on in Chapter 1. In the pagan world of *Cymbeline* the dirge for Fidele calls on these resonances, as, much more playfully, does the fairies' song in *Dream*.

In almost every way the function of 'You spotted snakes' is straightforward enough. As Titania enters she asks for a 'roundel and a fairy song' before her fairies go off on their various duties, then demands 'Sing me now asleep' (2.2.7), and the fairies duly oblige. There is general agreement that the song should be performed as a solo and refrain. The form of the song is not strictly a *rondel*, and no instruction makes clear whether the fairies dance before the song, or during its refrain, or even not at all. Music and dance characterize the fairy world, and the lyric of this song, in warding off threats from snakes, hedgehogs, newts and blind-worms, spiders, beetles, worms, and snails, identifies them with the natural world, and continues the emphasis on their diminutive size begun in Titania's speech where she requests, for example, the collection of bats' wings to 'make my small elves coats' (2.2.5). And thereupon hangs a major practical question attending on this song.

It is generally assumed that the fairies would be played by boys, and the song therefore sung by them. If this were to be the case, however, it would mean that the play called for significantly more boy actors than was usual – a fact which has led some to speculate that the play was written for a special occasion where boys, perhaps from one of the chapels, were brought in as extras. William Ringler first suggested that the only way of casting the play within the normal establishment of the theatre company was to have the fairies played by the same actors who play the 'mechanicals'.[87] He saw this as creating a comic disparity between what is said of the fairies and the 'large lumbering actors' who took the parts. Peter Holland accepts the hypothesis of the doubling, but rightly remarks: 'The result need have nothing to do with "grotesquerie", only with the metamorphic world shared by the fairies and the practice of theatre itself. Adult fairies, as Peter Brook's production showed, can be disconcertingly strange and threatening; they need not be in the least awkward.'[88]

No original music survives, but Duffin's setting of it to the ballad tune 'Robin Goodfellow'[89] is a particularly felicitous conjecture – the tune's movement from a steady 4/4 rhythm for the verse to a livelier 6/4 for the refrain works extremely well in suggesting both the ritual formality of a charm, and the playfulness of its fairy performers. Whether or not this (or any other tune) would have been accompanied instrumentally, this choice demonstrates that an entirely appropriate effect could be derived from music that is relatively undemanding of its singers. There is, nonetheless, a significant difference between the sound of high and low-pitched voices – the effect of etheriality is more easily achieved by the former.[90] But, whether boys or men, it is surely important that this song does indeed sound with some delicacy – it must be a complete contrast to Bottom's 'Ousel cock' (3.1.119), a popular ballad sung in the lower register to keep his spirits up, and must persuade us that it is indeed a lullaby. The immediate irony, of course, is that while the song works to send Titania to sleep, its musical magic is unable to prevent the immediate entry of Oberon and the anointing of the queen's eyes.

The fairies' song in *A Midsummer Night's Dream*, like all the others we have been considering in this section, has a ritual function. All are marked by some degree of gravity, and none directly advances the plot of its play; some might be cut in performance, but all use the impersonality of choral song to persuade us of the solemnity of the moments they accompany. The final trio of songs in this category, however, celebrate rituals of very different kinds. The first of them is the riotously unsolemn song of the fake fairies in *Merry Wives of Windsor*. It is vitally important to the final action of the play, where it serves both to humiliate Falstaff, and as a cover for the 'elopement' of Ann Page and Fenton. Apparently utterly different from the ceremonial songs so far discussed, it is, however, precisely their antithesis, a carnivalesque shaming ritual, and a subversive means of thwarting the will of the father – as Evans calls it: 'admirable pleasures and ferry honest knaveries' (4.4.79–80).

It also, incidentally, re-opens the question of the number of boy actors the company might have had, since the 'fairies' must be played by the children Evans says he will instruct, and which the stage direction at 5.5.102 requires; the number is not specified, but since two are stolen away along with Ann Page during the performance of the song, yet Falstaff addresses his remark 'And these are not fairies' (5.5.120) to boys remaining on-stage, there must be at least four. A minimum of seven boy actors are therefore required by the play – a number which would enable the *Dream* fairies also to be played by juveniles. More important for the dramatic action, if Evans, Pistol, and Mistress Quickly (possibly played by an adult rather than a boy) participate in the song, then a full vocal canvas would be available, implying the socially collective nature of the ritual they enact. No music survives, but the lyric seems to invite a musical contrast between the sententiousness of its first eight trochaic lines, and the dactylic triple time of the final two lines.[91] We are told that the whole scripting and rehearsing of the scene has been done by the parson, Sir Hugh Evans. Earlier in the play he had cut a comic figure, singing fearfully a mish-mash of psalm and Marlowe in 'To shallow rivers' (3.1.15–25), a comedy which would be increased if the cleric's words 'were put to the psalm-tune throughout; the provision of sacred parodies, edifying words written to popular tunes ... was a practice much favoured during and after the Reformation, and for a parson spontaneously to invert the process would be a hilarious reversal'.[92] Similar humour might derive from a setting of 'Fie on sinful fantasy' which played off a solemn, psalm-like tune for the first eight lines against a dance-like triple-time final section to accompany the pinching of Falstaff. This is, of course, pure speculation – and some modern productions have elaborated the humiliation of Falstaff in scenes of phantasmagorical menace – echoing the critical readings which have characterized it as a scene of ritual scapegoating.[93] This may be to press too hard on the comedy of the play's conclusion,[94] but the function of music in generating and emphasizing communal solidarity in the quasi-ritual response to the threat that Falstaff embodies is vitally important.

The second of the songs celebrating a less than solemn ritual is the drinking song 'Come, thou monarch of the vine', from *Antony and Cleopatra*, 2.7. It might seem that this song should simply be placed along-side other drinking songs, but ostensibly at least it serves a quasi-ritual function in cementing the friendship between the Roman triumvirs and their erstwhile enemy, Pompey.[95] It is, however, a distinctly odd song in a number of ways. Throughout the play revelry has been characterized as Egyptian, rather than Roman; and here Antony answers Pompey's 'This is not yet an Alexandrian feast' with the comment: 'It ripens towards it' (2.7.95–6). Enobarbus introduces the song itself with the comment 'Shall

we dance now the Egyptian bacchanals / And celebrate our drink'
(2.7.103–4). Paradoxically, then, the only actual example of 'Egyptian'
revelry in the play takes place in a Roman context. By the time the song
arrives Lepidus has already been carried off drunk, and Caesar has
confessed that he could 'well forbear' further drinking (2.7.97). Yet Antony
proposes the song as a symbolic assertion of amity: 'Let's all take hands
/ Till that the conquering wine hath steeped our sense / In soft and delicate
Lethe', and Enobarbus orders the ceremony:

> All take hands
> Make battery to our ears with the loud music.
> The while I'll place you, then the boy shall sing,
> The holding every man shall beat as loud
> As his strong sides can volley. (2.7.112–17)

As instruction for performance this is remarkably unclear. Earlier, the
scene has opened with the instruction '*Music plays*' as servants enter with
the banquet. It is not specified what kind of music this might be, although
if it is to continue under the servants' dialogue it presumably is a sociable consort, not the loud music of trumpets or hoboyes, which, however,
sounds as the banquet's guests are brought in. It is this loud music that
Enobarbus seems to request while he arranges the dance; but if a boy is
to sing solo then the song itself must be more modestly accompanied, at
least until the others enter with 'the holding'. This term is itself obscure.
It is usually glossed simply as a 'refrain', which would then distinguish
the singing of the boy from the refrain of the others – probably to the
repeated last line 'Cup us till the world go round'. Duffin, however, suggests that it might imply the 'holding of a part' in a round, and gives two
alternative settings, each of which would require the boy to begin, and
then the others to join in.[96] Attractive though this suggestion is – for
drunken companionship is explicitly signalled by the singing of a round
in *Twelfth Night* and *The Tempest* – it would seem to me more piquant
to contrast a solo boy's piping of 'Come thou monarch' with the lower,
drunken voices of the adult males.

It must also be a question whether, or with what enthusiasm, the
various characters participate in this musical emblem of togetherness.

Caesar's line immediately following the song is 'What would you more? Pompey, good night', which scarcely suggests that he has been a very enthusiastic singer, and his remark to Antony that 'Our graver business frowns at this levity' (3.1.119–20) firmly re-establishes his contempt for such revelry. How this song is staged is, then, very much a matter of choice – although quite a number of productions have taken the opportunity expansively to elaborate it.[97] In theatrical terms it is surely right that, for a time at least, the music must be allowed to work, and that Caesar's comment that 'The wild disguise hath almost / Anticked us all' (3.1.123–4) be taken to indicate that for a while even his cold blood has been warmed to song. As a political statement it is a doomed failure, but as a theatrical event it must work positively. Drunkenness is, of itself, unattractive or at best comic; the function of the song, however, by encouraging the audience to identify with and participate in it, is to suspend moral judgement and persuade them of the attractiveness of the scene's 'Egyptian' revelry. We then are contemptuous of Lepidus's failure to take his drink, and find Caesar's censoriousness inappropriate and unattractive. Menas' attempt earlier in the scene to persuade Pompey to murder his enemies comes from a man who has kept himself from the cup. We recognize, of course, that this is no way for the triple pillars of the world to behave, and are fully aware that the friendship they ostensibly celebrate is a fraud – but if we are involved in and by the song, we may wish briefly that it were otherwise. In this way the scene of the song enacts in miniature the oscillation of an audience's sympathy between Roman severity and Egyptian excess that characterizes the play as a whole.

The final example of a ritual song is very much less complicated in its purpose and effect – although, like those in *Merry Wives* and *Antony and Cleopatra*, it is open to varying degrees of theatrical elaboration. This is the interlude of the huntsman's song in *As You Like It*, 4.2. Without warning Jaques and assorted lords enter; Jaques asks who killed the deer, suggests that he be presented to the Duke 'like a Roman conqueror' and asks 'have you no song, forester, for this purpose?' (4.2.3–6). A song, 'What shall he have that kill'd the deer' (4.2.10–19), is duly sung, which represents the successful huntsman wearing the skin and horns of the deer, and goes on, with double entendre, to suggest that there is no dishonour in wearing the horn, otherwise and familiarly a sign of cuckoldry. Though the song seems to derive from ancient ritual tradition, its function in the play is primarily one of theatrical necessity – to provide an interlude between two scenes involving Rosalind, and thereby to suggest the passing of time. It is not exactly irrelevant to the play for, in our first encounter with the forest of Arden and its inhabitants in 2.1, Duke Senior lamented the necessity of hunting, and the First Lord reported Jaques's moralizing upon a dying deer, but the song does not pick up on the resonances of these earlier scenes. One might argue that its easy tolerance of cuckoldry adds another voice to the debates about love that form the substance of the play as a whole, and its celebration of upper-class bonding (for deer-hunting was very much an aristocratic sport) suits with the picture of the 'co-mates and brothers in exile' (2.1.1) that we have been offered from the beginning. In the end, however, it is a scene that can easily be cut without obvious detriment to the play – and has sometimes been omitted in the course of the play's performance history.[98]

It is, however, one of the few songs for which a tune survives that might well have been used in its first performance. A version was published in John Hilton's *Catch as Catch Can* (1652), but Ross Duffin has discovered a manuscript version from about 1625, whose text 'matches that of the play more closely than does Hilton's version', and this might therefore suggest that it derives directly from it.[99] What both versions have in common is the omission of the third line of the Folio text: 'Then sing him home: the rest shall bear this burden'. While editors once felt that this disqualified the setting from being that of the original performance, others plausibly argue, conversely, that its absence 'makes that line seem likely to be an invitation by Jaques to join in the round as just demonstrated by the leading voice'.[100] This neatly fulfils the way Jaques's initial request for a song is directed to an individual forester (who might well have been Amiens, the singer of the earlier songs in the play), but is followed by the demand that ''Tis no matter how it be in tune, so it make noise enough' (4.2.8–9). As a performed event, then, it partakes of the communality of the catch as the tune is picked up successively by four voices, and its festive solidarity is emphasized by this musical setting. The song then reaches out to involve the audience, for, as is true of all catches, the repetitiveness of the music implies that we could ourselves easily get hold of the tune, and the very fact of its successive entries suggests that we too might enter into it. Extraneous to the plot it undoubtedly is, but it helps to establish a note of celebration that prepares for the transformations of the play's fifth act.

In its attractive superfluity the hunters' catch is very like the other songs in the play – to which we now turn to conclude this chapter. *As You Like It* calls for more music than Shakespeare had ever previously demanded, yet, compared with almost all the songs so far discussed, those in this play have a curiously inessential quality. In part this is a consequence of the fact that most of them are (probably) performed by a character, Amiens, who has no other function than to sing. The songs, therefore, are in no way expressive of the personality of the individual who performs them. They are the purest example of the 'performed' song in the whole Shakespearean canon, and despite Amiens's conventional modesty about his singing abilities it is absolutely essential that they are well sung. Unlike the songs of other modest singers, such as Balthasar in *Much Ado* and Pandarus in *Troilus and Cressida*, however, Amiens's songs are much less integrated into the play's dramatic action. They neither derive directly from events nor does anything happen because of them.

Why, then, are they there? It may be that a significant spur to their inclusion was the popularity of songs in plays performed by the children's companies. Songs were expected, and plentiful, in their comedies,[101] and Shakespeare might well have wished to show that the King's Men could compete, and, fortuitously or not, his company must have acquired about this time an actor capable of rendering them sufficiently expertly. More important, however, is the generic impulse that comes from *As You Like It*'s pastoral setting. Singing is what characterizes literary shepherds, and pastoral was currently popular. Philip Sidney's influential prose romance, *Arcadia*, for example, included at the end of each book a series of set-piece song contests that trace their origin back through continental romances to classical pastoral, and songs are included in Lodge's *Rosalynde*, Shakespeare's immediate source for this play, as well as in other continental and English pastoral romances. Lyly's pastoral comedies are suffused with songs.

In *As You Like It* it is not shepherds who sing, but 'many Renaissance stories are not primarily about shepherds and shepherdesses but about people who arrive amongst them'.[102] The banished Duke Senior and his companions are not in the Forest of Arden by choice, but in the report of the wrestler, Charles, 'there they live like the old Robin Hood of England. They say many young gentlemen flock to him every day, and fleet the time carelessly, as they did in the golden world' (1.1.112–15). The important words here are 'like' and 'as'; Duke Senior is living a simile, self-consciously adapting his enforced banishment into literary tradition. He does so not without effort, and Amiens praises him in the first of the Arden scenes for his capacity to 'translate the stubbornness of fortune / Into so quiet and so sweet a style' (2.1.19–20). A major part of the endeavour of the songs in the play is to effect precisely this 'translation'. It is significant, however, that the songs belong to the courtiers; Touchstone, the fool, who might have been expected to sing, has but one brief quotation of a popular song 'O sweet Oliver', at the end of the comic scene with Sir Oliver Martext (3.3.91–7). Neither the shepherd, Corin, with his blunt awareness of the realities of rural life, nor the precious figures of Phoebe and Silvius, is musical. The confinement of music to the aristocrats, and, perhaps, the musical style they adopt, contributes significantly to the political conservatism of the play.

At the same time, however, the literary pastoral conventionally sets up its rural vantage point in order to critique the vanities and excesses of the urban world and the court; this is the purpose of pastoral which Spenser, for example, developed in his *Shepheardes Calendar* (1579) and *The Faerie Queene*, Book 6 (1596), and which, in the years after *As You Like It* was written, became a dominant mode for poets such as Browne and Drayton who were critical of the court of King James. This is the position adopted by Duke Senior in his opening speech, where the rural world may be harsh, but it is better than the 'envious court' and its false flatterers. It is the topic which animates Touchstone's dispute with the 'real' shepherd, Corin in 3.2, and Amiens's songs, too, participate in this moralizing.

The self-conscious literariness of the pastoral means that it not only presents endless opportunities for formal debate, but also offers a gallery of literary styles and forms. Sidney's shepherds' eclogues are generally cast as contests presenting opposing views of or perspectives upon a variety of topics, and at the same time they, like Spenser's shepherds in the *Shepheardes Calendar*, essay a wide variety of poetic forms. These are unmistakeable features of Shakespeare's play, where exchanges of wit between Rosalind and Orlando, Touchstone and Corin, are supplemented by the stylistic variety of poems on trees, Phoebe and Silvius's arch rhetoric, Touchstone's witty prose, and the high formality of language in the play's final movements; and all are presented to an audience for their delighted, knowing assessment. It is in this highly-wrought environment that the songs make sense. They are validated, not by their contribution to the plot, nor by their expression of an individual singing consciousness, but by their participation in the stylistic display that the pastoral genre demands.

This is very evident in the first set of songs, in 2.5. The previous scene has ended with Celia asserting: 'I like this place, / And willingly could waste my time in it', and Corin literally bringing her down to earth as he says 'If you like upon report /The soil, the profit and this kind of life, I will your very faithful feeder be' (2.4.93–4, 96–8). The next scene opens immediately with Amiens singing 'Under the greenwood tree', which invites him 'who loves to lie with me' to 'come hither'. It replays Corin's invitation to Celia in a different mode, and at the same time its gesture in the opening line to a tradition of Robin Hood ballads links back to Charles's comment upon the life of the exiled Duke. At the end of the stanza Amiens sings, 'Here shall he see / No enemy / But winter and rough weather' (2.5.6–8), connecting directly with Duke Senior's praise of the rural life at the beginning of 2.1. Amiens, then, translates into the sweetness of song thematic elements we have already encountered in the play. Furthermore, the obliqueness of the song's address invites the audience themselves to 'come hither' and participate in the pastoral game. The invitation Amiens issues can scarcely be directed to the lords who accompany him – they are already there – and for them the song is a self-validating confirmation of what they like to believe about their enforced retreat. The impersonality of Amiens's singing voice means that its target is not only the characters on stage but the audience who watch; songs of this kind are both inside and outside the play-world and we are invited to experience them as 'framed' events, to participate in the feelings the musical setting of the song arouses, but at the same time to assess their performance in exactly the same way as we are invited to judge Orlando's poems pinned to trees as variously (in)competent essays in conventional romantic rhetoric.

Thus far it is assumed that Amiens sings this stanza as a solo song, an assumption that Jaques's subsequent comments and requests for more endorses, although the Folio direction is simply 'Song'. Whether or not he is accompanied, by himself or another, is not specified, but on his next singing appearance the Duke orders 'Give us some music, and, good cousin, sing' (2.7.174), the separate commands probably indicating 'that Amiens was accompanied by one or more musicians'.[103] No tune survives, and it is of course possible that Shakespeare himself either wrote the words to fit an existing tune, or that he took over the whole song, words as well as tune, from the popular repertory; although the form is by no means a usual one for popular song, and the tune Duffin offers, *Sir Eglamore*,[104] sounds, to my ear, less convincing than many of his other conjectures, which might just suggest that the song, music as well as words, was specifically composed for the play.

The Folio stage direction for the second stanza, which follows after some banter between Jaques and Amiens, reads '*Song. Altogether here*'. Quite what this might mean is unclear – either all the lords sing the whole of the stanza (which also picks up motifs from Duke Senior's first speech), or else, and perhaps more probably, they join in the refrain lines 'Come hither, etc.'. Whatever the detail, the participation of the other lords signals their assent to Amiens's conventional, if slightly gloomy, version of the pastoral idyll. But then Jaques follows their singing with the line: 'I'll give you a verse to this note that I made yesterday' (2.5.43–4). We need not ask how Jaques comes to know the 'note' of this song (although it suggests that this is one of Amiens's regularly performed repertoire); what he has done is produce words which fit to an existing tune in exactly the way that Shakespeare himself might have done here and certainly did elsewhere.

There is some confusion about what exactly happens next. Amiens says that he will 'sing it', and the First Folio gives his name as the speech heading for the next line 'Thus it goes', prints the song in italics, and then adds another speech-heading for Amiens at the line which immediately follows:

'What's that "ducdame?"' (2.5.55). The Second Folio (which, of course, has no independent authority) changed the second speech heading to 'Jaques', and, by implication, then has him singing, or, more likely, speaking the lyric 'If it do come to pass', with Amiens responding with his puzzled question at the end. This is the version that has been preferred by modern editors and most theatrical directors. Seng, however, has defended the original text, commenting that 'it is entirely possible that Jaques hands the lyrics of the parody to Amiens who obligingly sings them. Additional evidence that the parody is sung, not recited, is the fact that it is set in italics like the first two stanzas of the song which were certainly sung.'[105] It seems to me, however, that the argument for Amiens' singing of the stanza is dramatic, rather than merely textual. He has just mouthed obediently Duke Senior's perspective upon the pastoral life; Jaques slips him his parody, which asserts:

> If it do come to pass
> That any man turn ass,
> Leaving his wealth and ease
> A stubborn will to please
> Ducdame, ducdame, ducdame.
> Here shall he see
> Gross fools he,
> And if he will come to me. (2.5.47–54)

We might imagine Amiens launching confidently into his rendition, only to sing with growing unease as he begins to recognize not only that the sentiments are the opposite of those he has just been giving voice to, but that in place of their generalized address this lyric is aimed directly at himself and his fellows. If the parody is sung by the same voice to the same tune as 'Under the greenwood tree' and 'Who doth ambition shun', then it economically but powerfully acts as a dramatic emblem of the way in which pastoral is the product of a subjective interpretation of circumstance. The original and its opposite become, if Amiens sings both, two sides of the air's coin. His question at the end, 'What's that "ducdame?"', might then emerge as a rather petulant demand of Jaques, an attempt to reassert some sort of control. Jaques's answer, ''Tis a Greek invocation to call fools into a circle', particularly if, as is common theatrical practice, it is addressed to lords who have clustered round him to hear his answer, becomes the sharp reinforcement of his message.

The point that must be emphasized, however, is that the songs in this scene do not merely exist to convey a 'colour of scene and sense of atmosphere'.[106] Instead they function as generic marker (we are in the pastoral world where songs are supposed to happen); they recast in another form sentiments we have already heard, and so partake of the play's bravura stylistic display; crucially, because of Jaques's parody, they also illustrate the staging of debate and alternatives of interpretation within the pastoral world that are refracted throughout the play's verbal action.

The next song Amiens sings, 'Blow, blow thou winter wind' in 2.7, accompanies the meal which had been in preparation during the earlier scene, and had presumably been left in view during the intervening episode where Orlando and Adam enter, fainting for lack of food. At the very simplest level, the singing of a song as an adjunct to a meal conforms to social practice in upper-class households of the period, suggesting the way the Duke maintains his courtly standards even in the forest (and illustrated by the lutenist who accompanies an outdoor meal in Figure 17). But in the context here, where we have just before it heard Jaques's disconsolate view of the seven ages of man, and witnessed the distress of Orlando and Adam, the darkly coloured amplification of Duke Senior's moralization of the winter's wind which 'bites and blows upon my body' (2.1.7), seems entirely appropriate. It is the moment when 'The Duke, confronted with someone who has suffered an injustice similar to his own, drops his pro-pastoral humbug and admits that, for him, exile to the forest of Arden is a suffering.'[107] The lyric's final lines, 'Then hey-ho the holly; This life is most jolly' (2.7.192–3), ring hollowly – and this insistent invocation of seasonal harshness has persuaded a number of directors in the last half-century or so to set the first half of the play in a bleak and wintry landscape. But while the song is not inappropriate, it is not commented on by any of the characters on stage. It simply happens, covering Adam and Orlando's feeding and commenting in shorthand on their plight. The lack of direct reaction to the song reinforces the sense of

FIGURE 17 Jost Amman, 'Picnic'. A lutenist accompanies an outdoor feast.

its being an optional add-on, appropriately decorative and amplificatory, but little more.

The final song I want to consider (since the hunter's chorus and the hymn to Hymen have been dealt with elsewhere) is perhaps the most adventitious song in the whole Shakespeare canon. A brief scene, 5.3, begins with Audrey and Touchstone completing the quartet of couples whose marriage is shortly to be solemnized, and then 'two of the banished Duke's pages' enter, sing the song 'It was a lover and his lass', and then leave. We may have seen the pages before in the Duke's retinue, and they might reappear to assist in the final song, but essentially they, even more than Amiens, exist only to sing.[108] It is probable that they perform the opening lines antiphonally, before joining in the final refrain, bearing out their promise that they will perform 'both in a tune, like gipsies on a horse'. Thematically this song in praise of rural love, with its injunction to 'take the present time' and its celebration of spring, suits the moment, as the play decisively turns its back on the wintry winds of exile which had figured in the imagery of earlier songs. It is, then, appropriate to its place in the play, but it is so only in the most general terms. Indeed, one suspects that it is there primarily because this little scene (like the huntsmen's chorus before it) is a necessary 'filler' allowing time to elapse between Rosalind's promise that she will meet the lovers again 'tomorrow' (5.2.113) and the final scene of the play when all is 'made even'. Something has to cover the transition, and in this pastoral comedy, it may as well be a song. This air, then, functions rather as songs frequently do in a modern musical comedy – there because the genre requires them – and it is perhaps not surprising that some productions have in various ways expanded the scene into a large-scale musical number involving many of the cast,[109] although to do so is to upset the delicate balance of the play's conclusion in which, as we have seen, ceremonial song and dance play a crucial part.

The most problematic feature of this song, however, is its provenance. *As You Like It* was written somewhere between 1598 and 1600; a delightful setting of this song by the distinguished composer, Thomas Morley, appeared in his *First Book of Ayres* published in 1600 (in a version which prints the stanzas in an order different from, but preferable to, that of the First Folio). If Morley's setting were the one used in the original performances, then this would make it the only known specially composed setting of a song in a Shakespeare play before Robert Johnson's songs for the last plays. It is not impossible that Shakespeare or his company did ask Morley to provide the setting, and that the composer saw fit to include it speedily thereafter in his published collection. The proximity between writing and printing should not disqualify the possibility – after all, Shakespeare was quite capable of moving very swiftly in the other direction when, in *Twelfth Night*, he quotes from a song that was published very close to the assumed date of the writing of the play. Equally it might be that Morley saw the play, say in 1599, liked the lyric, borrowed it, and set it in time for his own publication (after which the King's Men might well have borrowed it back). It is also possible that the song was already circulating in manuscript independently of the play, and that, faced with the necessity of finding something to fill up this scene, Shakespeare simply appropriated it for his purposes.[110] There is no way of resolving this uncertainty, but one would not want to be without Morley's setting, which is close to a popular style, yet gives it a wonderful 'lift' with the cross-rhythms introduced into the refrain. The more general, and perhaps uncomfortable, question is how far one might assume that Shakespeare wrote any of the lyrics for songs here or elsewhere, and it is a question that arises perhaps more insistently with *As You Like It* than most other plays. Attractive its songs are, and thematically appropriate to the parts of the play in which they are placed, but it would not be entirely surprising to discover that these performed songs were versions of already existing lyrics. It would have a crucial effect on the dynamic of the relationship between songs and audience if the songs were already familiar to them – but in the absence of any hard evidence, speculation is probably best avoided. It might be argued, however, that this is precisely the central characteristic of Shakespeare's deployment of songs in the plays – that he takes ingredients that an audience might have recognized, whether in tune, words, or situation, and develops them in dramatic contexts which make them work in ways that are often surprising, frequently subtle, and almost always serve to give the familiar a novel pointedness and freshness of effect.

Chapter Five

MUSICAL THEMATICS: *TWELFTH NIGHT* AND *THE TEMPEST*

In writing *As You Like It* Shakespeare significantly increased the quantity of music he demanded, but, as we have seen, though appropriate to the pastoral genre of the play and to themes raised within it, it is somewhat less than fully integrated into the dramatic action. The final two plays I want to consider take the deployment of music and its effects to a different level. Both *Twelfth Night* and *The Tempest* call for a wide variety of musics. Neither of them requires the trumpets and drums of history and tragedy, but in different ways they each integrate the variety of their musical events into larger thematic and dramatic preoccupations. This is most obviously true of *The Tempest*, Shakespeare's last single-authored play, written in 1610–11 after the musical establishment of the King's Men increased following the acquisition of Blackfriars. From beginning to end the play is suffused with musical sounds and the effects of music are a continuous dramatic and thematic subject. The earlier *Twelfth Night* (perhaps written immediately after *As You Like It*) is less ambitious musically; but, in its first half especially, music is much more than ornament. Taken together they provide a conspectus of most of the musical possibilities that Shakespeare entertained in the course of his career, and thus serve to bring together many of the threads which have run through this book.

TWELFTH NIGHT

Before embarking on a discussion of this play one textual issue needs briefly to be explored, for it significantly affects the way we might read the music in the play. Act 2, scene 4, opens with this dialogue:

ORSINO	Give me some music. Now good morrow friends.
	Now, good Cesario, but that piece of song,
	That old and antic song we heard last night;
	Methought it did relieve my passion much,
	More than light airs and recollected terms
	Of these most brisk and giddy-paced times.
	Come, but one verse.
CURIO	He is not here, so please your lordship, that should sing
	it.
ORSINO	Who was it?
CURIO	Feste the jester, my lord ...

The exchange is an awkward one. How might it be that Orsino has forgotten overnight who it was that sang the song he claims had such an effect upon him? Why begin the scene with this rather clumsily introduced wait for Feste to arrive? More significant, Orsino's opening speech seems to imply that he is requesting Viola/Cesario to sing 'but one verse' of the song; and, earlier in the play, when Viola decided to serve Orsino, she told the Captain: 'Thou shalt present me as an eunuch to him / [...] for I can sing, / And speak to him in many sorts of music' (1.2.56–8). These considerations have persuaded a number of scholars since the late nineteenth century that what we have is a revised text, and that in the original it was Viola, not Feste, who sang to Orsino in this scene. The argument then turns to the song that is now present in the text, 'Come away death', which, according to those who accept a theory of revision, does not accord with Orsino's description of it as 'old and antic', and so must have been substituted for a now lost song that Viola might have sung. The argument runs that the revision might have been necessitated by an actor's breaking voice, or by the arrival of a boy actor less competent as a singer.[1] Most recent editors have had little truck with the supposition. Wells and Warren, for example, roundly declare that 'the entire scene, in fact, is so unified that surely no one would suspect that anything was wrong unless they were looking for evidence of revision'.[2] They argue instead that Viola's earlier suggestion that she might sing was a first thought which Shakespeare simply abandoned in the course of the play's evolution (for Viola to appear as a eunuch would have had fairly disastrous implications for the plot, which requires Olivia to credit his masculine disguise and fall in love). They explain Orsino's speech at the beginning of this scene as an invitation to Cesario 'to listen to the song with him rather than asking him to sing it'. Neither side of this argument is absolutely compelling. Certainly, since the play was written either just before or just after *Hamlet*, the company had at that time a boy capable of singing Ophelia's songs, and the opening of the scene does seem clumsy. On the other hand, even if there were revision, the presumed 'original' is now irrecoverable and we must deal with what we have; and once past the opening, what we have makes very good theatrical sense.

It is, however, worth noting that in her declaration of intent Viola says that she can 'speak' as well as 'sing' music – and it is the music of her speech which we witness during the play. Orsino declares that 'Thou dost speak masterly' (2.4.22), and Olivia, falling in love with Viola, cries out:

> I bade you never speak again of him;
> But would you undertake another suit,
> I had rather hear you to solicit that,
> Than music from the spheres. (3.1.108–11)

This, indeed, is the only invocation of heavenly music in the play, and it is characteristic that it is disowned. The music of *Twelfth Night* is emphatically, exclusively, and distinctively earth-bound; it is notably 'free of even the scraps of traditional musical ideology that had been put to use in the plays preceding it'.[3]

One reason for the unmetaphysical quality of the music is precisely the fact of Shakespeare's change of mind that gives all the songs to the clown, Feste. He is a professional singer, the most developed representation of such a figure in the whole canon. Not for him the mock-modesty of Amiens or Balthasar; he, as he tells Orsino, takes pleasure in singing (2.4.68), although always ready to pocket the fee he deserves.[4] This has important consequence for our reactions to the songs we see him perform. When Feste sings, he calculates the appropriate song to offer to the audience in front of him – it is his job, as his epilogue song suggests, to 'strive to please'. When we watch him in action, therefore, we are not merely ourselves responding directly to the song as a musical event – nor attending only to the reactions of the characters on stage to his singing, measuring them against our own – but we are also assessing Feste's own calculation in offering that particular song at that moment. It is this layering of different perspectives that ensures that the songs are embedded in the action in a rich and suggestive fashion. Moreover, Feste is the one figure who moves between the different territories of the play; his ironic, detached perspective is important to the way we understand the text as a whole, and colours in particular our response to his songs.

The three territories of the play are Orsino's court, dominated by love, and the bifurcated household of Olivia in which she has renounced the world, while her kinsman, Sir Toby, though ostensibly occupied in securing Olivia as a match for his gull, Sir Andrew Aguecheek, is dedicated to the fleshly appetites of eating and drinking. In each of these worlds music – or its absence – plays a defining part.

The play opens with one of the most familiar of invocations:

> If music be the food of love, play on,
> Give me excess of it, that, surfeiting,
> The appetite may sicken, and so die.
> That strain again, it had a dying fall:
> O, it came o'er my ear like the sweet sound
> That breathes upon a bank of violets,
> Stealing and giving odour. Enough, no more;
> 'Tis not so sweet now as it was before.
> O spirit of love, how quick and fresh art thou,
> That notwithstanding thy capacity
> Receiveth as the sea, nought enters there,
> Of what validity and pitch soe'er,
> But falls into abatement and low price,
> Even in a minute! So full of shapes is fancy,
> That it alone is high fantastical. (1.1.1–15)

In staging this scene there are some important decisions to be made. Since the opening lines imply that music is already playing before the entry of Orsino and his courtiers, the question arises as to how long it should play before he appears; the same question then attends the musical punctuation of the speech – how long does Orsino give his musicians his attention, first before asking them to play a given phrase again, and then before he stops them? The way these questions are answered is crucial to our initial reading of Orsino's character. The dominant critical orthodoxy is that he is a man in love with love, impatient and self-gratifying, and that this impatience is figured in this opening speech, where music exists simply to feed his appetites, and is quickly disowned when it fails to work. But 'the combination of musical beauty and sensuous language is a crucial part of an audience's experience of the scene, and ... complicates any view that Orsino is being satirized or caricatured'.[5]

Because of its very familiarity we do not fully recognize how exceptional this opening is. There is no other Shakespearean play which begins with instrumental music other than the formal sound of a flourish or fanfare, and we need to ask what this might have signified to the original audience as they perhaps witnessed an individual or a group of musicians walk on stage and begin to play (the musician(s) could enter with Orsino, but the clear implication is that their music begins before his speech). To the more privileged amongst the playgoers it might have suggested that Shakespeare was taking a leaf out of the choirboy companies' book, since it is 'probable that opening music was a standard feature of the children's plays'.[6] More than that, such an ensemble – perhaps the mixed consort (see Figure 7 on p. 57) – would have suggested that we were being introduced to the household of a person of high rank, and might well have implied the prelude to a feast or banquet of some sort, since the association of music and feeding was commonplace. As Charles Butler observed: 'So kind [*appropriate*] is music at a feast, that it is compared to a rich jewel: and is preferred, at that time, even before wise speaking.'[7] It is just this association which Orsino picks up in his opening line; the music he requires, however, is not for a material banquet, but metaphorically to feed his love.[8] Again, these lines are so familiar that it is easy not quite to hear them fully, and in particular to overlook the force of the opening 'if' (there is, as Touchstone observes, 'much virtue in If' (*AYL*, 5.4.101)). Orsino is, of course, alluding in general terms to the commonplace notion that music can either salve a lover's melancholy, or else incite it further,[9] and the conditional 'if' suggests that on this occasion he wishes to indulge the delicious feelings of love, or else to hear no music. (Later, however, he commends the song 'Come away death' to Viola on exactly the opposite grounds that it 'did relieve my passion much' (2.4.4).) In the event, as the music continues, particularly if space is given for it to sound, it seems to have the opposite effect to that which he demanded – the melancholy cadence of the 'dying fall' allays rather than incites the feelings of love and provokes him to a poetic descant of which the music itself is the subject. There is then the opportunity once more either to let the music continue to sound, or else for it peremptorily to be brought to an end. Either way, however, the direction of Orsino's speech once the music stops shifts from feasting and indulgence to questions of repetition and change, of variety and instability, that are subsequently to be the subject of his conversations with Viola, and important for the play as a whole. If his speech begins by playing upon the social collocation of music and feasting, it ends with an assertion of the mind's quick changes which echoes the conventional aesthetic praise of music for its ability to move with variation and quick change from one mood to another.

Much, then, hangs on the pace of the staging in this opening; played quickly, with little space for the music, it becomes symptomatic primarily of an Orsino who is self-indulgent and capricious. Played more expansively its effect is to present us with a speech that itself becomes a meditation on the music that we hear (distantly related as a dramatic device, therefore, for all the difference of circumstance, to Richard II in Pomfret castle). Orsino, from this perspective, may be no less self-absorbed, but becomes a more interestingly introspective figure. The introduction of music at the play's opening is dextrous and economical in suggesting a whole range of potential meaning. At the realistic level it fixes the scene in an aristocratic household; as 'incidental' music it establishes a mood of pleasurable melancholy for the audience;[10] more specifically, the opening exploits the conventional associations of music with love and appetite which are to be central to the play's action. In a less tangible way, the music seems at one and the same time to image Orsino's mind, and yet to hint, even as he disowns it, at a harmony which is as yet beyond his reach.

The next musical event in Orsino's court comes in 2.4. If we take the scene as it now stands, then the music has a crucial role in its articulation and development, picking up and developing motifs from the play's opening. Orsino calls for a song he heard 'last night' (as in the opening scene he asked for a musical phrase to be repeated), and we ourselves hear the tune of the song more than once, first played instrumentally, and then sung by Feste. The song is framed by two discussions between Orsino and Viola which turn on questions of constancy, as had the latter part of Orsino's opening speech. The first such exchange takes place over the playing of the tune of 'Come away, death', a melody which Viola commends because it 'gives a very echo to the seat / Where love is throned' (2.4.21–2). During the conversation, Orsino first asserts that he is like 'all true lovers' in being constant only to the 'image of the creature / That is beloved' (2.4.19–20), and later concedes that men's affections are 'more giddy and infirm' than women's are (2.4.33). Viola begins, with all necessary indirection, to exhibit her own love for Orsino. The high artifice of the situation is both supported and ameliorated by the accompanying music. The halo of sound charges the tensely erotic atmosphere that builds up throughout this scene while at the same time softening the high poetic contrivance of the verbal exchange.

Feste then enters, and sings the song whose melody we have probably heard, by now, several times, perhaps with ornamentation from the instrumentalists. If it is somewhat fanciful to see this repeated music as an appropriate accompaniment to the verbal variation on conventional love-language that Orsino and Viola engage in, there is no doubt that its repetition functions subliminally to build the scene towards the moment when Feste finally gives words to the tune with which we have become familiar. It establishes the singing of the song as the goal of the first part of the scene, investing its words, therefore, with a particular importance. The lyric of 'Come away death', however, has not met with a great deal of approval from critics over the years. Its extravagant picture of the lover condemned to death by his 'fair cruel maid' and picturing his own funeral has often prompted the same kind of resistant realism that Rosalind offers in *As You Like It*: 'Men have died from time to time, and worms have eaten them, but not for love' (4.1.101–2). Since it is at Orsino's request that this particular song is sung, it has therefore been adduced as further evidence of his own self-indulgence in romantic cliché. Leah Scragg, for example, argues that 'Orsino's attitudes are life-denying, and the negative nature of his postures is expressed through the work of art he applauds'.[11] This, however, misses the essential point that we are hearing a song, not reading a poem. Certainly the conceit of the lover dying of love was well-worn by Shakespeare's time, and Donne, for example, played mischievous games with it in his lyric 'When by thy scorn, O murderess I am dead', which imagines not a ritual funeral but a ghostly and tormenting return. But songwriters, even the most distinguished of the period, were not above setting the most hackneyed of lyrics to eloquent music, and it is to the feeling of the music rather than the particularity of the words that we as auditors respond.

This song can be viewed from a number of different perspectives; Orsino, Viola, and Feste himself may each be hearing the song in different ways. Feste on the previous night had obviously chosen successfully a song he thought would appeal to Orsino. As a member of Olivia's household he is well aware of Orsino's doomed suit, and, given his role as fool and propensity for mockery, it is just possible that he might select this extravagantly exaggerated lyric with mischievous intent. Winifred Maynard takes this view, and suggests that 'If the original setting, now unknown, took up the cues for music of slightly over-languishing beauty, no one could achieve more deftly than Feste a performance combining musical pleasure and hinted parodic effect.'[12] This, I think, is much more difficult to achieve in practice than she implies. A singer, once launched into a song, generally must seem to mean what he or she sings; they may know that what they sing is self-indulgent, but they must appear precisely to be indulging themselves in it. Of course, by exaggerated vocal mannerism a singer may choose to send up what they sing, but even here – as for example in modern renditions of Victorian ballads that lend themselves to ridicule – the really successful performance comes from a singer who conveys pleasure in what (s)he guys.[13] The problem with anticipating a performance of this kind from Feste is that in such self-conscious renditions attention is focused on the performer, and our enjoyment derives from appreciating the way they steer a course between delighted exaggeration and mere parody. It is not impossible that this should be the case in a performance of this scene – but it would risk a great deal, in that it would not only critique Orsino's self-indulgence if he were to appear satisfied with a performance that the knowing audience recognized as ironically exaggerated, but potentially mock Viola, who is moved by the music, and for whom the possibility of dying without ever speaking her love is only too real. Orsino may have chosen the song, but it also speaks to and of Viola.

In the theatre we watch Feste singing, and observe the reactions of those to whom he sings. The responses of Viola and Orsino could well be rather different. Auden, who has a low opinion of the lyric in any case, observes:

> Shakespeare has so placed the song as to make it seem an expres-
> sion of the Duke's real character. Beside him sits the disguised Viola,
> for whom the Duke is not a playful fancy, but a serious passion. It
> would be painful enough for her if the man she loved really loved
> another, but it is much worse to be made to see that he only loves
> himself, and it is this insight which at this point Viola has to
> endure.[14]

This is a harsh reading, and requires an attentiveness to the lyric which I am not convinced either of the audiences, on-stage or in the auditorium, can command. Moreover, it resists the central fact that we are drawn by the music into the song; temporarily at least it casts us too in the role of melancholy lover as we identify with the situation the singer represents. In recent productions the song has often prompted the hesitant display of affection from Viola to Orsino, which is sometimes reciprocated. Much, of course, turns in the end on the nature and the quality of the music itself. No setting survives, and we cannot therefore know whether it was indeed sung to music 'old and plain', whether Orsino speaks true in calling it 'silly sooth', or whether it was rendered in a style nearer the powerful and fashionable melancholy of John Daniel or John Dowland.

This raises a general issue which has been hinted at earlier, but not fully explored, and it is one that is important for all of Feste's performances in this play. In Chapter 4 a distinction was offered between impromptu and performed song. There is, however, a further layer – for when a singer performs a song, at one level he or she is adopting a dramatic persona for whom the song he or she sings makes sense as an outburst of feeling. The 'I' of the lyric is not the 'I' who is the singer, and it is the music which renders it possible for an audience to accept the transformation of Feste the ageing jester into the lovelorn persona of 'Come away death'. Furthermore, the musically accompanied lyric requires that the audience position themselves, not as the addressee, but as the speaker of the song. As Mark Booth puts it: 'the singer's words are sung for us in that he says something that is also said somehow in extension *by* us, and we are drawn into the state, the pose, the attitude, the self offered by the song'.[15] He is writing here of lieder, of the song without dramatic context, and it is of course true that in theatrical song (as in opera) there are further complicating factors. Nonetheless, it is important to recognize the way in which a singer not only performs the music of a song, but in significant respects is performed by it. The musical setting is not simply contingent upon the words, but remakes and determines our response to them. As literary critics, and since the text is frequently all we have to discuss, we tend to simplify the potential relationships a song may have not only with its auditors, but also with the person who sings it, and crucially neglect the constitutive force of the music itself that is sung.

There can, of course, be no one 'right' reading of this song; if I am inclined to wish that the cumulative emotional effect of the repetition of the tune and its issue finally in song be taken to suggest a 'real' emotional intensity into which Feste enters as he sings, rather than undercutting it by self-parody, this is not to deny that at the same time we might register its solipsistic self-indulgence. Our response to the song is certainly complicated by the way, immediately it is over, Feste's caustic character-ization of the changeability of Orsino's mind, as 'a very opal' (2.4.75), directly confronts Orsino with a negative judgement of him. The motiva-tion of Feste's speech is not clear. It could be, as on the surface it appears, the product of a professional's irritation at having been summoned to perform, only to be quickly and summarily dismissed; but it seems to have deeper roots than this, which we cannot quite guess. It may be, of course, that it is some display of affection between Orsino and Viola during the song which prompts Feste to an accusation of Orsino for unfaithfulness to his own mistress.[16] Wherever it derives from, however, the critique immediately prompts Orsino both to return to the suit of Olivia and to protest his constancy in terms that flatly contradict his earlier admission to Viola of the giddy infirmity of men's affections. Feste has clearly hit upon a vulnerable nerve in Orsino's self-perception. This, in turn, incites Viola's rebuttal in which, again, she indirectly speaks to Orsino of herself in the figure of Patience on a monument, smiling at grief. Viola may not have sung the song, but in this last movement of the scene the musical enunciation of a death-directed love is transferred into her poetic voice, a voice which prompts Orsino's curiosity as he asks for more details of the story; thus, perhaps, replaying the sense of a mutual absorption that could have been hinted at in their response to the song itself. At the scene's end it is Viola herself who must recall Orsino to his mission as she enquires 'Shall I to this lady?', and Orsino seems to have to shake himself as he replies 'Ay that's the theme' (2.4.123). This scene is absolutely crucial to the emotional direction of the play, and music is essential to its conduct and to its effect. At a narrative level it is a scene (literally) of dead ends – Orsino imagining himself in his shroud of white; Viola figuring herself as Patience on her monument, her history a blank – and yet during it we see emotional doors begin to unlock, and it is music which oils the wards. The song's lyric may be one of self-indulgent love, yet it begins a movement towards a love of a very different temper.

'Come away, death' is the last love-song in the play, but it is not the first. In the preceding scene Feste had joined Sir Toby and Sir Andrew, and at their request (and on production of payment) had sung 'O mistress mine'. Whereas no tune survives for the later song, for this one various versions of a tune with the same title exist, although none exactly fits Shakespeare's lyrics. It is not necessary here to arbitrate on the arguments about which, if any, might be the version of the tune sung in the original play; it is probable that the tune, if not the lyric, pre-dated the play itself and was a melody 'reworked by various composers as they saw fit'.[17] It is also not clear whether Feste accompanies himself or, if he does so, what instrument he plays. In 3.1. he clearly enters playing music, and Viola's question 'dost thou live by thy tabor?' (3.1.1–2) implies that he uses the pipe and tabor,[18] for so long a badge of the comedian (see Figure 14 on p. 95), from

Tarlton through Kempe, and here perhaps employed by Kempe's successor, Robert Armin. This, however, would not serve to accompany the song, and he might demonstrate his musical versatility by playing on the lute. In his choice of song, however, Feste shows himself, as always, attentive to his audience. It is Sir Toby who requests a 'love song, a love song', but it is Sir Andrew who is actually the would-be lover of Olivia. At its most obvious level the song flatters Sir Andrew's hopes – hopes that in his first scene he had thought were gone, much to Sir Toby's alarm. It might be said, then, that Feste singing a love-song for Sir Andrew fits Sir Toby's purposes equally well; he needs to persuade Sir Andrew that there is some possibility of success if he is to keep him, and his money, available.

If the tune for the song is indeed a version of that employed by Morley and Byrd in their instrumental compositions of the same name, however, there is a tension between the positive tone of the lyric – with its suggestion that 'journeys end in lovers meeting' (2.3.43), and its encouragement of the lover to seize the day – and the melody, which has a melancholy tone, one which enforces the second stanza's awareness of the passing of time, rather than the optimism of the first. It is, I think, the particular character of this well-known melody which accounts in significant measure for the standard critical verdict, which was neatly formulated by John Moore as long ago as 1916: 'There is something pathetically human about the gross old knight and his withered dupe, sitting in the drunken gravity of midnight to hear the clown sing of the fresh love of youth.'[19] Auden concurs that the contrast between desire and the possibility of performance is the point, but views it much less tolerantly:

> True love certainly does not plead its cause by telling the beloved
> that love is transitory ... Taken seriously, these lines are
> the voice of elderly lust, afraid of its own death. Shakespeare forces
> this awareness on our consciousness by making the audience to the
> song a couple of seedy old drunks.[20]

Both of these readings make the music function rather as 'Sneak's Noise' does in the tavern scene in *2 Henry IV* discussed earlier, and they each depend on the assumption that both Toby and Andrew are past their prime.

This is not necessarily the case for Sir Andrew. He must be, at least in his own mind, a plausible suitor for Olivia, who, Sir Toby himself tells him, will 'not match above her degree, neither in estate, *years* nor wit' (1.3.106–7, my italics). The dynamic of this scene would be rather different if Andrew were significantly younger than his companions. Its emotional colouration would also be very much altered if the setting of the song were to reflect encouragement and incitement to action, rather than wistful contemplation of its impossibility.

Whatever the ages of the listeners, however, it is evident to the audience that the song is ironic; we know that Andrew has no hope of attaining Olivia, and placed immediately after their drunken entrance its gracefulness as a song points up the degree to which they have abdicated from the responsibilities of their social position in their behaviour. Here it is possible to imagine Feste looking at his on-stage audience with an ironic eye; he is giving them what they ask for, and must sing well, but he could well point up the absurdity of their dreams by exaggeration in a way that would be inappropriate in the following scene with Orsino and Viola. In most performances, however, the song provides an island in the scene's progress, and as is always the case with song, it is capable of making the audience briefly suspend judgement as they indulge in the feeling it generates. Although Hollander's view that the song is actually directed by Feste towards Olivia seems to me an overly prescriptive literal reading,[21] there is certainly a way in which the song might be held to critique the excess of her withdrawal from the world and from love. After this song, the scene quickly turns again to drunken revelry.

Toby calls again for a catch, and is enthusiastically supported by Andrew. The round they sing, 'Hold thy peace', certainly pre-existed the play and would likely have been known by the audience.[22] Its choice is, however, particularly felicitous. Not only does it permit some characteristic word-play from Feste, but its text is wittily inappropriate to a drunken celebration whose noise will prompt Maria to come and warn them of the likelihood of her mistress's disapproval. It is important, however, that although two of the three participants are the worse for drink, they should not therefore sing the catch disastrously badly. The sense of combined energy that a successful rendition of a round gives both to participants and to the audience is important as a springboard for the rest of the scene. Immediately afterwards Toby begins to spin off into characteristic drunken behaviour as he bawls out individual lines from popular ballads, and thus precipitates the key confrontation of the scene, with Malvolio.

As noted above, Malvolio's opening accusatory speech to the rioters resonates with the rhetoric of Puritan polemic, and his condemnation is of Toby and Andrew's betrayal of their social class by squeaking 'cozier's catches' (2.3.89) as in an alehouse. He warns Sir Toby that his niece is minded to expel him from her house if he does not mend his behaviour, and concludes 'If not, an it would please you to take leave of her she is very willing to bid you farewell' (2.3.98–9). Sir Toby immediately responds by picking up his final word as a prompt to sing 'Farewell dear heart, since I must needs be gone'. The characteristic behaviour of the inebriated in fastening on a word as a musical cue is deployed to comic effect in the case of Shallow in *2 Henry IV*, but here it is wonderfully elaborated as Feste continues with the next line of the song, which is not the popular ballad one might expect, but a song by Robert Jones only recently published in his *First Book of Songs or Airs* (1600).[23] How far Shakespeare might have expected his audience to pick up on the quotation of so recent an air is an open question (although some lute-songs do appear to have become well-known remarkably quickly, and many may have circulated in manuscript before publication), but they must have recognized the relative sophistication of the music, even if they could not have registered the improvisatory wit with which the singers convert Jones's lyric to their present purposes. Shakespeare takes the first part of the opening stanza, and combines it with the latter part of the second, and the wit is evident if one sets Jones's lyric alongside Shakespeare's version:

> Farewel, dear love, since thou wilt needs be gon,
> mine eies do shew my life is almost done,
>> nay I will never die,
>> so long as I can spie.
> .....
>> Shall I bid her goe

> What and if I doe?
> Shall I bid her go and spare not,
> O no, no, no, no, I dare not.[24]

Shakespeare's lyric (shorn of interruption) reads:

TOBY	Farewell dear heart, since I must needs be gone.
FESTE	His eyes do show his days are almost done.
TOBY	But I will never die.
FESTE	Sir Toby, there you lie.
TOBY	Shall I bid him go?
FESTE	What an if you do?
TOBY	Shall I bid him go and spare not?
FESTE	O no, no, no, no, you dare not. (2.3.100–11)

Shakespeare transforms the solo song of a lover determined not to be deterred by his mistress's desertion into a dialogue, and neatly stitches the first part of the opening stanza to the latter part of the second. In the process, the conversion of pronouns from first to second or third persons enables Toby and Feste to conduct an exchange ostensibly with one another, but directed largely at Malvolio. It is he, not the lover, whose eyes are aged, and he, not the beloved, who may be bidden to go. The third and fourth lines briefly chime with the sentiments of the song Feste sang earlier, as he deflates Toby's boast that he will 'never die' in the most radical departure from the original lyric, thus continuing the sense of time's pressure expressed in his earlier song, and distantly hinting, perhaps, at the melancholy realism of his final epilogue song.

If the song is sung to Jones's tune, then its melodic structure fits the escalation of the taunting of Malvolio, since it begins with stately movement of minims and crotchets before quickening to quavers on 'Shall I bid her goe', and maintaining that quicker movement to the end. The effect is to weave 'a magic net of sound in which the helpless Malvolio can only flounder and gasp'.[25] Sir Toby immediately follows the song with the contemptuous observation: 'Dost thou think because thou art virtuous there shall be no more cakes and ale' (2.3.113–14), accusing Malvolio of the Puritan condemnation of popular feasting at Church-ales, an accusation

Maria confirms a few lines later, when she observes 'sometimes he is a kind of puritan'. As Headlam Wells succinctly puts it: 'with his natural suspicion of music and its powers of exciting the passions, the puritan is here symbolically trapped and caught by what he most deprecates'.[26] This metaphorical musical entrapment is later to be further emphasized as Feste taunts the actually imprisoned Malvolio in 4.2, first by announcing his entrance with the old song 'Ah Robin',[27] which twists the knife in Malvolio's wounds with its suggestion that 'My lady is unkind, perdie ... She loves another', and then in his exit song 'I am gone sir' which pointedly ends 'Adieu, good man devil'. That Feste identifies himself to the imprisoned Malvolio by singing may in some ways actually lighten the potentially dark atmosphere of the scene, but at the same time it emphasizes the way in which this contest between the fool and the Puritan turns on a fundamental antipathy as well as personal grudge.

In characterizing Malvolio's mean-spiritedness through his hostility to music Shakespeare not only alludes to the stereotypical characterization of Puritan attitudes, but draws more generally on the philosophy outlined in Lorenzo's speech analysed earlier, with its condemnation of the man who has no music in his soul. He had used the same trope in representing Shylock in *Merchant of Venice*, 2.5.27–34, where he orders Jessica to 'stop my house's ears – I mean my casements. / Let not the sound of shallow fopp'ry enter / My sober house'. But the effect in *Twelfth Night* is rather more complicated than a simple opposition between love and hatred of music. It is not just that our contemporary sensibility finds the tormenting of Malvolio in 4.2 distinctly uncomfortable, even if we are happily prepared to go along with his musical humiliation in 2.3; but, as with all the musical moments in this play, there is, even in this scene, an ambivalence in our response. Sir Toby's fondness for the bottle is something that Feste himself judges excessive, as he tells Maria: 'If Sir Toby would leave drinking, thou wert as witty a piece of Eve's flesh as any in Illyria' (1.5.27–8), and, as in other drinking scenes, the complicity that music engenders does not finally obscure the unattractiveness of Sir Toby's dedication to excess. Music orchestrates this scene with great subtlety, engendering a tonal variety which manipulates the audience's perspective upon and response to the sub-plot as the succeeding scene does for the main action.

It is one of the curiosities of *Twelfth Night* that the music so pervasive in its first two acts disappears from the last three, save for the prison scene. It does, however, return in Feste's epilogue song, 'When that I was and a little tiny boy'. This musical ending is a far cry from the dances that conclude *A Midsummer Night's Dream*, *As You Like It* or *Much Ado about Nothing*. It is no invocation of social, let alone cosmic, harmony; but appears a weary, even disconsolate characterization of the course of a man's life. In its apparent discordancy with the spirit of comic conclusion it reaches back to the other sung epilogue in the canon in *Love's Labour's Lost*. There, however, the anticipated comic ending in marriage had already been frustrated by Marcade's entrance with the news of the King of France's death, and had been postponed by the ladies' setting of a year of tasks for their would-be lovers. The ambivalences of the epilogue sort well with the atmosphere at the end of the play's action. The first stanza of the dialogue-song, 'When daisies pied' complicates its seasonal picture by characterizing the cuckoo's song, the conventional harbinger of spring, as a 'word of fear / Unpleasing to a married ear', and the second stanza, 'When icicles hang by the wall' invokes an appropriately wintry picture, ending with the unlikely claim that the owl's call is a 'merry note'. Whereas these tensions do correspond to the provisional quality of *Love's Labour's Lost*'s ending, it is more difficult to argue the same for Feste's epilogue.

This song, however, raises a number of problems. In the first place, it is by no means certain that it was written specifically for the play; although concordances have not been identified it could have been an already existing ballad. More important, given the theatrical practice which saw plays concluded by a song or dance not connected in any way with the drama which had preceded it, we cannot assume that this song was expected by its original audience to be integrated with the play itself (or that additional action might not have accompanied it), nor that it necessarily followed every performance of the play. Many commentators in the eighteenth and nineteenth centuries felt it to be an inappropriate and extraneous addition, assuming that it was 'evidently one of those jigs, with which it was the rude custom of the Clown to gratify the groundlings',[28] and that it was inconceivable that it should have come from Shakespeare's pen.

Not everyone, even in the nineteenth century, agreed. Charles Knight called it 'the most philosophical Clown's song upon record'.[29] The same antithetical positions persist into the twentieth century.[30] The temper of the argument used to validate the song, however, changes significantly. The original Arden edition in 1929 spoke of it as embodying 'the philosophy of human life', and reminding us 'that we must return to realities'. In more recent years it has become customary to see its narrative of the ages of man as a drunkard's or a lecher's progress, and to emphasize the possibility of sexual innuendo in the 'foolish thing' that in childhood is 'but a toy'. For Robin Headlam Wells:

> the world evoked in this balladeer's version of the ancient *topos*
> of the four ages of man is a bleak and loveless world in which
> human beings do not gain wisdom with age and in which the only
> principle of constancy is the rain that raineth every day.[31]

This is a long way from Weiss's 1876 encomium on a song where 'the world's fierce, implacable roar reaches us … sifted through an air that hangs full of the Duke's dreams, of Viola's pensive love, of the hours which music flattered',[32] measuring the degree to which sensibilities have shifted over time. What all these attempts to integrate the song with the play share, however, is a focus upon interpreting the lyric's verbal content and a determination to make it fit thematically into an overall view of the play.

Yet it is, of course, a song. And as a sung, not spoken event, its meaning and the ways in which we might receive its statement are crucially affected by the nature of the music to which it is set and the manner of its performance. The 'traditional' tune – one of the best-known of all melodies to a Shakespeare lyric – first appeared in the late eighteenth century, attributed to Joseph Vernon. Whether or not it may have earlier origins, or even be an orally transmitted version of the song that Armin might have sung, its minor key and restricted melodic compass encourages a performance of insistent melancholy.[33] The tune to which Duffin sets the words, however – the ballad tune 'Tom Tinker', in the major key and with a jaunty 6/4 rhythm[34] – generates a quite different effect, altogether more confident, laughing at rather than oppressed by the human folly it catalogues (an impression which might be even stronger if Feste interspersed the verses with pipe and tabor interludes). It is partly a matter of melody, partly the manner of performance, which in turn raises the question of the status of the singer in the song.

Who is the 'I' of this song? At one extreme, it is possible, if one thinks of this as a song detachable from the play, that Feste has in effect disappeared, replaced by the actor fulfilling the formal requirement for a concluding song or jig. If we assume, as we are almost certain nowadays to do, that this is indeed a kind of epilogue, then it is an unusual one in that 'whereas the speakers of other Shakespearian epilogues like Rosalind in *As You Like It* or the King of France in *All's Well That Ends Well* step out of character to ask for applause, Feste simply presents the audience with a song which may or may not be a reflection of his own life'.[35] The suggestion that this is in an autobiographical song is not particularly plausible, since little we have heard of Feste in the play prepares us to read it this way. Furthermore, to assume that Feste speaks of himself, or even for himself, is to assume that for the first time in the play he sings a song which is directly expressive of his own state of mind (a kind of parallel to Ariel's 'Where the bee sucks' which will be considered shortly). Yet it is much more likely that this professional performer, who has always offered the songs appropriate to his audience within the play, is now giving us the song he thinks we need to hear. The significance and impact of this final song, then, is profoundly contingent on decisions about the music to which it is to be set, the degree to which Feste stays in character as he sings, and the nature of the address to the audience that he adopts. If most productions now insist on stressing the contrast between the lovers' happiness and the 'harsher reality in the "wind and the rain"',[36] that perhaps reflects our contemporary predilections. The problem it leaves is the turn to the final stanza, in which Feste tells us 'We'll strive to please you every day', which, in any production which emphasizes Feste's isolation and has him sing in melancholy vein, is a distinctly underpowered invitation to applause. Many productions of *As You Like It* have converted songs into triumphant ensemble pieces; I have never seen a production of *Twelfth Night* which made the same attempt with this song – although, paradoxically enough, if this indeed is a version of the jig at the end of the play, it might have more justification.

Putting that unlikely (and no doubt misguided) prospect to one side, however, it is characteristic of this play that its final appeal to us should be in a song, and a song whose precise import is difficult to pin down. Music has invited us equally to share the love-melancholy of Orsino and the drunken hilarity of Sir Toby and Sir Andrew; it has underpinned the erotic and tormented the Puritan; yet at every stage it has been surrounded with intimations of its limitations and of its capacity to endorse illusion. It is, then, appropriate that the play should end with a ballad that sweetens with music a view of life that, taken without such softening, might almost seem to endorse the moral censoriousness of the Malvolio who storms out of the play's conclusion. From one perspective the song offers us a sketch of a 'real' world which points up the limitations of the comedy we have just been watching and turns us out from the theatre to workaday reality; but delivered differently, it might actually celebrate the fact that the play has actually eluded the grimness of the everyday of which its lyric speaks.

THE TEMPEST

The Tempest,[37] like Twelfth Night, uses music to characterize its different worlds. The low-life characters sing unaccompanied ballads and a catch; Prospero is accompanied by harmonious instrumental sound and courtly song; the lords are buffeted by tempest and thunder, before finally recovering their wits to 'heavenly music'. But whereas the earlier comedy largely excludes the symbolic significance which music might carry in the period, the later romance subjects precisely those conventional notions to searching interrogation.

For many critics over the years it has been The Tempest's exemplification of the neoplatonic view of music's power which has been central to their readings of the play. Evidence for such an approach is not far to seek. We have already remarked on the way Ferdinand represents music's power to draw him after it in 1.2, and for him the invisibility of the music intensifies his sense of its celestial origins. So too, at the latter end of the play Prospero addresses the frantic lords gathered before him:

A solemn air and the best comforter
To an unsettled fancy, cure thy brains
(Now useless) boiled within thy skull. (5.1.58–60)

He invokes the curative power of music that we have seen in *Lear* and *Pericles*, and as the lords return to sanity over a musical accompaniment we are invited to assent to the capacity of musical sound to bring harmony to their disordered faculties. In between we have witnessed a masque of heavenly deities ushered in by 'soft music' (4.1.58), which culminates in a song of blessing and a dance, in a more elaborate version of the myth-laden ceremonial that had seen Hymen bless the lovers in *As You Like It*. Conversely, the villainy of Antonio and Sebastian is emblematically conveyed as they, in 2.1, simply do not hear the 'solemn music' that Ariel plays which charms all the others on-stage to sleep. Even more obviously than Malvolio these are characters in whose soul there is no music, and who therefore certainly cannot be trusted, as they immediately demonstrate by plotting the death of Alonso. In more general terms, the fact that Prospero's music is allied with his magical powers means that it is perfectly possible to take it as consequence and symbol of the learning he has been at such pains to acquire (see Figure 18), and to invest it with intimations of the 'myth of the musician-king'. From this perspective one might agree that '*The Tempest* offers its audiences a vision of social harmony in which discords are resolved by the magical power of "solemne musicke"'.[38] More consistently and continuously than any other Shakespearean play, *The Tempest* demands that we read its musical events in the light of the philosophical understanding of music's power that is summarized in Chapter 1. But considered as a work in the theatre, the safely insulated view of Prospero's celestial music which such an understanding seems to afford the literary critic is put under considerable pressure from different directions.

At first sight the music of the low-life characters in the play seems marginal; the Arden 3 editors claim that 'compared to Ariel's songs, the rest of the music ... is entertaining but of scant importance to the plot'.[39] I would argue, however, that it is of considerable relevance to the audience's experience of the play, and to the way in which music structures

FIGURE 18 Alchemist's laboratory, from Heinrich Kuhnrath, *Amphitheatrum sapientae aeternae* (1609). The instruments and music book on the table demonstrate the importance of music as one of the means of reaching higher truths.

the drama as a whole. Stephano enters singing 'I shall no more to sea, to sea / Here shall I die ashore', and breaks off, commenting 'This is a very scurvy tune to sing at a man's funeral' (2.2.42–4). After a further drink he sings a ballad of the choosy prostitute, Kate, who refused sailors in favour of the tailor. That Stephano sings is symptomatic of his drunkenness, and we can easily be amused at the most basic level by the ballads' content. As with all such impromptu songs, however, his ballads invite a level of involvement with the singer; and we recognize that Stephano is singing them not merely out of intoxication, but out of a very real fear at his isolation in this strange place. Shakespeare chooses his lyrics carefully here. Stephano's belated recognition that the first ballad which pops into his mind speaks of death ashore is only partly comic, and it is not surprising that his second ends with the wish to depart 'to sea boys, and let her go hang!' (2.2.54). Neither song comforts him much, and he turns to his bottle again. Dramatically the songs which announce Stephano's arrival offer an antithetical parallel to the song of Ariel which brought Ferdinand before our eyes. One character enters surrounded by instrumental sound and courtly melody, the other sings unaccompanied ballads of bawdy content.

The scene ends with Caliban singing 'drunkenly' a song of freedom,[40] which resonates rather differently from Stephano's. At one level it marks Caliban's swift degeneration as a result of his introduction to 'celestial liquor', and Trinculo comments dismissively on him as 'A howling monster, a drunken monster' (2.2.176). In the arc of the scene's development, however, it registers the way in which Caliban's fearful sense of inhibition by Prospero's magic power in his opening speech is dissolved through alcohol, and the fact that he sings his rebellion – and perhaps does so to a well-known tune – invites our participation in his sense of release. As Booth observes: 'songs of protest do not appeal to an audience as jury but invite the already sympathetic into collective accusation'.[41] At this point popular music becomes oppositional, rather than merely antithetical. This is continued in 3.2, where rebellious energy again finds expression in musical form. Towards the end of the scene Caliban, elated at his apparent success in persuading Stephano to murder Prospero, demands: 'Let us be jocund. Will you troll the catch / You taught me but whilere' (3.2.118–19), and Stephano, Trinculo, and (perhaps) Caliban launch into 'Flout 'em and scout 'em'.

This catch (for which no contemporary setting has been identified) is, like the other catches we have already discussed, firmly associated with the world of the tavern and 'low life' and, as always, the musical form is one which has a strong potential to command the complicity of the audience in its conspiratorial combination. Compared to the catch in *Twelfth Night*, however, the nature of the performance itself and its situation within the dramatic action is much less clear. Stephano asks Trinculo to sing, and the text proceeds as follows:

> Flout 'em and scout 'em,
> And scout 'em and flout 'em,
> Thought is free.

CALIBAN   That's not the tune.

Ariel plays the tune on a tabor and pipe.

STEPHANO   What is this same?

TRINCULO   This is the tune of our catch, played by the picture
            of Nobody. (3.2.122–8)

Caliban's line here can be taken in a variety of ways. He could be commenting on the collapse of the catch itself (in which he might, or might not, have attempted to participate), or else be reacting to Ariel's intervention – failing at first to recognize that he plays the tune they have been singing. If the catch is, for a time, allowed to work musically, then it gives a potency to the conspirators' ambition. More important, if Ariel takes up the same tune, it becomes a powerful dramatic image of the way Prospero co-opts and transforms this rebellious music. Their catch declares that 'thought is free'; Ariel's presence, and his conversion of their song, demonstrate that in this play it most certainly is not.

Before, however, the conspirators leave the stage to follow Ariel, Caliban reassures his fellows:

> Be not afeard. The isle is full of noises,
> Sounds and sweet airs that give delight and hurt not.
> Sometimes a thousand twangling instruments
> Will hum about mine ears; and sometimes voices,
> That if I then had waked after long sleep,
> Will make me sleep again; and then in dreaming,
> The clouds, methought, would open and show riches
> Ready to drop upon me, that when I waked
> I cried to dream again. (3.2.136–44)

Dramatically, this haunting set-piece speech halts the onward movement of the scene; thematically it connects to the rest of the play in a complex fashion. In its tone of wonderment it echoes Ferdinand's account of the music that crept by him on the waters, subliminally reinforcing the way in which Caliban, the would-be rapist of Miranda, is the dark double for the prince who intends to marry her. The contrast between Caliban's response to the music and Stephano's crudely materialistic 'This will prove a brave kingdom to me, where I shall have my music for nothing' (3.2.145–6) has often been taken to suggest a 'civilization' in Caliban as opposed to the loutishness of his companions. Such a reading, however, risks sentimentalizing him, for the myths of music's power emphasize precisely that brute beasts, like the 'unhandled colts' of which Lorenzo speaks (*MV*, 5.1.72), are sensitive to its influence. From this perspective it is precisely Caliban's *lack* of civilization which renders him open to music as Stephano (and Antonio and Sebastian) are not. To attempt to control our response to Caliban at this moment by invoking musical theory will not, however, contain the disturbing quality this speech has, and not only in its capacity to make us feel for and with Caliban; for the narrative he offers is one of disappointment, of illusory riches that fade in dreams. His account prefigures only too accurately the way in which the music he invites his fellows to approve is actually to be the means by which Prospero leads them to a stinking pool, and at the same time its narrative of fading dream is one which, as we will see, is reflected at every social level in the play.

This powerful dramatic moment, then, connects with the central issues of the relationship of music and power, of symbolic and material politics, that run through the play. We have already seen in Chapter 1 how the play's first song, 'Come unto these yellow sands', ensures that Ferdinand is in the right place, and the right state of mind, to meet Miranda, as Prospero's plan requires. The next song, which follows very shortly afterwards, is 'Full fathom five thy father lies' (1.2.397). Robert Johnson's setting of this song survives, unmistakeable evidence that Shakespeare was not writing words to fit an existing tune, but, perhaps directly as a consequence of the King's Men's acquisition of the indoor Blackfriars theatre, was able to call upon the services of the royal lutenist and composer to set lyrics specifically written for their place in the play.[42] It is a grave, but relatively uncomplicated setting, existing in a number of manuscript versions, and finally published in John Wilson's *Cheerful Ayres* (1660).[43]

Considered as a lyric, and interpreted symbolically, this song has frequently been taken as an image of the transformative possibilities that the play is held ultimately to embody. In it, death is imaged as a change 'into something rich and strange' and generations of critics have seen this as proleptic anticipation of Alonso's moral metamorphosis. Winifred Maynard stands for many when she writes that 'Ariel's second song too is to be symbolically understood', and concludes, 'through suffering, estrangement and understanding Alonso is made anew'.[44] Auden, for whom *The Tempest* was a particularly important play, and whose extended descant upon it in his *The Sea and the Mirror* is one of the most thoughtful and provocative of the many re-writings and responses the play has engendered,[45] suggests that the song is transformative in a more immediate fashion:

> Ferdinand listens to [Ariel] in a very different way from that in which the Duke listens to *Come away, come away, death*, or Mariana to *Take, O take those lips away*. The effect on them was not to change them but to confirm the mood they were already in. The effect on Ferdinand ... is more like the effect of instrumental music on Thaisa: direct, positive, magical.

He goes on to emphasize that the effect of 'Full fathom five' is

> not to lessen his feeling of loss, but to change his attitude towards his grief from one of rebellion ... to one of awe and reverent acceptance ... Thanks to the music, Ferdinand is able to accept the past, symbolized by his father, as past, and at once there stands before him his future, Miranda.[46]

Persuasive though these accounts might be of the immediate psychological and dramatic effect of the songs on Ferdinand, it must still be acknowledged that at a literal level the lyric of 'Full fathom five' is simply untrue. Ferdinand comments that 'the ditty does remember my drowned father' (1.2.406), yet Alonso is not dead, although it is essential to Prospero's purposes that Ferdinand think him so. From this perspective the song is an example of the manipulative use to which Prospero continuously puts music throughout the play. It is 'magical' in its effect, but we are at the same time fully aware of the contrivance that underlies and even enables that magic.

What, however, of this song as it is experienced by a theatre audience? It is likely that no audience hearing the song for the first time would be able fully to register the symbolic possibilities which are open to the reader of the lyric; they necessarily experience a musical event in which the character of the musical language takes precedence over the detail of verbal meaning. Both Howell Chickering and Jacquelyn Fox-Good provide close musical analyses of Johnson's setting, the former suggesting that 'the melody … expresses a sense both of continuity and continuing transformation, which perfectly suits the paradoxical poetic imagery',[47] the latter that 'the song's music does not refer to or summarise "sea change" but rather enacts it (melodically/harmonically) involving the hearer in that process with more immediacy'.[48] The critique which both offer of too reductive a *reading* of the lyric is just; but the problem is that they instate Robert Johnson's setting as an authoritative performance of the song. The effects they derive from its melodic and harmonic structures are therefore inevitably contingent on this particular setting and will be constituted very differently by another musical realization of the lyric.

The choice that faces the composer is analogous to the choice which faces the director – whether to emphasize the general magical atmosphere the song might help to support, or to underline its specific address to Ferdinand. The question of address is important for both of the songs in 1.2, for although they are structurally similar, both requiring a burden or refrain to answer the solo voice of Ariel, there are important differences between them. 'Full fathom five' is sung directly to Ferdinand, and in this respect is like Ariel's later song of warning to Gonzalo, 'While you here do snoring lie' (2.2.301–6). We, as auditors, are positioned outside the immediate exchange in which Ariel, on Prospero's behalf, speaks directly to characters within the play. Our interest, then, like our interest in Balthasar's 'Sigh no more, ladies', or Marina's song to Pericles, is significantly focused on the effect these songs have in the evolving action of the play and on the people to whom they are sung. The address of 'Come unto these yellow sands', however, is much more elusive. At first we might hear it as directed towards Ferdinand, whom it leads on-stage, and understand the invitation to 'take hands' to be directing him towards Miranda. The imperative verb, however, like the 'come hither' of Amiens' song in the Forest of Arden, seems equally to be directed outwards to include us in its invitation, and the song therefore to be characterizing the island just as Amiens's airs did the enforced rural retreat of Duke Senior. As the lyric evolves we belatedly recognize that it speaks neither to Ferdinand nor to us, but to disembodied spirits, the executants of the magic charm which Ferdinand tells us was able to calm the waters and his despair. These spirits respond with burdens of cocks crowing and dogs barking which might, depending on the setting, disturb the serenity of Ariel's air. He sings of 'watch-dogs', potentially threatening guardians, and we might later be reminded of their faint menace as spirit-dogs are materially embodied to chase out the conspirators at the end of Act 4. A lot will indeed depend on the setting – for where Maynard sees 'a song which is ceremonial, orderly, restrained' symbolically drawing Ferdinand 'to a wooing in which impulse is controlled and courtesy and reverence prevail',[49] Chickering hears it as containing 'images of two kinds of music heard later in the play – the mythological dance of the masque in 4.1. and the cacophonous singing of Trinculo and Caliban'.[50] I would want to hear it as also hinting at the capricious, even malevolent side of Prospero's magic and its instruments. Obviously such variation in reading depends not only on the overall perspective of an individual critic upon the play, but crucially on the character of the music itself.

In whatever way one wants to read these songs of Ariel, one of the most obvious and striking differences between them and the later songs of Stephano and Caliban is not merely their different musical vocabulary, but the fact that the first-person pronoun does not figure in their lyrics, so that, unlike the popular songs, they do not invite us to adopt the position of the singer, but place us passively as recipients of their address and observers of their effect. However much the music itself speaks to us as an aesthetic event and involves us in its emotional affect, it reaches us in a fashion quite distinct from the immediate, impromptu singing of the low-life characters. There is a world of difference, then, not only between the vocabulary and instrumentation of these opposed musics, but between the fundamental nature of the relationship they set up between song and theatre audience.

One of the principal reasons for the elusiveness of these songs is the fact that they are sung by Ariel. As a musician the actor playing Ariel needs to be accomplished. As he leads Ferdinand on stage he enters *playing and singing* (1.2.375) – if he accompanied himself in Johnson's air it was presumably upon the lute. In 3.2 he plays the tabor and pipe, and he must also play *solemn music* at 2.1.184. As a singer, however, Ariel is like no other in the whole Shakespearean canon.

> Ariel is neither a singer, that is to say, a human being whose vocal gifts provide him with a social function, nor a nonmusical person who in certain moods feels like singing.[51]

Ariel's role is further complicated by his androgyne nature (he is dressed as a sea-nymph when he sings to Ferdinand, as Ceres when he sings in the masque), which destabilizes the gendered perception of song and singer that we have remarked so frequently elsewhere. One might, however, want to argue that the female dress he adopts to entice Ferdinand invokes as its dark shadow the myth of the dangerous siren (it is not entirely coincidental that the seductive sea nymph metamorphoses, in 3.3, to the accusing harpy – see Figure 4, p. 45). Even more important, Ariel, until his final song, is singing airs which are neither scripted nor chosen by himself, but by Prospero. Throughout the play he is the magician's agent and executant; the nature of the investment that Ariel himself brings to his singing is therefore ill-defined. So long as critics assumed that the spirit, after an initial outburst, was a willing servant to Prospero, it was not too difficult to accept a straightforward continuity between Prospero's purposes and their execution through the songs of his 'delicate' Ariel; but many recent productions have seen their relationship as one of tension, and have emphasized in a variety of ways Ariel's reluctant servitude.[52] Whatever the merits of such readings of the role, the effect on his musical performances is further to detach them from the performer and to emphasize their instrumentality in the prosecution of Prospero's designs. This is in accord with the general turn in *Tempest* criticism over the last thirty-five years or so, which, concentrating on the politics of the play, has converted Prospero from benign magus to imperialist despot. To debate such approaches would take us well beyond the scope of this study; but

I would want to argue that the music in the play actually problematizes any such monocular critical perspective upon it.

This is in no small measure due to the way in which the conflict between 'symbolic' and 'political' readings of the music of *The Tempest* echoes the way in which thinking about music in the period itself was in transition, and the understanding of the source of its effectiveness was moving from a metaphysical to a rhetorical foundation.[53] The tension between these two perspectives upon musical power is precisely caught in the moment when Prospero declares:

> But this rough magic
> I here abjure; and when I have required
> Some heavenly music (which even now I do)
> To work mine end upon their senses that
> This airy charm is for, I'll break my staff,
> Bury it certain fathoms in the earth,
> And deeper than did ever plummet sound
> I'll drown my book. (5.1.50–57)

Calling for music is the last 'magical' action that Prospero performs and its 'airy charm' will effect the curing of the lords' addled wits. The stage direction '*Solemn music*' recalls the '*solemn music*' which put the lords to sleep in 2.1, and the '*Solemn and strange music*' which accompanied the apparition of the '*strange shapes*' in 3.3. While the precise terminology of the stage directions may well be that of the scribe Ralph Crane rather than Shakespeare, the consistent association of this instrumental sound – delivered, presumably, by musicians hidden from view in the music room above the stage which by now was a feature of both the playing spaces of the King's Men – is with magic and the otherworldly. But the imperson-ality of the musical sound, which could certainly to a Renaissance audience suggest a 'heavenly' music, has in its earlier manifestations enabled the conspiracy of Antonio, and taunted the lords with an illusory banquet. Here in Act 5 the symbolic is juxtaposed with Prospero's declaration that the music will 'work mine end upon their senses'. This is music with a purpose, and that purpose is Prospero's own. We are at this moment uncomfortably reminded of the bitter outcry of Prospero himself against the usurping brother who was able to 'set all hearts i'th'state / To what tune pleased his ear' (1.2.84–5).

Politically, then, this 'heavenly' music is no different from the invisible music of pipe and tabor which diverted Stephano, Trinculo, and Caliban from their rebellious purpose; and, if one is so minded, it can readily be claimed that its seductiveness for audience and on-stage characters alike performs an ideological aestheticization of the political power that Prospero embodies. The play itself, however, will not quite be contained by such a simple interpretation. While it is possible to emphasize the way in which Prospero deploys music to mislead – Ferdinand, the lords, and Caliban and his compeers alike – and to read Caliban's account of music's false promise of riches as a melancholy miniaturization of the progress of his relationship with Prospero from apparent love to enslavement, it must be recognized that it is not only Caliban for whom music's harmonious promise is elusive or delusory.

The masque in Act 4 gestures generically to the literary kind which in the period offered the most thorough-going embodiment of neoplatonic theory harnessed to monarchical power. Ben Jonson and Inigo Jones had, by the time *The Tempest* was written, firmly established the court masque as a spectacle of state, one which

> presents the triumph of an aristocratic community; at its center is a belief in the hierarchy and a faith in the power of idealization. Philosophically, it is both Platonic and Machiavellian; Platonic because it presents images of the good to which the participants aspire and may ascend; Machiavellian because its idealizations are designed to justify the power they celebrate.[54]

Prospero introduces his masque for Miranda's betrothal specifically in magical terms – it is a 'vanity of mine art' (4.1.41), and Ferdinand is adjured 'Hush and be mute, / Or else our spell is marred' (4.1.126–7). It builds to a musical climax, first with the hymn of Ceres and Juno, and then with the emblematically appropriate fusion of male heat and female wateriness in the '*graceful dance*' of nymphs and reapers (4.1.138). The dreamlike illusion is, however, shattered in '*a strange hollow and confused noise*' (4.1.138.3–4). The immediate cause of the masque's dissolution is

Prospero's recollection of Caliban's 'foul conspiracy' (4.1.139), but when he moralizes the spectacle for the benefit of Ferdinand and Miranda he draws attention to the fact that the actors 'were all spirits and / Are melted into air' (4.1.149–50), and compares his 'insubstantial pageant' to 'the great globe itself' which 'shall dissolve'. Structurally the abrupt ending of the masque echoes the pattern of the previous scene, where the lords' banquet is snatched away in the thunder of Ariel's appearance as a harpy. Both scenes extend and amplify the pattern of disappointment which has attended not only Caliban's account of the 'sounds and sweet airs', but also Gonzalo's vision of a golden-age commonwealth (2.1.144–69). Prospero's Biblically inflected vision of the end of all things (recalling 2 Peter, 3.12) makes us aware that he, as much as anyone else, is fully aware of the limitations of all art and of its – and his – power to command.

It is precisely that awareness of art's limits that is dramatically embodied in Ariel's final song, 'Where the bee sucks' (5.1.88–94). The song accompanies Prospero's robing of himself as he was 'sometime Milan' before he confronts his erstwhile enemies, but yet seems a strange ditty to assist in the preparation of Prospero's moment of triumph. Where the song speaks of a life of hedonistic idleness, Prospero is about to resume the cares of ducal authority in Milan; where the narrative is focused upon Prospero's action, the lyric speaks entirely of Ariel. The apparent collision between action and song has often prompted directors to move the song elsewhere in the play, or else to have Ariel perform it without reference to Prospero. During the nineteenth century it was, for example, often placed at the very end of the play, bolstering an optimistic view of its conclusion. Yet I would argue that the awkwardness of the match of lyric to action directs us to the heart of *The Tempest*'s analysis of music.

It does so in a number of different ways. First, because it is the single example of Ariel using the first-person pronoun in song it is the only one of his performances which asks the audience to identify directly with him as singer. Robert Johnson's setting, responding to the metrical change in the last two lines into a triple-time metre, underlines the sense of release of which the lyric speaks. It is, therefore, a high-art version of Caliban's song of freedom in 2.2, and at one level underlines the similarity of the position of both Prospero's servants, since for both of them it is in music that they are able to image and celebrate the possibility of release. In many recent productions of the play it has been important to a political reading that Ariel and Caliban both be seen as the oppressed servants of Prospero, and the similarity of their songs seems to assist such an interpretation.

The two characters, however, are crucially distinguished not only in the kind of music they sing, but in the fact that when Prospero came first to the island, the only sounds to be heard were the 'groans' of Ariel, imprisoned by Caliban's mother, Sycorax, in a pine-tree, which 'did make wolves howl and penetrate the breasts of ever-angry bears' (1.2.288–9). Music becomes possible at all only when Ariel is freed. Although Prospero uses his release of Ariel to demand from him a period of service, and although during that time he is able to ask his spirit to deploy his music to work his own ends upon those who come to his island, his control over his spirit is fragile and temporary. Sometimes Caliban's speech on the sounds and sweet airs is taken to indicate that the music is that of the island where he was once sole king, a further instance of Prospero's colonialist appropriation. This seems to me simply wrong: the music of the island is neither Prospero's nor Caliban's but Ariel's.

'Where the bee sucks', from another perspective, offers a clear sense of the implication and consequence of Prospero's abjuration of magic. Once his 'art' is abandoned, then Prospero must lose control of Ariel and of his singing. Once that control is gone, and Ariel sings in his own insouciant voice, he does so in an utterly solipsistic song. This reaches to central issues in the period's debates about music. The traditional philosophical defence of music located the source of music's power in its intrinsic mathematical harmonies, and in their reflection of celestial order. Musical humanism, however, wished to control music's dangerous energies by subordinating it to words. These are precisely the views that are tested here. Throughout the play, music has been used for the moral purposes that its neoplatonic defenders argued were central to its validation, and in order to accept its curative function in the final act, we must at some level assent to that tradition. But at the same time we have been made aware that the ends music serves are dictated by Prospero's human ambition expressed in the words of the songs he gives Ariel to sing. When Ariel finally sings for himself, the self-indulgence of his lyric opens up the possibility that music itself is morally neutral, that its effects ultimately depend upon the uses to which it is put. This does not, for a moment, deny the attractiveness of this final song as a performed event in the play, nor fail to recognize that for the audience in the theatre as well as for the Ariel who sings it, the delight of its celebration of a freedom that the spirit has so earnestly desired throughout is powerfully expressed. But the vital recognition that attends the song is that just as Caliban could only cry to dream again, so Prospero will 'miss' his musical adjutant as he returns to a Milan where 'every third thought shall be my grave' (5.1.313).

After this song, although Ariel assists in the tidying-up of the play's action, there is no more music. Indeed, of all the late plays this is the one whose ending is most provisional. Just as he had failed to hear music at all in 2.1, Antonio remains unrepentant to the last. When Prospero for the first time produces a 'wonder' entirely without benefit of magic or music, Miranda somewhat inauspiciously accuses her husband of cheating, and her delighted contemplation of the 'brave new world' now available to her is ironically undercut by Prospero's ''tis new to thee' (5.1.185). As Auden observes: '*The Tempest* is full of music of all kinds, yet it is not one of the plays in which, in a symbolic sense, harmony and concord finally triumph over dissonant disorder.'[55] Almost Prospero's last words in the play are to Ariel: 'Then to the elements / Be free, and fare thou well'. The parting of Ariel and Prospero can be played in many different ways, ranging from an Ariel reluctant to leave his erstwhile master through to an Ariel who contemptuously spits in Prospero's face, as in Simon Russell Beale's performance at Stratford in 1993; although perhaps either impassive indifference, or even the absence of Ariel himself at the play's end, most painfully underscores the sense of loss that begins with Prospero's response to 'Where the bee sucks', and continues into his epilogue.[56]

Like any epilogue, this speech might not have been delivered at every performance of the play, and is not essential to it.[57] As in *Twelfth Night*'s closing song, it is not absolutely clear who it is that stands before us – Prospero, the actor playing the part, or a figure for the dramatist himself.[58] In the present context, however, the most significant juxtaposition is of the final plea to 'set me free' (Ep. 20) with the earlier statement: 'Now I want / Spirits to enforce, art to enchant' (Ep. 13–14). 'Want' here, of course, means simply 'lack'; yet it is impossible not to hear behind it the sigh of desire for control that motivated Prospero's magical studies, and the note of regret at their necessary abandonment. It is that complex of feeling which Auden so memorably elaborates and explores in *The Sea and the Mirror*, where Prospero's address to Ariel begins:

> Stay with me, Ariel, while I pack, and with your first free act
> > Delight my leaving; share my resigning thoughts
> As you have served my revelling wishes: then brave spirit,
> > Ages to you of song and daring, and to me
> Briefly Milan, then earth.[59]

Ferdinand, like Caliban, responds enthusiastically to Prospero's musical magic in his praise of the 'most majestic vision, and / Harmonious charmingly', and exclaims 'Let me live here ever!' (4.1.118–19, 122). But for him, as for Caliban, and ultimately for Prospero himself, the desires that music induces and the plenitude it promises cannot be sustained.

Lorenzo, poetically but ultimately complacently, had assured Jessica that 'whilst this muddy vesture of decay / Doth close it in' (*MV*, 5.1.64–5) we cannot hear the music of the spheres. *The Tempest* explores more fully, more richly, and more ambiguously than any other play, the wish that we might.

Appendix

GLOSSARY OF MUSICAL INSTRUMENTS

In the period instruments were thought of very much in their 'families', and that is how they are grouped here. References are given to figures where they are depicted.

PLUCKED STRINGS

bandora (also *pandora*) A bass instrument, with a flat back and scalloped outline, invented in England during the sixteenth century. It had six double courses of wire strings, and was a required member of the mixed consort (see Figure 7 on p. 57).

cittern Wire-strung, usually, in England, with four double courses. It is very shallow, with a flat back, and a pear-shaped body. Generally played with a plectrum, rather than with the fingers. Although demanding solo music was written for the instrument, and it was a constituent of the mixed consort, it was also associated with popular music, and instruments were hung up in taverns and barber's shops for customers to play (see Figure 7 on p. 57).

lute The most important of all the plucked stringed instruments, with a long history. It had gut strings, generally with six courses, and was played with the fingers. It had a rounded back made of thin ribs of wood and a pear-shaped body, with the peg-box characteristically turned back. The soundhole or 'rose' on the front was frequently elaborately carved. There were various sizes of lute, and various tunings. A solo instrument with a considerable virtuoso repertoire, and also the most frequently used for accompanying solo songs in the later sixteenth and early seventeenth centuries. Ensembles of up to twenty-four lutes of various sizes might be assembled to accompany the court masques (see Figure 17 on p. 196).

mandora (mandore) Strictly a term for a small treble lute, usually with four strings, and found particularly in French music. The only use of the term in this book is in Gerschow's report on music at Blackfriars, and he is probably using it to describe the cittern.

orpharion Like the bandora, which it resembles in shape, this instrument was invented in the late sixteenth century, again in England. It was smaller than its cousin, and was essentially treated as a wire-strung lute.

KEYBOARD INSTRUMENTS

virginal(s) The name was used in England to cover all keyboard instruments in which strings were plucked by jacks, rather than struck with hammers as in the modern piano. Differentiated from the harpsichord by its oblong shape, with the strings parallel to the keyboard (where the harpsichord is shaped and strung roughly like a modern grand piano) it was an important domestic instrument, and perhaps derived its name from its association with female performers.

BOWED STRINGS

fiddle The term is confusingly used in the early modern period for any bowed string instrument, including the viol and violin and smaller instruments with a long prehistory, such as the *rebec* (a pear-shaped small instrument) or the *kit* (a small, narrow, violin-like instrument, sometimes with three strings, which was used especially by dancing-masters). The fiddle was often used to accompany dancing (see Figure 9 on p. 61).

viol Viols came in various sizes, together making up a consort. The viol is differentiated from the violin family by its flat back and sloping shoulders and has a fretted fingerboard (as does the modern guitar and all the plucked instruments described above). It usually had six strings (though sometimes five or seven). Unlike the violin, it was bowed under-hand and usually held downwards, resting on the player's knees (hence the name 'viol da gamba'). It was played both domestically and by pro-fessionals. Introduced into England probably in the reign of Henry VIII, it remained an important instrument, especially in England, until well into the seventeenth century. Its sound is reedier and quieter than that of the violin (see Figure 7 on p. 57).

violin The violin, in its modern form, evolved during the sixteenth cen-tury, and first appears in England about 1540. Originally used as the name for instruments of different sizes playing in consort rather than only, as now, for the treble instrument.

WIND INSTRUMENTS

cornett (cornet, cornetto) An instrument with a cupped mouthpiece (like a trumpet), and finger-holes (like a recorder or flute), and not to be con-fused with the modern brass instrument, the cornet. It was usually made of leather-covered wood, and its commonest form is gently curved, although the *mute cornett* was straight, with a built-in, rather than detachable mouthpiece, and the tenor cornett, or *lizard*, had two bends (see Figure 8 on p. 59). The cornett was one of the most versatile of wind instruments, capable both of a brilliant, almost trumpet-like sound and of a quieter singing tone; and its finger-holes meant that, unlike the trumpet, it could play fully chromatic music over a wide range. A difficult instrument to master, it was the preserve of professionals, but could be deployed in many different contexts, includ-ing accompanying voices in church or in secular environments, in both of which it was often played in consort with *sackbuts* providing the lower parts. It seems to have been used in the indoor theatres in place of the louder trumpet.

fife A flute with a narrow bore, giving a shrill sound. It is almost always associated with martial contexts (see Figure 15 on p. 97).

flute The name could be applied in the period either to the precursor of the modern transverse flute, held sideways to the mouth, or else to the recorder. In the sixteenth century the flute was made in one piece, with a cylindrical bore, and had no keys to cover the finger-holes. The sound of the Renaissance flute is 'cooler' than its modern equivalent. Instruments were made in various sizes, but the treble flute was by far the commonest instrument, and it, or the recorder, was a required member of the mixed consort (see Figure 7 on p. 57).

hautboy Another name for the *shawm*.

pipe The name for a number of different instruments with a whistle mouthpiece, but in the period (and in this book) it is used most often for a three-hole duct flute, with a thumb-hole at the back and two holes on the top, which, by overblowing, could achieve a range of one and a half octaves. It could be held in one hand, leaving the other free to beat the 'tabor' or drum, and is indelibly associated with dancing and with the theatrical clown (see Figures 9 and 14 on pp. 61 and 95).

recorder Perhaps the most familiar of all early instruments because of its revival during the twentieth century as an instrument suitable for teaching in schools. The recorder with which we are now familiar, however, is based on a later, Baroque design. In the Renaissance the cylindrical bore in the upper part of the instrument, the inverted conical bore below and the slight flare at the end produced a sound notably warmer and fuller than the later instrument, although more restricted in range. Recorders were produced in a number of sizes, and consorts are found in royal and noble households throughout the sixteenth century; it could also form part of the mixed consort.

sackbut The early trombone. As with other brass instruments, the sound of the Renaissance instrument, because of its narrower bore, was lighter than its modern successor. The slide meant that it was fully chromatic, and provided the lower parts in ensembles of diverse kinds, accompanying trumpets, cornetts, and shawms in particular. It was produced in a number of different sizes (see Figure 8 on p. 59).

shawm Also often, and interchangeably, called the *hautbois* or *hoboy* (with many variant spellings); this prompts confusion with the modern oboe, which actually developed in the later seventeenth century. The shawm is altogether louder, and is of different construction. Apart from the absence of keys (except for one on the larger *bombard*), the most distinctive difference from the modern oboe is that the double reed is wider and stubbier, and is not generally held between the lips. Instead, it is fitted into a cup, or 'pirouette', against which the player rests his or her lips so that the reed vibrates freely in the mouth. It may still be heard in popular celebration in various parts of Europe. Arbeau notes that 'hautboys have some resemblance to trumpets', and that the combination of a larger and smaller instrument 'is excellent for making a tremendous noise, such as is required at village fêtes or large gatherings'.[1] (See Figure 6 on p. 54.)

DRUMS

Drums in this period as in every other came in a variety of sizes; *kettle-drums* could be played on horseback, *side-drums* might be the large instrument depicted in Figure 15 on p. 97, or the smaller *tabor* which accompanied the pipe (Figure 14 on page 95). Arbeau describes the 'French' side-drum as being 'two and a half feet deep' and 'about two and a half feet in diameter' making 'a great noise when the skins are beaten with two sticks',[2] whereas the tabor is 'about two small feet long and one foot in diameter'.[3]

NOTES

INTRODUCTION

1. *The Tempest*, 1.2.375–95. The quotation is taken from my New Cambridge Shakespeare edition (Cambridge, 2002), since textual questions are relevant to what follows. This passage is 1.2.376–96 in the Arden edition, from which all subsequent quotations are taken.

2. A glossary of musical instruments is to be found in the appendix to this volume.

3. On this scribe's tendency to elaborate stage directions, see John Jowett, 'New Created Creatures: Ralph Crane and the Stage Directions in *The Tempest*', *Shakespeare Survey*, 25 (1983), 107–20; Trevor Howard-Hill, *Ralph Crane and Some Shakespeare First Folio Comedies* (Charlottesville, 1972); and 'Shakespeare's Earliest Editor: Ralph Crane', *Shakespeare Survey*, 44 (1992), 113–30.

4. Bryan N.S. Gooch and David Thatcher (eds), *A Shakespeare Music Catalogue*, 5 vols (Oxford, 1991).

5. I discuss the editorial problems of this song in my edition of *The Tempest* (Cambridge, 2002), 247–9.

6. See David Lindley, *Shakespeare at Stratford: The Tempest* (London, 2003), Chapter 6, for an extended consideration of music in the history of the play's production at Stratford since 1945.

7. But Martin White disagrees: 'After experimenting extensively with music, language and action in a range of plays ... I am certain that music would have been used ... in a manner not dissimilar to the way it was used to accompany action in early cinema and in film scores today.' *Renaissance Drama in Action* (London, 1998), 154.

8. Compare Oberon's description of hearing 'a mermaid on a dolphin's back / Uttering such dulcet and harmonious breath / That the rude sea grew civil at her song' (*MND* 2.1.150–52).

9. Thomas Morley, *A Plain and Easy Introduction to Practical Music*, ed. R. Alec Harman (London and New York, revised edition 1963), 101.

1: MUSICAL THEORY

1. In using the speech as my 'text' I follow the lead of James Hutton, in his valuable article, 'Some English Poems in Praise of Music', *English Miscellany*, 2 (1951), 1–64, although my elaboration takes a different course. This seminal essay is reprinted in James Hutton, *Essays on Renaissance Poetry*, Rita Guerlac (ed.) (Ithaca and London, 1980).

2. See, for example, Gretchen Ludke Finney, *Musical Backgrounds for English Literature: 1580–1650* (Westport, Conn., 1962); John Hollander, *The Untuning of the Sky: Ideas of Music in English Poetry, 1500–1700* (Princeton, 1961; New York, 1970); Frances Yates, *French Academies of the Sixteenth Century* (London, 1947); Robert M. Isherwood, *Music in the Service of the King* (Ithaca and London, 1973).

3. That this is empirically not the case did not prevent the story being endlessly recycled.

4. A convenient summary can be found in James Haar's article, 'Pythagorean Harmony of the Universe', in the *Dictionary of Ideas* (New York, 1973–4), accessible in the electronic edition at http://etext.lib.virginia.edu/DicHist/dict.html. Again, technically, these Pythagorean intervals are more complex than can be indicated here, and there were heated arguments in the Renaissance about the precise mathematical basis of musical intervals.

5. Penelope Gouk, *Music, Science and Natural Magic in Seventeenth-Century England* (New Haven and London, 1999).

6. Plato, *The Republic*, trans. H.D.P. Lee (Harmondsworth, 1955), 397.

7. Aristotle, *De Caelo*, 2.9.291.

8. Macrobius, *Commentary on the Dream of Scipio*, translated with introduction and notes by William Harris Stahl (New York and London, 1952).

9. See Kathi Meyer-Baer, *Music of the Spheres and the Dance of Death: Studies in Musical Iconology* (New York, 1984), for a detailed consideration of the evolution of the pictorial tradition.

10. Hollander, *The Untuning of the Sky*, 152. The commentaries in both Arden2, ed. John Russell Brown (London, 1955) and Oxford, ed. Jay L. Halio (Oxford, 1993) occlude Shakespeare's unconventionality by mistakenly citing as a parallel Montaigne's account in *Essays*, 1.23, where the inaudibility of the music of the spheres is expressly accounted for by the fact that their sound is so insistently present that we become indifferent to it.

11. See Hutton, 'Some English Poems', 34–5, on the problems of interpreting the speech, problems which recent editors have largely ignored.

12. John Carey and Alastair Fowler (eds), *The Poems of John Milton* (London, 1968), 159.

13. See Nan Cooke Carpenter, *Music in the Medieval and Renaissance Universities* (Oklahoma, 1958; reprinted New York, 1972).

14. Quoted in David C. Price, *Patrons and Musicians of the English Renaissance* (Cambridge, 1981), 41.

15. Oliver Strunk, *Source Readings in Music History* (revised edition by Leo Treitler) (New York and London, 1998), 140–1.

16. Walter R. Davis (ed.), *The Works of Thomas Campion* (London, 1969), 48.

17. Susan Snyder (ed.), *The Divine Weeks and Works of Guillaume de Saluste Sieur du Bartas*, 2 vols (Oxford, 1979), 1.487.

18. Thomas Elyot, *The Boke Named the Governour*, ed. Henry Herbert Stephen Croft, 2 vols (London 1883), 1.42. It should be noted, however, that this only comes after much negative comment on the possibility that music can lead to wantonness and abandoning of serious duties.

19. *Certayne Sermons appoynted by the Quenes Maiestie, to be declared and read ...* (London, 1559), sig. R4r. The text may be accessed in the 1623 edition, edited by Ian Lancashire, at http://www.library.utoronto.ca/utel/ret/homilies/bk1hom10.html.

20. Strunk, *Source Readings*, 141.

21. John Dowland, *Andreas Ornithoparcus His Micrologus*, ed. Gustave Reese and Steven Ledbetter (New York, 1973), 121.

22. George Herbert, 'Man', 13–22 (*The Works of George Herbert*, ed. F.E. Hutchinson, Oxford, 1941, 91).

23. Snyder (ed.), *Divine Works*, 1.274.

24. Sir Thomas Browne, *Religio Medici*, Part 1, Section 34.

25. These lines are part of a passage found only in the Quarto text of the play.

26. Gary Tomlinson, *Music in Renaissance Magic* (Chicago and London, 1993), 50.

27. D.P. Walker, ed. Penelope Gouk, *Music, Spirit and Language in the Renaissance* (London, 1985), 8.147.

28. Strunk, *Source Readings*, 124.

29. Alluded to in *Tem*, 2.1.87–8.

30. See Fletcher's famous song in *H8*, 3.1.3–14, 'Orpheus with his lute'. The myth is comically dramatized in Fletcher's *The Mad Lover*, 4.1.

31. Plato, *The Republic*, trans. H. D. P. Lee (Harmondsworth, 1995), 139. To use the term 'mode' for the Greek *harmonia* is musicologically inexact, but the conflation of the Greek with the church modes of the Middle Ages became a standard, if confused, part of later writings.

32. Tomlinson, *Renaissance Magic*, 71.

33. Thomas Wright, *The Passions of the Minde in Generall*, reprinted with an introduction by Thomas O. Sloan (Urbana, Chicago and London, 1971), 163.

34. Wright, 168.

35. Wright, 168–71.

36. Richard Hooker, *Of the Laws of Ecclesiastical Polity*, 5.38 in W. Speed Hill (ed.), *The Folger Library Edition of the Works of Richard Hooker*, vol. 2 (Cambridge, Mass., 1977), 151.

37. Robert Burton, *The Anatomy of Melancholy*, 1.2.2, ed. Thomas C. Faulkner, Nicolas K. Kiessling, Rhonda L. Blair, 6 vols (Oxford, 1989–2000). (I give the part, membrum, section and (where used) subsection numbers which Burton used, in order that readers can find the references in other editions, including the more widely available Everyman edition by Holbrook Jackson, London, 1932.) For a lucid description of Renaissance physiology, J.B. Bamborough's *The Little World of Man* (London, 1952) is still useful.

38. On the attitudes to sound's penetration through the ear see Wes Folkerth, *The Sound of Shakespeare* (London, 2002), Chapters 2 and 3.

39. See Charles Edelman (ed.), *Shakespeare in Production: The Merchant of Venice* (Cambridge, 2002), 248; Miriam Gilbert, *Shakespeare at Stratford: The Merchant of Venice* (London, 2002), 149.

40. Timothy Bright, *A Treatise of Melancholy* (London, 1586). The quotation is from the 1613 edition, 301.

41. See Penelope Gouk, 'Music, Melancholy, and Medical Spirits in Early Modern Thought', in Peregrine Horden (ed.), *Music as Medicine: The History of Music Therapy since Antiquity* (Aldershot, 2000), 195–212.

42. The traditional spelling of the name as 'Imogen' is now generally taken to be an error, and all recent editions, including the forthcoming Arden 3, adopt 'Innogen'. I have therefore used this spelling throughout.

43. Linda Austern, 'Musical Treatments for Lovesickness', in Hordern, *Music as Medicine*, 227.

44. For a fuller discussion, see pages 202–4.

45. Burton, *Anatomy*, 2.2.6.3; Oxford edition, 2.116.

46. Gouk in Horden, *Music as Medicine*, 174.

47. Marsilio Ficino, *Three Books on Life [De Vita]*, ed. and trans. Carol V. Kaske and John R. Clark (New York, 1989), 255, 259.

48. These effects were explicable in the same way as music's power over human affections, for all of nature was infused with 'spirit' – but stones and trees possessed only the lowest, or 'vegetable' spirits.

49. Strunk, *Source Readings*, 465. For other examples see D.P. Walker's ground-breaking articles on musical humanism, collected by Penelope Gouk in *Music, Spirit and Language in the Renaissance* (London, 1985).

50. Yates, *French Academies*, 48.

51. Strunk, 524.

52. Walker, ed. Gouk, I.291.

53. Ficino, *Three Books*, 359.

54. Hooker, *Ecclesiastical Polity*, 5.151.

55. See James Anderson Winn, *Unsuspected Eloquence* (New Haven and London, 1981), Chapter 4: 'The Rhetorical Renaissance'.

56. See Derek Attridge, *Well-Weighed Syllables: Elizabethan Verse in Classical Metres* (Cambridge, 1974).

57. Henry Peacham, *The Complete Gentleman*, ed. Virgil B. Helzel (Ithaca, New York, 1962), 115, 109, 116. In the last quotation he marries technical terms from music and rhetoric in metaphoric exchange. German theorists in particular attempted to describe musical composition in rhetorical terms – see Joachim Burmeister's *Musica Poetica* (1606), of which an extract is printed in Strunk, 467–71. See also Brian Vickers, 'Figures of Rhetoric/Figures of Music', *Rhetorica*, 2 (1984), 1–44, and *In Defence of Rhetoric* (Oxford, 1988), 360–74.

58. Vickers, *In Defence*, 368.

59. Yates, *French Academies*, 240, 247.

60. James M. Saslow, *The Medici Wedding of 1589* (New Haven and London, 1996), 130.

61. Saslow, *Medici Wedding*, 31.

62. C. H. Herford, Percy and Evelyn Simpson (eds), *Ben Jonson*, 7 (Oxford, 1941), 189. Henceforward referred to as Herford and Simpson.

63. Robert Kruger (ed.), *The Poems of Sir John Davies* (Oxford, 1975), 94. The tone of this often-cited poem has been much discussed, and its seriousness questioned.

64. Elyot, 1.235–6.

65. Elyot, 1.269. On the theory of dance see James Miller, *Measures of Wisdom: The Cosmic Dance in Classical and Christian Antiquity* (Toronto, 1986); Alan Brissenden, *Shakespeare and the Dance* (London, 1981).

66. Elyot, 241.

67. Herford and Simpson, 7, 488–9.

68. Yates, 59.

69. On the neoplatonism of the Stuart masque, see the various essays on masques in D.J. Gordon, *The Renaissance Imagination*, Stephen Orgel (ed.) (1975); Stephen Orgel and Roy Strong, *Inigo Jones and the Theatre of the Stuart Court* (London and Berkeley, 1973).

70. Yates, 23. The full French text of the statutes is given in her Appendix 1.

71. See David Lindley, *Thomas Campion* (Leiden, 1986), 192–4.

72. Walter R. Davis (ed.), *The Works of Thomas Campion* (London, 1969), 250.

73. Herford and Simpson, 7, 534.

74. Herford and Simpson, 7, 404.

75. See David Lindley, 'The Politics of Music in the Masque', in David Bevington and Peter Holbrook (eds), *The Politics of the Stuart Court Masque* (Cambridge, 1998), 273–95.

76. Thomas Middleton, *Women Beware Women*, ed. J.R. Mulryne (Manchester, 1975), 5.2.171–2.

77. *The Praise of Musicke* (1586), 79. He actually goes on to attempt some defence of both. The authorship of this treatise was at one time attributed to John Case, who published the *Apologia musices* in 1588, but the attribution is not now accepted.

78. Plato, *Republic*, 139.

79. These lines may be part of an addition by Middleton; but they express a Renaissance commonplace.

80. On this debate see Percy A. Scholes, *The Puritans and Music in England and New England* (Oxford, 1934); Peter Le Huray, *Music and the Reformation in England, 1549–1660* (London, 1974).

81. William Prynne, *Histriomastix* (1633), 275.

82. Lodowick Lloyd, *The Pilgrimage of Princes* (1607 edition), 98.

83. Stephen Gosson, *The School of Abuse* (1587), ed. Edward Arber (London, 1869), 18–19.

84. Philip Stubbes, *Anatomy of Abuses* (1579), ed. Frederick J. Furnivall (London, 1877–9), 163, 171.

85. Francis Beaumont and John Fletcher, *The Maid's Tragedy*, ed. T.W. Craik (Manchester, 1988), 1.1.41–3.

86. Linda Phyllis Austern, '"Sing Againe Syren": The Female Musician and Sexual Enchantment in Elizabethan Life and Literature', *Renaissance Quarterly*, 42 (1989), 423. See also her '"Alluring the Auditorie to Effeminacie": Music and the Idea of the Feminine in Early Modern England', *Music and Letters*, 74 (1993), 343–54.

87. *Praise of Musicke*, 58.

88. Cornelius Agrippa von Nettesheim, *The Vanity of Arts and Sciences* (English translation of the original *De incertitudine et vanitate scientiarum et artium* of 1530; 1684 edition), 59.

89. Gosson, *The School of Abuse*, 16.

2: MUSIC IN PRACTICE

1. See John Stevens, *Music and Poetry in the Early Tudor Court* (London, 1961), Chapter 13; and on the terms 'minstrel' and 'musician', see Elizabeth Baldwin, *Paying the Piper: Music in Pre-1642 Cheshire* (Kalamazoo, 2002), 14–20.

2. See A.L. Beier, *Masterless Men: The Vagrancy Problem in England, 1560–1640* (London, 1985).

3. For a parallel instance of travelling players objecting to being called 'rogues', see Siobhan Keenan, *Travelling Players in Shakespeare's England* (London, 2002), 5.

4. James M. Osborn (ed.), *The Autobiography of Thomas Whythorne* (modern-spelling edition; Oxford, 1962), 193–4, 203. For further examples of contempt see Linda Phyllis Austern, *Music in English Children's Drama of the Later Renaissance* (Philadelphia, 1992), 147–9.

5. Walter L. Woodfill, *Musicians in English Society from Elizabeth to Charles I* (Princeton, 1953), 109.

6. Woodfill, 27, 113.

7. Craig Monson, 'Elizabethan London', in Iain Fenlon (ed.), *Man and Music: The Renaissance* (London, 1989), 304.

8. The shawm was also known in England as a 'wait', or 'wait-pipe' from its association with the waits. For descriptions of these and other instruments see the glossary of musical instruments in the appendix to this volume.

9. Richard Rastall informs me that the myth derives from a misreading of a paragraph in E. K. Chambers, *The Medieval Stage*, 1.51, perpetuated in the later literature. See his article 'Waits' in L. Macy (ed.), *Grove Music Online* (accessed 15.06.04), http://www.grovemusic.com. This revises the entry in the printed *Grove Dictionary of Music and Musicians* (ed. Stanley Sadie and John Tyrell, 2nd edition, Oxford, 2001). Throughout I cite from the online edition, which offers annual updates, although the printed text in almost all cases is identical.

10. Much of what follows is derived from Woodfill, *Musicians*, Chapter 2.

11. Thomas Heywood, *A Woman Killed with Kindness*, ed. R.W. van Fossen (London, 1961), 1.1.80–4.

12. Thomas Morley, *The First Book of Consort Lessons* (London, 1599), sig. A2r. Reproduced in the edition by Sydney Beck (New York, London and Frankfurt, 1959).

13. In addition to Woodfill, Chapter 4, see Elizabeth Baldwin, *Paying the Piper*; L.G. Langwill, 'The Waits: A Short Historical Study', *Hinrischen's Musical Year Book*, 7 (1952), 170–83; James Stokes, 'The Waits of Lincolnshire', *Early Theatre*, 1 (1998), 75–111; Cheryl Glenn Seitz, 'Sounds and Sweet Airs: City Waits of Medieval and Renaissance England', *Essays in Medieval Studies*, 4 (1987), 119–42; John C. Coldewey, 'Some Nottinghamshire Waits: Their History and Habits', *Records of Early English Drama Newsletter*, 1 (1982), 40–9.

14. Beaumont and Fletcher, *The Knight of the Burning Pestle*, ed. Sheldon P. Zitner (Manchester, 1984), Induction, 98–108.

15. Lynne M. Hulse, 'The Musical Patronage of the English Aristocracy', unpublished Ph.D., King's College, London (1992), 95–7.

16. Hulse, 'English Aristocracy', 101.

17. The Venetian ambassador, reporting on Elizabeth's coronation day, quoted in Peter Holman, *Four and Twenty Fiddlers: The Violin at the English Court, 1540–1690* (Oxford, 1993), 118.

18. Holman, 114.

19. Holman 115.

20. Andrew Ashbee, *Records of English Court Music*, 9 vols (Snodland, Kent, 1986–1996). In contrast to the musicians of the Chapel Royal, and to the London waits, many of the members of the royal music were of foreign extraction. The families of Lupo, Bassano, Galliardello, Ferrabosco, and Lanier were all represented over several generations.

21. The lord mayor's shows also employed up to thirty-two trumpeters in the Jacobean period; from whence they gathered such a number is not clear, but it points to the prominence of the instrument in the aural world of London.

22. The most comprehensive account of the music of the masque is Peter Walls, *Music in the English Courtly Masque 1604–1640* (Oxford, 1996).

23. Walter R. Davis (ed.), *The Works of Thomas Campion* (London, 1969), 223.

24. C.H. Herford, Perry and Evelyn Simpson (eds), *Ben Jonson*, 10 (Oxford, 1950), 529–30. Henceforward referred to as Herford and Simpson.

25. Woodfill, *Musicians in English Society*, 187.

26. Osborn, *Thomas Whythorne*, 203. Part of the reason for the decline was also that noble families no longer retained choirs for their domestic religious observances.

27. For a brief survey see Beat Kümin, 'Music in the English Parish, c. 1400–1600', in Fiona Kisby (ed.), *Music and Musicians in Renaissance Cities and Towns* (Cambridge, 2001), 70–81. For more detailed treatment of the subject, see Peter Le Huray, *Music and the Reformation in England, 1549–1660* (first published 1967, corrected edition Cambridge, 1978); Nicholas Temperley, *Music of the English Parish Church*, 2 vols (Cambridge, 1979).

28. The Injunction is printed in Le Huray, 32–3.

29. Monson, 'Elizabethan London', 308.

30. See Le Huray, especially Chapter 2.

31. James Saunders, 'Music and Moonlighting: The Cathedral Choirmen of Early Modern England, 1558–1649', in Kisby (ed.), *Music and Musicians*, 157–66.

32. Thomas Morley, *A Plain and Easy Introduction to Practical Music* (1597), ed. R. Alec Harman (London and New York, revised edition 1963), 293.

33. But see Roslyn Lander Knutson, *Playing Companies and Commerce in Shakespeare's Time* (Cambridge, 2001) for a challenging re-interpretation of the nature of the relationships between the theatrical companies in the period.

34. Robert Greene, *The Second Part of Cony-Catching* (1592), in Gamini Salgado (ed.), *Cony-Catchers and Bawdy Baskets* (Harmondsworth, 1972), 211.

35. Temperley, I, 76.

36. Quoted in Temperley, I, 43.

37. Joanna Moody (ed.), *The Private Life of an Elizabethan Lady: The Diary of Lady Margaret Hoby, 1599–1605* (Stroud, 1998), 38, 106.

38. Hulse, 'English Aristocracy', 274.

39. Kümin, 81.

40. 'Puritan' is a hotly contested label; here it is being used in its widest sense.

41. Stubbes, *Anatomy of Abuses* (1579), ed. Frederick J. Furnivall (London, 1877–9). 125–6.

42. Moody (ed.), *Margaret Hoby*, 56.

43. Percy M. Scholes, *The Puritans and Music* (Oxford, 1934).

44. Stubbes, 128.

45. Stubbes, 118–19.

46. Thomas Lovell, *A dialogue between custom and vertue concerning the use and abuse of dauncing and minstrelsie* (1581), sig. A4v. See Nicholas Bownd, *The Doctrine of the Sabbath* (1595) for the extreme sabbatarian position.

47. On the changing nature of popular festivity see David Cressy, *Bonfires and Bells* (Berkeley and Los Angeles, 1989); Ronald Hutton, *The Stations of the Sun* (Oxford, 1996).

48. *The Kings Maiesties declaration to his subjects, concerning lawfull sports to be used* (1618), known as the *Book of Sports*, 10–11. The proclamation had wider political purposes, and has been extensively discussed in Leah Marcus, *The Politics of Mirth* (Chicago, 1986).

49. *Book of Sports*, 7, 8.

50. Stubbes, *Anatomy of Abuses*, 123.

51. Peter Clark, *The English Alehouse: A Social History, 1200–1800* (London, 1983), 29.

52. Stubbes, 128.

53. Anon., *Pasquils Palinodia and His progresse to the Taverne* (1619), sig. B2v. See Woodfill, *Musicians in English Society*, 28–9.

54. John Earle, *Micro-cosmographie Or, A peece of the world discouered*, first published 1628; this and subsequent quotations are from the edition of 1630. The Trumpeter is Character Number 57.

55. Earle, Character 69.

56. W.S., *The Puritaine or the widdowe of Watling-streete* (1607), H2r. (The play was, in 1664, included amongst the Shakespearean apocrypha.)

57. Earle, Character 24.

58. See Clark, *English Alehouse*, 'Introduction'.

59. Clark, 152.

60. Clark, 155.

61. George Puttenham, *The Arte of English Poesie* (1589), 69.

62. Katherine Duncan-Jones (ed.), *Sir Philip Sidney* (Oxford, 1989), 231.

63. *Praise of Musike* (1586), 44.

64. Thomas Deloney, *Jack of Newbury*, in Paul Salzman (ed.), *An Anthology of Elizabethan Prose Fiction* (Oxford, 1987), 348–54.

65. Discussed by Bruce R. Smith, *The Acoustic World of Early Modern England* (Chicago, 1999), 170–73.
66. Printed in Morrison Comegys Boyd, *Elizabethan Music and Musical Criticism* (Philadelphia, 1940, revised edition 1962), 39.
67. Boyd, 53–4.
68. They are called 'broadsides' because most were printed on one side of a single large sheet of paper.
69. Tessa Watt, *Cheap Print and Popular Piety, 1550–1640* (Cambridge, 1991), 11, 42.
70. Nicholas Bownd, *The doctrine of the sabbath* (London, 1595), 241–2.
71. Chapman, Jonson and Marston, *Eastward Ho*, ed. R.W. van Fossen, (Manchester, 1979), 5.5.52–109.
72. Smith, *Acoustic World*, 202–203, lists versions of plays as diverse as *Titus Andronicus*, *Doctor Faustus* and *Romeo and Juliet*. See also his essay 'Shakespeare's Residuals: The Circulation of Ballads in Cultural Memory', in Stuart Gillespie and Neil Rhodes (eds), *Shakespeare and Elizabethan Popular Culture* (London, 2005).
73. Adam Fox, *Oral and Literate Culture in England, 1500–1700* (Oxford, 2000), 1–6 and Chapter 6.
74. Smith, *Acoustic World*, 177.
75. Claude M. Simpson, *The British Broadside Ballad and its Music* (New Brunswick, NJ, 1966), xv.
76. See Watt, 33–5.
77. Fox, 319.
78. Fox, 320.
79. See Margaret Spufford, *Small Books and Pleasant Histories* (Cambridge, 1981), which, though it concentrates principally on the later seventeenth century, has much information about the making and selling of popular fictions and ballads in the earlier period.
80. Watt, 23.
81. Robert Wilson, *The stately morall* (1591), sig. C.1r-v. (The scene goes on to lament the recent death in 1588 of Richard Tarlton, the famous clown, and member first of Sussex's Men and then of the Queen's Men.)
82. Henry Chettle, *Kind-harts Dreame* (1593), sig. C1r. Watt, 27–9, suggests that Chettle may have been right to point to the ballad-seller as young – she calculates that two-thirds were under the age of twenty-one.
83. Richard Brathwaite, *Whimzies, or a new cast of characters* (1631), 9.
84. Herford and Simpson, 6 (Oxford 1938).
85. Wye Saltonstall, *Picturae loquenter. Or pictures drawne forth in characters* (1631), no. 21.
86. Brathwaite, 9, 11.

87. British Library MS Royal 18B 19, fol. 7r-v. The treatise dates from c. 1625.

88. Hulse, 'English Aristocracy', 28; but she suggests also that the number may have been small, and in the absence of records that the claim 'cannot be verified' (58).

89. Jonathan P. Wainwright, *Musical Patronage in Seventeenth-century England: Christopher, First Baron Hatton (1605–1670)* (Aldershot, 1997).

90. Edward Doughtie (ed.), *Lyrics from English Airs* (Cambridge, Mass., 1970), 260.

91. Davis (ed.), *Thomas Campion*, 133.

92. Quoted in David C. Price, *Patrons and Musicians of the English Renaissance* (Cambridge, 1981), 192.

93. Woodfill, *Musicians in English Society*, 59. He was in the service of the Kytson family of Hengrave Hall, Suffolk.

94. Hulse, 'English Aristocracy', 40.

95. Lynn Hulse, 'The Musical Patronage of Robert Cecil', *Journal of the Royal Musical Association*, 116 (1991), 24–40.

96. Hulse, 'Robert Cecil', 26.

97. Stevens, *Music and Poetry*, 270.

98. Baldassare Castiglione, *The Book of the Courtier*, trans. Sir Thomas Hoby, edited with introduction by W.H.D. Rouse (London, 1928), 75.

99. Henry Peacham, *The Complete Gentleman*, ed. Virgil B. Heltzel (Ithaca, New York, 1962), 111.

100. Morley, *Consort Lessons*, 9.

101. Price, *Patrons and Musicians*, 109.

102. F. G. Emmison, *Tudor Secretary: Sir William Petre at Court and Home* (London, 1961), 212. The Petre family became patrons of William Byrd.

103. Joan Simon, *Education and Society in Tudor England* (Cambridge, 1967), 364.

104. Boyd, *Elizabethan Music*, 15–16.

105. Boyd, 16.

106. Richard Mulcaster, *Positions* (1581), 36, 37.

107. Boyd, 16.

108. Quoted in Nan Cooke Carpenter, *Music in the Medieval and Renaissance Universities* (Oklahoma, 1958; reprinted, New York, 1972), 172.

109. William Bathe, *A briefe introduction to the skill of song* (1596), sig A3v. (Reprinted with introduction by Bernarr Rainbow, Kilkenny, 1982.)

110. J. Alford, *A briefe and easye instruction* (1568); F.K., gentleman, *A brief and plaine instruction* (1574).

111. William Barley, *A new Booke of Tabliture* (1596), sig. A3v. The production of instruction books such as Thomas Robinson's *The Schoole of Musicke* (1603), continued in the seventeenth century.

112. Robert Dowland, *Varietie of lute-lessons* (1610), sig. B1r.

113. Price, *Patrons and Musicians*, 22–31.

114. Hulse, 'English Aristocracy', 158–60.

115. Price, 22.

116. J. B. Leishman (ed.), *The Three Parnassus Plays* (London, 1949). In *The Second Part of the Return from Parnassus*, 5.1 the desperate students become fiddlers (349–52).

117. Hulse, 'English Aristocracy', 153.

118. John Harper, 'Ensemble and Lute Music', in Roger Bray (ed.), *Music in Britain: The Sixteenth Century* (Oxford, 1995), 272.

119. Diana Poulton, *John Dowland* (London, 1972, revised edition 1982), 186.

120. See Mary Chan, 'Music Books', in John Barnard and D.F. McKenzie (eds), assisted by Maureen Bell, *The Cambridge History of the Book in Britain Volume 4, 1557–1695* (Cambridge, 2002), Chapter 5.

121. Peter Holman with Paul O'Dette, 'John Dowland', in *Grove Music Online*, L. Macy (ed.) (accessed 14.01.04), http://www.grovemusic.com.

122. Nicholas Yonge, *Musica Transalpina* (1588), sig. A2r.

123. Price, *Patrons and Musicians*, 113–14.

124. See Michael G. Brennan, 'Sir Charles Somerset's Music Books (1622)', *Music and Letters*, 74 (1993), 501–518.

125. Hulse, 'English Aristocracy', 111.

126. Peacham, *Complete Gentleman*, 112.

127. Woodfill, *Musicians in English Society*, 217.

128. How well or badly Balthazar actually sings is a matter of debate. See Sheldon P. Zitner (ed.), *Much Ado about Nothing* (Oxford, 1993), 44–5, and p. 176 below.

129. Castiglione, 101.

130. Castiglione, 75.

131. Doughtie (ed.), *Lyrics*, 284–5.

132. Robert Burton, *The Anatomy of Melancholy*, 3.2.3.1, ed. Thomas C. Faulkner, Nicolas K. Kiessling, Rhonda L. Blair, 6 vols (Oxford, 1989–2000), 3.187–8.

133. Cited in David Scott, 'Queen Elizabeth' in *Grove Music Online*. She was still keen to know from the Scottish ambassador whether she played better than her rival Mary Queen of Scots.

134. Roy Strong, *Portraits of Queen Elizabeth* (Oxford, 1963). Later Lady Mary Wroth was to be depicted standing beside a theorbo (a large lute with additional bass strings). (See Gavin Alexander, 'The Musical Sidneys', *The John Donne Journal*, forthcoming, for a detailed account of the musical knowledge, expertise and patronage of this influential family.)

135. Burton, *Anatomy*, 3.2.3.1, Oxford edition, 3.188.

136. Stephen Orgel has provided a provocative re-investigation of the cultural implications of this general rule in *Impersonations* (Cambridge, 1996).

137. Virtually nothing is known of either woman, though Roy Booth suggests that Madame Coniack was the subject of Thomas Randolph's poem 'Upon a very deformed gentlewoman, but of a voice incomparable sweet' ('The First Female Professional Singers: Madam Coniack', *Notes and Queries*, 242 (1997), 553). See also Suzanne Gossett, '"Man-maid be gone": Women in Masques', *English Literary Renaissance*, 18 (1988), 96–113.

138. Hulse, 'English Aristocracy', 293.

139. On this revival see Harry Haskell, *The Early Music Revival: A History* (London, 1988, revised edition New York, 1996).

140. Samuel Rowlands, in the 6th Satire of *The Letting of Humors Blood* (1600), line 73, refers to 'the great organ-pipe in *Poules*', but by the standards of Bach's organ, let alone the later Victorian instrument, it was small.

141. Bruce R. Smith, *The Acoustic World of Early Modern England* (Chicago, 1999), 49.

142. See Siobhan Keenan, *Travelling Players*, 15–17.

143. E. D. Pendry (ed.), *Thomas Dekker: Selected Prose Writings* (London, 1967), 100.

144. Pendry, 98.

145. Richard Hosley, 'Was there a Music-Room in Shakespeare's Globe', *Shakespeare Survey*, 13 (1960), 113–23.

146. See Andrew Gurr, *The Shakespearean Stage, 1574–1642*, 3rd edition (Cambridge, 1992), 147–9.

147. Linda Phyllis Austern, *Music in English Children's Drama of the Later Renaissance* (Philadelphia, 1992), 32–3. See also Michael Shapiro, *Children of the Revels: the Boy Companies of Shakespeare's Time and their Plays* (New York, 1977).

148. Austern, *Children's Drama*, 311.

149. Hosley, 119, suggests that the addition of the stage direction in the Folio *A Midsummer Night's Dream* for the four lovers to '*sleep all the Act*', not present in the earlier quarto, is a mark of changed practice by the King's Men after the acquisition of Blackfriars.

150. Andrew Gurr, *The Shakespearian Playing Companies* (Oxford, 1996), 368.

151. The 'cornets' which are called for in *MV* 2.1 and 2.7, appear only in the Folio SDs (stage directions), and are not specified in the Quarto. In both plays the mention of cornetts is most likely to reflect later, indoor theatre practice.

152. See Stanley Wells and Gary Taylor, *William Shakespeare: A Textual Companion* (Oxford, 1987, reprinted with corrections, New York, 1997), 492.

153. Peter Thompson, *Shakespeare's Theatre* (London, 1983), 89.

154. Quoted in David Daniell (ed.), *Julius Caesar* (London, 1998), 12.

155. Still the fullest account of the stage jig is Charles Read Baskerville, *The Elizabethan Jig and Related Song Drama* (Chicago, Ill., 1929). See especially Chapters 3 and 4.

156. R.A. Foakes (ed.), *Henslowe's Diary* (2nd edition, Cambridge, 2002), 101, 130.

157. Foakes, 102, 122.

158. Carol Chillington Rutter (ed.), *Documents of the Rose Playhouse* (Manchester, 1984), 136. The inventory was transcribed by Malone in 1790, from an MS now lost.

159. Woodfill, *Musicians in English Society*, 30.

160. *The Dramatic Works of Thomas Heywood*, 6 vols (London, 1874), 1.316.

161. J. S. Manifold, *The Music in English Drama, Shakespeare to Purcell* (1956), 58–9.

162. Musical accompaniment to dumb shows was traditional – though here the fact that no music seems to play during the show itself might be a sign of limited musical resources.

163. Manifold, 42.

164. Alan C. Dessen and Leslie Thomson, *A Dictionary of Stage Directions in English Drama, 1580–1642* (Cambridge, 1999).

165. See John Jowett, 'From Print to Performance: Looking at the Masque in *Timon of Athens*', in *From Performance to Print in Early Modern England*, Peter Holland and Stephen Orgel (eds) (London, Forthcoming, 2005) for a valuable discussion of the association of lute-playing and whoredom.

166. Manifold, 79.

167. Manifold suggest that 'solemn music' indicates the organ – which was available in the indoor theatres – but this is probably too rigid a reading of the instruction.

168. In a chapter in his forthcoming book on the English consort.

169. See Gurr, *Shakespearean Stage*, 103–14. In *Playing Companies*, 83–5, he suggests that by the 1630s longer runs might have become customary. See also Neil Carson, *A Companion to Henslowe's Diary* (Cambridge, 1988), 67–79 for a detailed discussion of the repertoire of Henslowe's companies.

170. Christine Eccles, *The Rose Theatre* (London, 1990), 144.

171. See T.J. King, *Casting Shakespeare's Plays: London Actors and their Roles, 1590–1642* (Cambridge, 1992); David Bradley, *From Text to Performance in the Elizabethan Theatre: Preparing the Play for the Stage* (Cambridge, 1992).

172. Carson, *Henslowe's Diary*, 30.

173. Carson, 36.

174. I am grateful to Richard Rastall for this observation.

175. Scott McMillin and Sally-Beth McLean, *The Queen's Men and their Plays* (Cambridge, 1998), 63.

176. Woodfill, *Musicians in English Society*, 30.

177. Holman, *Four and Twenty Fiddlers*, 36.

178. Michela Calore and Christopher R. Wilson, *Dictionary of Music in Shakespeare* (London, forthcoming 2005), sv. 'Trumpet'.

PRELUDE

1. John Hollander, *The Untuning of the Sky: Ideas of Music in English Poetry 1500–1700* (Princeton, 1961; New York, 1970), 148.
2. The musical image is inaccurate, wrongly using the term 'jacks' for the keys upon which the mistress plays, rather than for the plectra which pluck the strings.
3. Deryck Cooke, *The Language of Music* (Oxford, 1959); Leonard B. Meyer, *Emotions and Meaning in Music* (Chicago, 1956); Peter Kivy, *The Corded Shell* (Princeton, 1980).
4. Patrice Pavis, *Analyzing Performance*, trans. David Williams (Ann Arbor, 2003), 141.
5. F.W. Sternfeld, *Music in Shakespearean Tragedy* (London, 1963), 117.

3: INSTRUMENTAL MUSIC AND DANCE

1. See Roger Savage's excellent article on 'Incidental Music' in *Grove Music Online*, L. Macy (ed.) (accessed 25.06.04), http://www.grovemusic.com.
2. The SD at *1H6* 3.4.27: 'Sennet. Flourish' implies some difference between them, but it is not clear what this might be. Michela Calore and Christopher R. Wilson, *Dictionary of Music in Shakespeare* (London, forthcoming, 2005), suggest that the 'flourish' is an improvised call, where the Sennet is associated specifically with the entry and exit of only those of the highest status. The 'tucket' is the least well-defined of fanfares.
3. On the signals of war, see Paul A. Jorgensen, *Shakespeare's Military World* (Berkeley and Los Angeles, 1956), Chapter 1; Frances A. Shirley, *Shakespeare's Use of Off-Stage Sounds* (Lincoln, NE, 1963) covers a wide range of instrumental musical cues.
4. See Peter M. Wright, 'Stage Directions for Music and Sound Effects in *2–3 Henry VI*: "No Quarrel but a Slight Contention", in Grace Ioppolo (ed.), *Shakespeare Performed: Essays in Honor of R. A. Foakes* (Newark, 2000), 72–87, for a discussion which includes the relationship between Quarto and Folio stage directions in these plays.
5. Jorgensen, 4.
6. Sidney, *Arcadia*, ed. Victor Skretkowicz (Oxford, 1987), 340. See Jorgensen, Chapter 1, for examples of the discourse of war, as well as its action, conceived in musical terms.
7. Gervase Markham, *The Souldier's Accidence* (1635), 100. Earlier (16) he had suggested that the drum might equally give a number of very specific signals, which it was the business of the soldier to learn.
8. John M. Ward, 'Points of Departure', *Harvard Library Bulletin*, 2.4 (1991), 10.

9. Edward Burns (ed.), *King Henry VI Part 1* (London, 2000), commentary, suggests, following the Grove dictionary entry on 'march', that there would not be much difference between these marches, and that it may have been instrumentation which made them distinct – but the quotation does suggest that there was at least some differentiation in the drumming itself.

10. The same might be true for the '*Danish March*' which the Folio text specifies for the entrance of Claudius and his court in *Hamlet*, 3.3.

11. Markham, 64.

12. The stage direction is simply '*Trumpet sounds*', but it must have been a parley, as King Philip a few lines later announces 'Our trumpet calls you to this gentle parle'.

13. Charles Forker in the Arden 3 edition (London, 2002) adds a trumpet to the Folio stage direction, but, as will become apparent, this seems to me mistaken.

14. The Quarto text simply has '*The Trumpets sound, Richard appeareth on the walls*'. One of the marks of the theatrical origin of the Folio as against the authorial manuscript assumed to lie behind Q is precisely the addition of greater detail to musical cues throughout.

15. In the Folio SDs in 1.3 '*The trumpets sound*' for Richard's entry at line 5, and then for Bolingbroke at 25. Forker adds an additional call to the first SD, arguing that 'a separate fanfare should announce Mowbray', but this perhaps diminishes the way the scene sets up the opposition specifically as one between the king and Bolingbroke.

16. In the Folio text; the Q text has Edgar enter on the third call, without issuing a response.

17. Forker chooses to add a '*flourish*' to Richard's entry as he descends from the castle walls at line 185, which might reinforce the irony of his powerlessness, but which would perhaps lessen the ambivalence of the scene's ending.

18. Jorgensen, *Shakespeare's Military World*, 25–6, suggests that Londoners could become familiar with martial musical signals through their acquaintance with the drilling of citizen soldiers at Mile End.

19. The same is true at 3.1.141 where it is Paris who recognizes the sound that signals the end of the day's fighting.

20. Once again the differences between Quarto and Folio texts make this a moment not straightforwardly to be interpreted. Q has the retreat, but no flourish; in both texts Richard and Richmond enter and fight; no instruction is given for Richmond to leave the stage, but he is described as 'entering' after Richard's death. Jowett suggests plausibly, in his edition (Oxford, 2000), that Richmond should leave the stage, with Richard's body alone, before entering again with Stanley bearing the crown. If this staging is adopted then the differentiated trumpet calls do a good deal of work.

21. Calore and Wilson, *Dictionary*, under 'dirge'. Cowling's assertion that funeral music was rarely heard on the Elizabethan stage, quoted by Brockbank in his Arden2 edition of *Coriolanus* (London, 1976), is simply wrong. The examples given in Dessen and Thompson can be supplemented by many more.

22. In the Quarto version of the text the effect is even stronger as the murdered body of Humphrey of Gloucester is revealed at the opening of the scene, then simply curtained off as Henry enters.

23. This is the assumption that is made by Bevington in Arden3 (London, 1998), who has the musicians entering with Paris and Helen, presumably in part so that they can accompany Pandarus in his song later in the scene. This, however, is not the only possible realization.

24. See above, p. 56.

25. Compare the music which accompanies the appearance of Helen in both the A and B texts of Marlowe's *Doctor Faustus*, and that which surrounds the entry of Antiochus's daughter in *Pericles* – see below p. 139.

26. For a discussion of the song, see below, pp. 171–2.

27. It is an open question how many of the original audience would have understood a song in Welsh; for most, however, it presumably was incomprehensible and therefore functioned almost as pure sound.

28. Wes Folkerth, *The Sound of Shakespeare* (London, 2002), 29–30. His suggestive analysis of the sound-world of the plays goes well beyond my focus on specifically musical events.

29. Daniell, Arden3 edition, commentary.

30. See F.W. Sternfeld, *Music in Shakespearean Tragedy* (London, 1963), 81. He suggests Dowland's 'Weep you no more sad fountains' might be a better substitute, while remarking, properly, 'any sleepy tune' would serve (21).

31. Forker notes that Mahood's suggestion that the sympathetic Groom is the offstage musician has been taken up in production.

32. It is possible that an ensemble performed – though this would seem to contradict Richard's singular pronoun when offering 'blessing on his heart who gives it to me' (64).

33. Both 'time' and 'proportion' are technical musical terms, the latter indicating the relationship between groups of notes.

34. See Pierre Iselin, 'Myth, Memory and Music in *Richard II, Hamlet* and *Othello*', in A.J. Hoenselaars (ed.), *Reclamations of Shakespeare* (Amsterdam, 1994), 173–86.

35. Robert Burton, *The Anatomy of Melancholy*, 2.2.6.4, ed. Thomas C. Faulkner, Nicolas K. Kiessling, Rhonda L. Blair, 6 vols (Oxford, 1989–2000), 2.116. He quotes also Plutarch '*musica dementat quam vinum*' ('music maddens more than wine').

36. Throughout the eighteenth and nineteenth centuries the final entrance of Fortinbras was usually cut, in part, no doubt, to keep attention focused upon the pathos of Hamlet's death. See Robert Hapgood (ed.), *Hamlet* (Shakespeare in Production: Cambridge, 1999), 275.

37. That 'cornetts' are specified almost certainly indicates that the instructions were added in the light of later stage-practice.

38. Later in the speech is becomes clear that her other feminine accomplishments include weaving and embroidery. Compare with this narrative of competition between Marina and Philoten Helena's account of her childhood with Hermia in *MND*, 3.2.201–08 which included singing songs together.

39. It is just possible that Viola was originally intended to sing. See below, pp. 199–201.

40. Desdemona similarly delights Othello, in that she 'sings, plays and dances well' (3.2.188), though we only see her sing in anticipation of her death (see below, pp. 150–51).

41. Although Stanley Wells and Gary Taylor in the *Complete Works* (Oxford, 1988) introduce a scene of his singing from the sources (Scene 8a).

42. Peter R. Seddon (ed.), *Letter of John Holles*, 3 vols (Nottingham, 1975–86), 1.54.

43. Sidney, *Arcadia*, 71.

44. Compare Hamlet's rejection of the idea that he can be played upon like a recorder.

45. These lines are usually attributed to Shakespeare's collaborator, George Wilkins.

46. Thomas Elyot, *The Boke Named the Governour* (1531), ed. Henry Herbert Stephen Croft (London, 1883), 2 vols, 1.236–8.

47. Alan Brissenden, *Shakespeare and the Dance* (London, 1981), 49–50.

48. They may be carrying no more than the tabor which accompanies the pipe – but perhaps something larger is implied.

49. This refusal to participate was echoed in the real world when, in 1612, Frances Howard and her sister refused to dance with the masquers in *Love Restored*, so that the men were forced to dance with one another.

50. A drum is not specified in the opening SD of 1.4, but is called for at line 112.

51. Brissenden, 64.

52. Jill Levenson (ed.) (Oxford, 2000), commentary, following P.C. McGuire, 'On the dancing in *Romeo and Juliet*', *Renaissance and Reformation*, N.S. 5 (1981).

53. It was probably the firing of cannon in this scene which caused the fire which burnt down the first Globe theatre in 1613.

54. It is possible, however, that Leonato is not disapproving, but rather suggesting that lovemaking, for which dance is an emblem, will follow marriage.

55. The essay 'Hands, Feet and Bottoms: Decentering the Cosmic Dance in *A Midsummer Night's Dream*', *Shakespeare Quarterly*, 44 (1993), 325–42 is followed up by *The Politics of Courtly Dancing* (Amherst, 1998).

56. 'Decentering', 326.

57. Harry Berger, Jr, 'Against the Sink-a-Pace: Sexual and Family Politics in *Much Ado About Nothing*', *Shakespeare Quarterly*, 33 (1982), 302–13.

58. Brissenden, *Shakespeare and Dance*, 45; Walter Sorrel, however, argues that although it was a popular dance it was not necessarily clumsy or parodic (cited in Peter Holland (ed.), *A Midsummer Night's Dream*, Oxford, 1994, commentary on 5.4.316).

59. See above pp. 59–60.

60. See Katherine M. Briggs, *The Anatomy of Puck* (London, 1959), 44–70; Linda Phyllis Austern, *Music in English Children's Drama of the Later Renaissance* (Philadelphia, 1992), 161–3.

61. However, this is further complicated if the suggestion that the fairies and the mechanicals were played by the same actors is accepted. See below p. 185.

62. There is some uncertainty about what exactly happens at this point. The Folio SD (not in Q) is '*Musicke Tongs, Rurall Musicke*'. Harold Brooks thinks this an error 'contrary to Shakespeare's intention' (Arden2, London, 1979) while Holland comments: 'Titania's next line might seem to deny Bottom his music but F's SD ... is likely to have prompt-book authority', arguing that this 'rough music' is the first of a variety of musics that punctuate this scene.

63. 'Still' here signifies 'quiet' music. See Dessen and Thomson, *Dictionary of Stage Directions*, under 'still', for other examples of the use of the term in stage directions.

64. Anne Barton, '*As You Like It* and *Twelfth Night*: Shakespeare's "sense of an ending"', reprinted in *Essays Mainly Shakespearean* (Cambridge, 1994), 104.

65. See Robert Smallwood, *Shakespeare at Stratford: As You Like It* (London, 2003), Chapter 7, 'Rustic Revelry'. Cynthia Marshall (ed.), *Shakespeare in Production: As You Like It* (Cambridge, 2004), 244, briefly notes a number of alternative renditions.

66. Judith Anderson, quoted by Gordon McMullan, in the Arden3 edition (London, 2000), 123. See also 132–6.

67. See above, p. 31.

68. John Marston, *Iacke Drums entertainment: or The comedie of Pasquill and Katherine* (1601), sig. H4v.

69. Foakes suggests in his commentary to the scene (Arden3, London, 1997) that the music was cut in order to get rid of the extra character of the doctor.

70. Roger Warren and his music editor James Walker suggest the addition of a number of musical cues in the Oxford edition of the play (Oxford, 1998).

71. Warren (ed.), 273.

72. Dessen and Thompson, *Dictionary of Stage Directions*, under 'solemn'.

73. Firecrackers, however, were probably not used in the indoor playhouses, where instrumental sound – perhaps of drums – was most likely substituted.

74. It should be noted that some recent feminist critics have treated the resurrection of Hermione less sympathetically, and have read the whole final scene as demonstrating Leontes' resumption of unproblematic masculine control. It is a response I, and countless theatregoers, do not share.

75. Stephen Orgel, in an excellent succinct discussion of the scene in his edition (Oxford, 1996, 62), concludes that Paulina's 'demand for a suspension of disbelief, her invocation of wonder, and most of all, her claims for the therapeutic quality of her performance sound much more like Renaissance apologias for theatre than like any version of religious experience'.

76. See the footnote and Long Note in Suzanne Gossett's Arden 3 edition (London, 2004). F. Elizabeth Hart has striven mightily to validate the reading of 'rough' by linking it to the Phrygian music of the cult of Cybele/Diana in 'Cerimon's "Rough" Music in *Pericles*, 3.2.', *Shakespeare Quarterly*, 51 (2000), 313–31. But Bevington's suggestion that 'Cerimon may be apologizing for the only music he can provide at short notice' (quoted in Hart, 314, fn.5) seems to me perfectly adequate justification for the reading.

4: SONG

1. Ross Duffin, *Shakespeare's Songbook* (New York, 2004), 32. His book is an extremely useful and suggestive resource, to which frequent reference will be made. He collects the relatively few cases where original music survives, and also suggests, for the majority where it does not, popular song tunes to which the words can be accommodated.

2. W.H. Auden, 'Music in Shakespeare', in *The Dyer's Hand* (London, 1962), 511, 522.

3. Mark W. Booth, *The Experience of Songs* (New Haven and London, 1981), 118.

4. Dekker and Middleton, *The Honest Whore, Part 1*, 1.1.75–7, in Fredson Bowers (ed.), *The Dramatic Works of Thomas Dekker*, 4 vols, 2 (Cambridge, 1955). See Fox, *Oral and Literate Culture*, (Oxford, 2000), 306–07, for other examples.

5. The same tune is recalled by Margaret in *Much Ado*, 3.2.41, and Beatrice seems immediately aware of its implication of female unchastity as she puts it by with a witty rebuke.

6. Duffin, *Shakespeare's Songbook*, 89.

7. Peter J. Seng, *The Vocal Songs in the Plays of Shakespeare: A Critical History* (Cambridge, Mass., 1967).

8. Armado actually translates the ballad into his egregious high style in the letter intercepted in 4.1.66–79. It is Shakespeare's most frequently mentioned
   ballad, with five citations in four different plays (see Duffin, 235–40).

9. 'Noise' is a term for a band of musicians. It is not necessarily pejorative,
   although perhaps usually associated with civic and itinerant bands, rather
   than with a courtly ensemble.

10. Duffin, 435. Though only the first line is given in the text, it is entirely pos-
    sible that this might be a cue for the actor to continue a little further with a
    well-known song.

11. See A.H. Bullen (ed.), *The Works of Thomas Middleton*, 8 vols (London, 1885),
    3.146. I am grateful to John Jowett for alerting me to this reference.

12. Duffin, 192.

13. Robin Headlam Wells, 'Falstaff, Prince Hal and the New Song', in
    Elizabethan Mythologies: Studies in Poetry, Drama and Music (Cambridge, 1994),
    55.

14. Wells, 56.

15. On the significance of ballads as 'documents of memory', see Bruce R. Smith,
    'Shakespeare's Residuals: The Circulation of Ballads in Cultural Memory', in
    Stuart Gillespie and Neil Rhodes (eds), *Shakespeare and Elizabethan Popular
    Culture* (London, forthcoming, 2005).

16. See below, pp. 199–201.

17. E.A.J. Honigman, *The Texts of 'Othello' and Shakespearian Revision* (London and
    New York, 1996), 40.

18. On text and music see F.W. Sternfeld, *Music in Shakespearean Tragedy*
    (London, 1963), 23–52; Duffin, 467–70.

19. Rosalind King, 'The music and structure of *Othello*', *Shakespeare Survey*, 39
    (1986), 157.

20. King, 157.

21. Sternfeld, 34.

22. 'Set down the pegs' means to turn the tuning pegs to which the strings of a
    musical instrument such as lute or violin are attached, slackening the strings
    and thus rendering the instrument out of tune.

23. Tempting though it might be, as King argues (154) to see some significance
    in the variation, which substitutes a monarch who presided over civil war
    for the victorious Henry, the recollection of the same version by Trinculo in
    The Tempest suggests that there was simply more than one version of the
    words in circulation.

24. King, 155.

25. Lawrence J. Ross, 'Shakespeare's "Dull Clown" and Symbolic Music',
    Shakespeare Quarterly, 17 (1966), 107–28.

26. Ross, 125.

27. The musical metaphor of the bells is not very exact – but she presumably contrasts the orderly procession of bells chiming one after the other in the peculiarly English custom of change ringing, with their being sounded all together, which is the signal of an alarm. The *Grove Music Online* entry on 'change ringing' dates its beginnings to the latter part of the sixteenth century, and notes that during the early seventeenth century it was an entirely secular activity, practised on every day *but* Sunday.

28. The Second Quarto SD is simply '*Enter Ophelia*' (4.5.20); F has '*Enter Ophelia distracted*'. The status of the First Quarto has been much debated – but the stage direction must, at the very least, represent a contemporary staging possibility.

29. See Maurice Charney and Hanna Charney, 'The Language of Madwomen in Shakespeare and His Fellow Dramatists', *Signs*, 3 (1977), 451–60.

30. See Carol Thomas Neely, *Distracted Subjects: Madness and Gender in Shakespeare and Early Modern Culture* (Ithaca and London, 2004), Chapter 2.

31. See Michael MacDonald, *Mystical Bedlam: Madness, Anxiety and Healing in Seventeenth-Century England* (Cambridge, 1981), 27.

32. Elaine Showalter, 'Ophelia: the Responsibilities of Feminist Criticism', in Patricia Parker and Geoffrey Hartman (eds), *Shakespeare and the Question of Theory* (New York, 1985), 86, notes that by the Victorian period 'the iconography of the romantic Ophelia had begun to infiltrate reality, to define a style for mad young women seeking to express and communicate their distress'. See Dolly MacKinnon, '"Poor Senseless Bess, Clothed in her Rags and Folly": Early Modern Women, Madness and Song in Seventeenth-Century England', *Parergon*, 18 (2001), 119–51, for the evolution of the mad song genre.

33. The most detailed treatment of texts and tunes is in Seng, *Vocal Songs*, 131–62.

34. Auden, *Dyer's Hand*, 522.

35. Harold Jenkins (ed.), *Hamlet* (1982), 4.5.20, commentary.

36. Robert Hapgood (ed.), *Shakespeare in Production: Hamlet* (Cambridge, 1999), 231.

37. Exactly the same strategy was adopted in the RSC performance in 2004.

38. See Kent Cartwright, *Shakespearean Tragedy and its Double: The Rhythms of Audience Response* (Pennsylvania, 1991), 3: 'Playing dead constitutes one of the few challenges in acting (fainting and madness are two others) where the performer must always pretend and not "be".'

39. These lines are given to Horatio in the Second Quarto; in F they are spoken by Gertrude – a reading I rather prefer.

40. Jenkins (ed.), 349–50.

41. Lesley C. Dunn, 'Ophelia's Songs in *Hamlet*: Music, Madness, and the Feminine', in Lesley C. Dunn and Nancy A. Jones (eds), *Embodied Voices: Representing Female Vocality in Western Culture* (Cambridge, 1994), 58.

42. So Sternfeld argues (*Music in Shakespearean Tragedy*, 54), but Seng disagrees (*Vocal Song*, 132–3).

43. The force of her indecorum is rendered the more marked by contrast with the Jailor's Daughter in *TNK*, whose transgressiveness is much less marked because of her lower social class.

44. See above, p. 98.

45. See, for example, Carroll Camden, 'On Ophelia's Madness', *Shakespeare Quarterly*, 15 (1964), 247–55, and pp. 31–2, above. Showalter's influential essay fascinatingly traces the changing representation of Ophelia's madness and sexuality – but makes little mention of music's contribution to that history.

46. Dunn, 'Ophelia's Songs', 59.

47. Jacquelyn A. Fox-Good, 'Ophelia's Mad Songs: Music, Gender, Power', in David C. Allen and Robert A White (eds), *Subjects on the World's Stage: Essays on British Literature of the Middle Ages and the Renaissance* (Newark, 1995), 233.

48. The tunes handed down in theatrical convention may or may not be those originally heard. But it is generally assumed that 'How should I' goes to the tune of Walsingham, a haunting modal melody whose downward leaps intensify its melancholy.

49. See Sternfeld, 151–5, for an account of the versions of the tune that survive (one a nineteenth-century transcription from a handwritten addition to an edition of *Tottel* that is now lost – evidence, if any were needed, for the chanciness of the survival of ballad tunes). Duffin, 211–14, prints the complete text of both lyrics, and a different conjectural reshaping of the surviving tune to fit the words.

50. Peter J. Seng, 'An Early Tune for the Fool's Song in *King Lear*', *Shakespeare Quarterly*, 9 (1958), 583–5. Duffin, however, objects that 'this is a round rather than a ballad setting and would not easily fit the ballad lyrics', and suggests instead the tune 'If Care Do Cause Men Cry' (*Shakespeare's Songbook*, 376–7).

51. For suggestions for tunes to the latter see David Greer, 'Sleepest or wakest, jolly shepherd', *Shakespeare Quarterly*, 45 (1992), 224–6; Duffin, 232–3.

52. Jay Halio (ed.), *The Tragedy of King Lear* (Cambridge, 1992), commentary on 2.2.238–43.

53. *Dyer's Hand*, 523.

54. See Bruce R. Smith, *The Acoustic World of Early Modern England* (Chicago, 1999), 63–70.

55. Duffin, 165.

56. Somewhat surprisingly, John Caldwell suggests that the song was accompanied by a regal, or small organ – which would probably not have been available to the actors at the Globe – saying that 'boys did not normally play the

lute' (*Measure for Measure*, N.W. Bawcutt (ed.), Oxford, 1991, 240). Yet we have the unambiguous example of Lucius in *Julius Caesar* to prove that it certainly was an accomplishment of boy actors.

57. There is some ambiguity as to the implication of the Duke's ''Tis good'. He might either be commending her use of music to temper her melancholy, or else approving of her contrition at having been found listening to music, which might suggest an inappropriate levity in her conduct.

58. See John Jowett and Gary Taylor, 'With New Additions: Theatrical Interpolation in *Measure for Measure*', in Taylor and Jowett, *Shakespeare Reshaped, 1606–1623* (Oxford, 1993). Evidence for revision of *Measure for Measure* is summarized in Gary Taylor, 'Shakespeare's Mediterranean *Measure for Measure*', in Tom Clayton, Susan Brock and Vicente Forés, *Shakespeare and the Mediterranean* (Newark, 2004), 243–69. The setting which survives, by John Wilson, certainly post-dates the play's first production in 1604.

59. It is precisely this quality which persuaded Alice Walker that it was a later addition; she asserts that: 'in a consistently ironic comedy, which makes no concession to the sentimental or romantic, the song is an artistic blunder and the following dialogue is clearly the work of an inexpert hand'. Quoted in Brian Gibbons (ed.), *Measure for Measure* (Cambridge, 1991) 4.1 commentary.

60. Sternfeld, 88.

61. Duffin, 258–9. Neither of the suggestions he offers seems to me very compelling.

62. Little is known about Jones, active 1597–1615, although along with Philip Rosseter and others he was a patentee for the 'Children of the Revels of the Queen' in 1610. There is no evidence that he had any other theatrical connection.

63. Edward Doughtie (ed.), *Lyrics from English Airs* (Cambridge, Mass., 1970), 129 (quotation marks added).

64. Sternfeld, 136–7.

65. Linda Phyllis Austern, *Music in English Children's Drama of the Later Renaissance* (Philadelphia, 1992), 126–9.

66. Duffin, 460.

67. Roger Warren (ed.), *Cymbeline* (Oxford, 1998), 271–2.

68. Transcribed in Ian Spink (ed.), *Robert Johnson: Ayres Songs and Dialogues*, 2nd edition (London, 1974), 55.

69. Warren (ed.), 2.3.19, commentary.

70. His name is given as 'Giacomo' in the Oxford editions.

71. Martin Butler (ed.), *Cymbeline* (Cambridge, forthcoming 2005).

72. Auden, *Dyer's Hand*, 517.

73. Many songs of the period exploit a distinct change of mood between their sections.

74. The song is given here in the layout of the First Quarto – how it is to be interpreted in musical terms has been the subject of debate. It is not clear whether 'reply, reply' is to be sung by another voice, or by 'All' as John Russell Brown suggests in his Arden edition (London, 1955), 2.3.63–72. See Seng, 42–3.

75. Russell Brown (ed.), commentary; see Seng, 36–40 for other contributions to the debate. Charles Edelman notes that since the 1920s it has become 'a strong performance tradition' in one way or another to emphasize the clues the song offers (*Shakespeare in Production: The Merchant of Venice*, Cambridge, 2002, 188).

76. Seng, *Vocal Songs*, 42.

77. William Empson, *Seven Types of Ambiguity* (1930); quoted in Seng, 39.

78. Winifred Maynard, *Elizabethan Lyric Poetry and its Music* (Oxford, 1986), 184.

79. J.S. Manifold, *The Music in English Drama, Shakespeare to Purcell* (London, 1956), 181.

80. See John F. Cox (ed.), *Much Ado About Nothing* (Shakespeare in Production, Cambridge, 1997), 224–5, although he also notes some recent productions which have responded more positively to it.

81. See Seng, 66–7.

82. Seng, 66.

83. Warren (ed.), *Cymbeline*, 45.

84. 'Polydore' and 'Cadwal' are the names by which the brothers are known at this stage, having been stolen from court by Belarius and brought up as his sons.

85. Stanley Wells and Gary Taylor, *William Shakespeare: A Textual Companion* (Oxford, 1987; reprinted with corrections 1997), 607–8.

86. Warren (ed.), 274.

87. William A. Ringler, Jr, 'The Number of Actors in Shakespeare's Early Plays', in G.E. Bentley (ed.), *The Seventeenth-Century Stage* (Chicago, 1968), 134.

88. Peter Holland (ed.), *A Midsummer Night's Dream* (Oxford, 1994), 24.

89. Duffin, 479–80.

90. In the CD accompanying Duffin's book the song is given to a solo female singer. See Bruce R. Smith, *The Acoustic World of Early Modern England* (Chicago, 1999), 225–37, for interesting speculation on the way 'volume and pitch shape the experience of stage plays'.

91. Duffin sets it to the tune of 'Packington's Pound' (143), but this works rather less convincingly than his setting for 'You spotted snakes'.

92. Maynard, *Elizabethan Lyric Poetry*, 181.

93. See, for example, Jeanne Addison Roberts, *Shakespeare's English Comedy: 'The Merry Wives of Windsor' in Context* (Lincoln, Nebr. and London, 1979); François Laroque, *Shakespeare's Festive World* (Cambridge, 1991), 264–6.

94. Both T.W. Craik and David Crane, the most recent editors of the play for Oxford (1990) and Cambridge (1997) respectively, have little time for such readings.

95. Some commentators have tried to give it an even more ritualistic function. Noble, followed by Sternfeld, suggested that its lyric was a pagan parody of the pentecostal hymn 'Come Holy Ghost', and that it was a celebration of 'the religious significance to a Roman of wine'. These notions are cited, and rightly dismissed, by Seng, 211–12.

96. Duffin, 109–10.

97. See Richard Madelaine (ed.), *Shakespeare in Production: Antony and Cleopatra* (Cambridge, 1998), 210–11.

98. Attempts in modern productions to elaborate the scene can, paradoxically, make its inessential nature only more obviously apparent.

99. Duffin, 233–4. See also Ross Duffin, 'Catching the Burden: A New Round of Shakespearean Musical Hunting', *Studies in Music* (2000–01), 19–20.

100. Duffin, 434.

101. See Austern, *Children's Drama*.

102. Alan Brissenden (ed.), *As You Like It* (Oxford, 1993), 45.

103. Brissenden (ed.), commentary.

104. Duffin, 415–17.

105. Seng, 72.

106. Noble, quoted in Seng, 76.

107. Auden, *Dyer's Hand*, 520.

108. This reflects choirboy company practice, where one finds just such anonymous singing pages in roles 'clearly designed for singers whose acting skills have yet to be developed' (Austern, *Children's Drama*, 23).

109. See Robert Smallwood, *Shakespeare at Stratford: As You Like It* (London, 2003), 167–88, for examples from post-war Stratford.

110. Seng, 89–90, reviews the competing positions.

5: MUSICAL THEMATICS: *TWELFTH NIGHT AND THE TEMPEST*

1. See 150 above for Honigman's argument that this circumstance also affected *Othello*.

2. Stanley Wells and Roger Warren (eds), *Twelfth Night* (Oxford, 1994), 75.

3. John Hollander, *The Untuning of the Sky: Ideas of Music in English Poetry, 1500–1700* (Princeton, 1961; New York, 1970), 161. He argues that it is indeed Viola's speech which provides the curative musical function of harmonious integration in the play.

4. His remark to Orsino is often interpreted as evincing some anger at being treated as one who simply sings for money. This seems to me an over-reading of the exchange, where his riposte to Orsino's 'There's for thy pains', 'No pains, sir, I take pleasure' may equally be another example of his refusal to let any opportunity for a corrective pun to pass him by.

5. Wells and Warren, 28–9.

6. Linda Phyllis Austern, *Music in English Children's Drama of the Later Renaissance* (Philadelphia, 1992), 82–3.

7. Charles Butler, *The Principles of Music* (1636), 124 (orthography normalized). See also Austern, *Children's Drama*, 115–18.

8. On *Twelfth Night* as a play which offers 'an analysis, as well as a representation of feasting', see Hollander, 153–61.

9. See above, pp. 31–2.

10. Musical melancholy was fashionable; although Dowland's *Lachrimae* were not published until 1604, his celebrated 'Flow my tears' was published in the *Second Book of Airs* in 1600, a collection which contains a number of tunes that would be ideally suited to this play.

11. Leah Scragg, *Discovering Shakespeare's Meaning* (London, 1988), 216.

12. Winifred Maynard, *Elizabethan Lyric Poetry and its Music* (Oxford, 1986), 202.

13. I am thinking here of performances of songs such as 'Excelsior' or 'Come into the garden, Maud' by Robert Tear and Benjamin Luxon.

14. W.H. Auden, 'Music in Shakespeare', in *The Dyer's Hand* (London, 1962), 522.

15. Mark W. Booth, *The Experience of Songs* (New Haven and London, 1981), 15.

16. If there is a display of homoerotic attraction between Orsino and Viola it perhaps also gives an additional reason for his abrupt, even embarrassed, paying off of Feste, and swift return to the business of wooing Olivia.

17. Peter J. Seng, *The Vocal Songs in the Plays of Shakespeare: A Critical History* (Cambridge, Mass., 1967), 97. The issues are quite different from those which attach to Morley's setting of 'It was a lover and his lass', discussed above, for that tune is evidently intended for those words, and there is no trace of other versions. That Morley's *Consort Lessons* is one of the sources for 'O Mistress Mine' has persuaded some that Shakespeare and Morley collaborated at this period, but the arguments are unconvincing.

18. The Arden *Complete Works* expands the Folio stage direction '*Enter Viola and Clowne*' with '*playing on pipe and tabor*' – but, strictly, the pipe isn't mentioned, and he may simply be drumming.

19. Quoted in Seng, 94.

20. Auden, *Dyer's Hand*, 521–2.

21. He argues that the song is 'a direct appeal to ... Olivia' and speaks of Viola-Sebastian 'the master-mistress of Orsino's and Olivia's passion' (quoted in Seng, 95).

22. Ross Duffin, *Shakespeare's Songbook* (New York, 2004), 200–201, prints both surviving versions, one of which certainly precedes the play; the other, and perhaps better-known, from Ravenscroft's *Deuteromelia* (1609), probably does. He has some interesting suggestions of possible performance patterns.

23. The song was to become 'one of the most successful of all the English lutenist songs', imitated and parodied in Scotland, and on the continent, and referred to in other plays. See David Greer, 'Five Variations on "Farewell Dear loue"', in John Caldwell, Edward Olleson and Susan Wollenberg (eds), *The Well Enchanting Skill* (Oxford, 1990), 213–30.

24. Edward Doughtie (ed.), *Lyrics from English Airs* (Cambridge, Mass., 1970), 126.

25. Robin Headlam Wells, *Elizabethan Mythologies* (Cambridge, 1994), 218.

26. Wells, 219.

27. A song from the court of Henry VIII, with words perhaps by Thomas Wyatt, music by William Cornish.

28. Quoted from Staunton's edition of 1858–60 in Seng, *Vocal Songs*, 124.

29. Seng, 124.

30. See Seng, 123–30.

31. Headlam Wells, 221.

32. Seng, 124

33. See F.W. Sternfeld, *Music in Shakesperean Tragedy* (London, 1963), 188–91. There is a later version of the tune printed by Chappell in 1859. In Vernon's original the tempo direction is 'Spiritoso', and there is some play between voice and orchestra on the words 'hey, ho', which gives it a very much less melancholy feel than the more usually employed unaccompanied singing of Chappell's version.

34. Duffin, 448–50.

35. Wells and Warren (eds), *Twelfth Night*, 70.

36. Wells and Warren.

37. Many of the ideas in this section were adumbrated in my 'Music, Masque and Meaning in *The Tempest*', in D. Lindley (ed.), *The Court Masque* (Manchester, 1984); I hope that their expression here has benefited from critiques offered by Robin Headlam Wells, Howell Chickering and Jacquelyn Fox-Good, among others.

38. Wells, 63.

39. Alden T. and Virginia Mason Vaughan (eds), *The Tempest* (London, 2000), 18.

40. There is a minor textual problem here, in that the stage direction is placed before the line 'Farewell master; farewell, farewell', but only the succeeding five-line stanza, beginning 'No more dams' is set in italic, the normal indication of a song. Orgel, in the Oxford edition, suggests that the SD may be misplaced; both the Vaughans and I simply reprint F. Duffin notes that 'five-line ballads are very rare' (274), but also tells me in a private communication that

there are no ballad lyrics with the rhyme scheme that would be produced by treating it as a six-line lyric. In some performances the final line 'Freedom, high-day' is also incorporated in the song, though not italicized in F.

41. Mark W. Booth, *The Experience of Songs*, 16.

42. It is possible, of course, that the Johnson settings were composed for performances of the play later than 1610/11, or that the surviving manuscript and printed versions preserve the melodies of the songs in a form modified from their theatrical origins for domestic consumption.

43. The Wilson publication of this setting, and that for 'Where the bee sucks' is photographically reproduced in the Arden 3 edition (19–20). Orgel's Oxford edition (223–5) reproduces the versions edited by Ian Spink in *Robert Johnson, Ayres, Songs and Dialogues* (London, 1974); my New Cambridge edition (252–3) prints tune and bass for both songs, but essays a conjectural three-part version of the refrain 'Ding, dong, bell' which might fit the requirement that Ferdinand hear the music continue around and above him.

44. Maynard, *Elizabethan Lyric Poetry*, 219.

45. W.H. Auden, *The Sea and The Mirror*, ed. Arthur Kirsch (Princeton and Oxford, 2003), which contains much useful information on Auden's developing responses to *The Tempest*.

46. Auden, *Dyer's Hand*, 525.

47. Howell Chickering, 'Hearing Ariel's Songs', *The Journal of Medieval and Renaissance Studies*, 24 (1994), 158.

48. Jacquelyn Fox-Good, 'Other Voices: The Sweet, Dangerous Air(s) of Shakespeare's *Tempest*', *Shakespeare Studies* (1996), 253.

49. Maynard, 218.

50. Chickering, 155.

51. Auden, *Dyer's Hand*, 524.

52. See Christine Dymkowski (ed.), *Shakespeare in Production: The Tempest* (Cambridge, 2000), 34–48; D. Lindley, *Shakespeare at Stratford: The Tempest* (London, 2003), Chapter 3.

53. See above, pp. 37–8.

54. Stephen Orgel, *The Illusion of Power: Political Theater in the English Renaissance* (Berkeley, Los Angeles and London, 1975), 40.

55. Auden, *Dyer's Hand*, 526.

56. On the variant stagings of the parting of Prospero and Ariel see Dymkowski, *The Tempest*, 326–30, and Lindley, *Shakespeare at Stratford*, 106–10.

57. It was generally cut throughout the nineteenth century, and only fitfully restored in the early part of the twentieth.

58. It was once commonplace, somewhat sentimentally and inaccurately, to see this as Shakespeare's farewell to the stage.

59. Auden, *The Sea and the Mirror*, 4.

APPENDIX: GLOSSARY

1. Thoinot Arbeau, *Orchesography* (1589), trans. Mary Stewart Evans (New York, revised edition 1967), 50.
2. Arbeau, 19.
3. Arbeau, 46.

SELECT BIBLIOGRAPHY

This is a selective bibliography, listing only some of the most substantial books and articles referred to in this study.

REFERENCE WORKS

Ashbee, Andrew, *Records of English Court Music*, 9 vols (Snodland, Kent, 1986–1996).

Dessen, Alan C. and Leslie Thomson, *A Dictionary of Stage Directions in English Drama, 1580–1642* (Cambridge, 1999).

Duffin, Ross, *Shakespeare's Songbook* (New York, 2004). Prints all the surviving music contemporary or nearly contemporary with the first performance, together with suggestions of popular tunes to fit those songs for which no music is extant.

Gooch, Bryan N.S. and David Thatcher (eds), *A Shakespeare Music Catalogue*, 5 vols (Oxford, 1991). A comprehensive listing of virtually all known music associated with Shakespeare, including detailed information on scores and songs from the seventeenth century to the present.

Sadie, Stanley and John Tyrrell, *The New Grove Dictionary of Music and Musicians*, 2nd edition (Oxford, 2001). The online version, L. Macy (ed.), *Grove Music Online* at http://www.grovemusic.com, is updated annually, and is the version cited in this book.

Seng, Peter J., *The Vocal Songs in the Plays of Shakespeare: A Critical History* (Cambridge, Mass., 1967). Summarizes all previous criticism of the songs up to 1964.

Simpson, Claude M., *The British Broadside Ballad and its Music* (New Brunswick, NJ, 1966).

Strunk, Oliver, *Source Readings in Music History* (revised edition by Leo Treitler) (New York and London, 1998).

Wilson, Christopher R. and Michela Calore (eds), *Dictionary of Music in Shakespeare* (London, forthcoming, 2005),

PRIMARY TEXTS

Anon. (attrib. to John Case), *The Praise of Musicke* (1586).

Burton, Robert, *The Anatomy of Melancholy*, ed. Thomas C. Faulkner, Nicolas K. Kiessling, Rhonda L. Blair, with commentary by J.B. Bamborough and Martin Dodsworth, 6 vols (Oxford, 1989–2000).

Castiglione, Baldassare, *The Book of the Courtier*, trans. Sir Thomas Hoby, edited with introduction by W. H. D. Rouse (London, 1928).

Earle, John, *Micro-cosmographie Or, A peece of the world discouered* (London, 1628).

Elyot, Thomas, *The Boke Named the Governour* (1531), ed. Henry Herbert Stephen Croft (London, 1883), 2 vols.

Gosson, Stephen, *The School of Abuse*, Edward Arber (ed.) (London, 1869).

Morley, Thomas, *A Plain and Easy Introduction to Practical Music* (1597), ed. R Alec Harman (London and New York, revised edition 1963).

Osborn, James M (ed.), *The Autobiography of Thomas Whythorne* (modern-spelling edition; Oxford, 1962),

Peacham, Henry, *The Complete Gentleman* (1622), ed. Virgil B. Helzel (Ithaca, New York, 1962).

Stubbes, Philip, *Anatomy of Abuses* (1579), ed. Frederick J. Furnivall (London, 1877–9).

Wright, Thomas, *The Passions of the Minde in Generall*, reprinted with an introduction by Thomas O. Sloan (Urbana, Chicago and London, 1971).

CRITICAL STUDIES

General studies of music in the period

Austern, Linda Phyllis, '"Sing Againe Syren": The Female Musician and Sexual Enchantment in Elizabethan Life and Literature', *Renaissance Quarterly*, 42 (1989), 420–48.

——, *Music in English Children's Drama of the Later Renaissance* (Philadelphia, 1992).

——, '"Alluring the Auditorie to Effeminacie": Music and the Idea of the Feminine in Early Modern England', *Music and Letters*, 74 (1993), 343–54.

Baldwin, Elizabeth, *Paying the Piper: Music in Pre-1642 Cheshire* (Kalamazoo, 2002).

Baskerville, Charles Read, *The Elizabethan Jig and Related Song Drama* (Chicago, Ill., 1929).

Booth, Mark W., *The Experience of Songs* (New Haven and London, 1981).

Boyd, Morrison Comegys, *Elizabethan Music and Musical Criticism* (Philadelphia, 1940, revised edition 1962).

Bray, Roger (ed.), *Music in Britain: The Sixteenth Century* (Oxford, 1995).

Carpenter, Nan Cooke, *Music in the Medieval and Renaissance Universities*, (Oklahoma, 1958; reprinted New York, 1972).

Fenlon, Iain (ed.), *Man and Music: The Renaissance* (London, 1989).

Finney, Gretchen Ludke, *Musical Backgrounds for English Literature: 1580–1650* (Westport, Conn., 1962).

Gouk, Penelope, *Music, Science and Natural Magic in Seventeenth-Century England* (New Haven and London, 1999)

Hollander, John, *The Untuning of the Sky: Ideas of Music in English Poetry, 1500–1700* (Princeton, 1961; New York, 1970).

Holman, Peter, *Four and Twenty Fiddlers: The Violin at the English Court, 1540–1690* (Oxford, 1993).

Horden, Peregrine (ed.), *Music as Medicine: The History of Music Therapy since Antiquity* (Aldershot, 2000).

Howard, Skiles, *The Politics of Courtly Dancing* (Amherst, 1998).

Hulse, Lynn, 'The Musical Patronage of Robert Cecil', *Journal of the Royal Musical Association*, 116 (1991), 24–40.

Hulse, Lynne M., 'The Musical Patronage of the English Aristocracy', unpublished Ph.D., King's College, London (1992).

Hutton, James, 'Some English Poems in Praise of Music', *English Miscellany*, 2 (1951), 1–64.

Kisby, Fiona (ed.), *Music and Musicians in Renaissance Cities and Towns*, (Cambridge, 2001).

Le Huray, Peter, *Music and the Reformation in England, 1549–1660* (London, 1978).

Manifold, J. S., *The Music in English Drama, Shakespeare to Purcell* (London, 1956).

Meyer-Baer, Kathi, *Music of the Spheres and the Dance of Death: Studies in Musical Iconology* (New York, 1984).

Price, David C., *Patrons and Musicians of the English Renaissance* (Cambridge, 1981).

Scholes, Percy A., *The Puritans and Music in England and New England* (Oxford, 1934).

Smith, Bruce R., *The Acoustic World of Early Modern England* (Chicago, 1999).

Temperley, Nicholas, *Music of the English Parish Church*, 2 vols (Cambridge, 1979).

Tomlinson, Gary, *Music in Renaissance Magic* (Chicago and London, 1993).

Vickers, Brian, 'Figures of Rhetoric/Figures of Music', *Rhetorica*, 2 (1984), 1–44.

Walker, D.P., ed. Penelope Gouk, *Music, Spirit and Language in the Renaissance* (London, 1985).

Walls, Peter, *Music in the English Courtly Masque 1604–1640* (Oxford, 1996).

Watt, Tessa, *Cheap Print and Popular Piety, 1550–1640* (Cambridge, 1991).

White, Martin, *Renaissance Drama in Action* (London, 1998).

Winn, James Anderson, *Unsuspected Eloquence* (New Haven and London, 1981).

Woodfill, Walter L., *Musicians in English Society from Elizabeth to Charles I* (Princeton, 1953).

Studies of music in Shakespeare

Auden, W.H., 'Music in Shakespeare', in *The Dyer's Hand* (London, 1962).

Brissenden, Alan, *Shakespeare and the Dance* (London, 1981).

Chickering, Howell, 'Hearing Ariel's Songs', *The Journal of Medieval and Renaissance Studies*, 24 (1994), 131–72.

Dunn, Lesley C., 'Ophelia's Songs in *Hamlet*: Music, Madness, and the Feminine', in Lesley C. Dunn and Nancy A. Jones (eds), *Embodied Voices: Representing Female Vocality in Western Culture* (Cambridge, 1994).

Folkerth, Wes, *The Sound of Shakespeare* (London, 2002).

Fox-Good, Jacquelyn A., 'Ophelia's Mad Songs: Music, Gender, Power', in David C. Allen and Robert A. White (eds), *Subjects on the World's Stage: Essays on British Literature of the Middle Ages and the Renaissance* (Newark, 1995).

——, 'Other Voices: The Sweet, Dangerous Air(s) of Shakespeare's *Tempest*', *Shakespeare Studies* (1996), 241–74.

Gurr, Andrew, *The Shakespearean Stage, 1574–1642*, 3rd edition (Cambridge, 1992).

Headlam Wells, Robin, *Elizabethan Mythologies: Studies in Poetry, Drama and Music* (Cambridge, 1994).

Hosley, Richard, 'Was there a Music-Room in Shakespeare's Globe', *Shakespeare Survey*, 13 (1960), 113–23.

Howard, Skiles, 'Hands, Feet and Bottoms: Decentering the Cosmic Dance in *A Midsummer Night's Dream*', *Shakespeare Quarterly*, 44 (1993), 325–42.

Iselin, Pierre, 'Myth, Memory and Music in *Richard II, Hamlet* and *Othello*', in A.J. Hoenselaars (ed.), *Reclamations of Shakespeare* (Amsterdam, 1994), 173–86.

King, Rosalind, 'The Music and Structure of *Othello*', *Shakespeare Survey*, 39 (1986), 149–58.

Lindley, David, 'Music, Masque and Meaning in *The Tempest*,' in David Lindley (ed.), *The Court Masque* (Manchester, 1984).

——, *Shakespeare at Stratford: The Tempest* (London, 2003).

——, 'Tempestuous Transformations', in Shirley Chew and Alistair Stead (eds), *Translating Life: Studies in Transpositional Aesthetics* (Liverpool, 1999), 99–120.

Maynard, Winifred, *Elizabethan Lyric Poetry and its Music* (Oxford, 1986).

Smith, Bruce R., 'Shakespeare's Residuals: The Circulation of Ballads in Cultural Memory', in Stuart Gillespie and Neil Rhodes (eds), *Shakespeare and Elizabethan Popular Culture* (London, forthcoming, 2005).

Sternfeld, F.W., *Music in Shakespearean Tragedy* (London, 1963).

Wright, Peter M., 'Stage Directions for Music and Sound Effects in *2–3 Henry VI*: "No Quarrel but a Slight Contention"', in Grace Ioppolo (ed.), *Shakespeare Performed: Essays in Honor of R.A. Foakes* (Newark, 2000), 72–87.

INDEX